T0289197

The Utah Prairie Dog

THEODORE G. MANNO

The Utah Prairie Dog
LIFE AMONG THE RED ROCKS

photography by
ELAINE MILLER BOND

foreword by
JOHN L. HOOGLAND

The University of Utah Press | *Salt Lake City*

The Defiance House Man colophon is a registered trademark of the University of Utah Press. It is based on a four-foot-tall Ancient Puebloan pictograph (late PIII) near Glen Canyon, Utah.

18 17 16 15 14   1 2 3 4 5

Library of Congress Cataloging-in-Publication Data

Manno, Theodore G.
The Utah prairie dog : life among the red rocks/Theodore G. Manno ; photography by Elaine Miller Bond ; foreword by John L. Hoogland.
        pages   cm
Includes bibliographical references and index.
ISBN 978-1-60781-366-8 (pbk. : alk. paper)—ISBN 978-1-60781-367-5 (ebook)
1. Utah prairie dog.
2. Utah prairie dog—Research—Anecdotes.
I. Title.
QL737.R68M3316 2014
599.36'709792—dc23   2014014483

All photos are by Elaine Miller Bond unless noted otherwise in the caption. Chapter 1 opener photo (page xviii) by Theodore G. Manno.

All artwork is by Elaine Miller Bond, except for the map of the Utah prairie dog geographic ranges, which is courtesy of Keith Day and the Utah Division of Wildlife Resources.

Printed and bound by Sheridan Books, Inc., Ann Arbor, Michigan.

for

BLACK-BUTT-9, DEUCEY, I-15, JUNIOR, TIC-TAC-TOE, WETSUIT,

and so many of our study animals.

Their descendants roam the valleys of Utah
unaware that they are among the last.
They taught us so much,
but we know so little.

CONTENTS

TABLES

FOREWORD

People frequently ask me, "Which is your favorite species of prairie dog?" I have no good answer, because I love 'em all. Indeed, I have studied the ecology and social behavior of four species (one at a time, each for at least seven years) over the last four decades. I nonetheless have a special fondness for the Utah prairie dogs that I studied at Bryce Canyon National Park (BCNP) for 11 consecutive years.

What's so special about Utah prairie dogs? For starters, the Utah prairie dogs at BCNP were more habituated to people, and therefore more user-friendly, than prairie dogs of other species that I have studied. Capturing and marking hundreds of them each year, and getting to know them as individuals, was therefore feasible and rewarding. I also enjoyed documenting that Utah prairie dogs are a good candidate for designation as a "keystone species," because they profoundly affect the biology of so many organisms. Their burrows provide homes for many vertebrates and hundreds of invertebrates, for example. And Utah prairie dogs serve as prey for American badgers, golden eagles, long-tailed weasels, northern goshawks, red foxes, and other predators.

User-friendliness, keystone status, and my concern for conservation were all important, but none of these factors, alone or in combination, was sufficient to lure me back to the Utah prairie dogs at BCNP every spring. Rather, it was my *insatiable curiosity* about the behavioral ecology of Utah prairie dogs that motivated me to sit in towers from dawn to dusk during unpredictable weather—usually frigid, and always windy—every day from early March through mid-July of every year from 1995 through 2005. Why was each female

sexually receptive for only five to six hours on a single day each year? Why did some females mate with as many as five males, and sometimes with close kin such as fathers and sons, during the short period of sexual receptivity? Why did males sometimes kill the offspring of females with whom they mated? Both males and females were almost always surrounded by offspring and other kin, so why did only females give alarm calls during attacks by American badgers and red foxes? We all understand why female mammals nurse their own offspring, but why did female Utah prairie dogs commonly nurse the offspring of *other* females as well? When over 50 percent of adult and juvenile Utah prairie dogs died each year, how did certain males and females manage to survive for as long as seven or eight years? These are only some of the mesmerizing questions that chained me to my tower each spring. Chained, yes, but *I was one happy prisoner who was not seeking parole*.

For the 2004 and 2005 field seasons, Theodore (Theo) Manno was another happy prisoner. During our collaboration, he sat in his own tower and followed the same schedule as described above: dawn to dusk, every day regardless of the weather, from before the first Utah prairie dog mating in March until the capture of the last weaned juvenile in July. For this reason, Theo is uniquely qualified to write this book intended for curious naturalists. I therefore endorse *The Utah Prairie Dog: Legend of the Red Rocks*, for which I have verified the accuracy of all aspects of the demography, ecology, and social behavior of Utah prairie dogs.

Elaine Bond joined me in 2005 for my final year of research at BCNP. Her sole objective was to document, with her camera, the riveting social behavior of Utah prairie dogs. Her dedication and attention to detail were phenomenal, and she therefore documented charity, malice, and mischief that have eluded all previous photographers. Stunning, indeed, are her images of aboveground matings, stealing of nest material, fights and chases, communal nursing, and predation. Gotta love those Utah prairie dogs!

Paint a number on his side, and a male Utah prairie dog instantly *comes alive*. He might become, for example, the stud who is the biggest bully in the colony, who runs two to three miles (3–5 km) per day during the mating season, and who mates with as many 10 females from his own and adjacent territories during a single mating season. A painted female might become the amicable one-year-old who suddenly turns incredibly nasty as soon as she obtains sufficient sperm, who collects hundreds of mouthfuls of nest material over the 29 days when she is pregnant, and who eventually weans seven offspring. By chronicling the lives of Utah prairie dogs with monikers such as Tic-Tac-Toe, Wetsuit, and Sweet-16, Theo accurately communicates the satisfaction and the excitement—and the sadness as well—that come from watching marked individuals over time.

The Utah prairie dog is the rarest of the five prairie dog species (the four that I have studied in the western United States, plus the Mexican prairie dog), and its persistence for future generations is in serious jeopardy. Theo and I disagree about the details regarding the best plans for conserving Utah prairie dogs, but we fully agree on two fundamental issues. First, the battle to save Utah prairie dogs from extinction is one that we can win, mainly because Utah prairie dogs are so incredibly resilient to threats such as shooting and poisoning. Information from our long-term research will contribute significantly to the victory. Second, we contend that conservation requires compromise. Consequently, realistic plans for the survival of Utah prairie dogs will completely satisfy neither ranchers nor prairie dog advocates.

Theo's passion for Utah prairie dogs is evident on every page of this book, and Elaine's affection is manifest in every eye-catching photograph. Enjoy viewing and reading about my "little people" at BCNP!

JOHN L. HOOGLAND, PHD
Center for Environmental Science,
Appalachian Laboratory
Frostburg, Maryland

PREFACE

Pioneers who ventured west found the expansive colonies of prairie dogs hard to ignore. So did a young scientist named John Hoogland, who decided in 1974 to study prairie dogs for his dissertation research after briefly observing their fascinating social behavior. Almost thirty years later, I also thought prairie dogs to be remarkable after I discovered them completely by accident. The rodents were tucked away in a yellow enclosure at a small zoo in Hershey, Pennsylvania, where I was volunteering while working a summer job as a musician in the nearby amusement park.[1]

The constant movement and social interaction of the prairie dogs was so compelling that I was inspired to major in biology upon return to my hometown in New Jersey for college. It seemed like a plan, but over the next two years, my communing with nature and alienation with the "college experience" would leave me with few meaningful job skills. So, in the spirit of immature college graduates everywhere, I pursued the only viable option available to me following commencement—graduate school.

All I needed was a dissertation adviser, and the search started with John Hoogland. Having conducted research on four species of prairie dogs over four decades, John was studying Utah prairie dogs that year. As it turned out, John did not take graduate students, but he needed research assistants. So a few months later, in March 2004, I packed my jalopy to the brim and drove 2,600 miles (4200 km) into southern Utah's prairie dog country, a place I would call home until John concluded his research there in summer 2005.

I conceived this book four years later. I originally dismissed it as a silly idea that

would never come to fruition because of other commitments. However, it eventually became clear that I could no longer ignore the absence of a book devoted completely to Utah prairie dogs. In the midst of such a crucial time for their conservation, I realized that it was my professional responsibility to help. My goals were simple, but ambitious—to write the definitive source on the species, and to make it widely accessible to interested laypeople and amateur naturalists, not just other biologists.

Since 2009, I have been almost completely ensconced in achieving these goals. It has been a long road, but the study animals and my colleagues have made this endeavor worthwhile. Many individuals have offered their assistance, their time, and most importantly, their inspiration.

Managing editor Glenda Cotter, acquisition editors Reba Rauch and John Alley, assistant editor Stephanie Warnick, and the entire editorial team at the University of Utah Press went outside the box and recognized the importance of this project. Without their vision, this book would have never come to fruition. They provided outstanding assistance with all aspects of preparing the manuscript, and I am grateful to all of them for their excellent work.

The sharp eyes of copyeditor Laurel Anderton spared readers of this book from various errors and improved my writing tremendously. Her attention to detail while criticizing this manuscript was exemplary, and I thank her for this thoroughness.

I cannot thank John Hoogland enough for having me as a member of his "Dog Squad" during 2004–2005, for mentoring me throughout my career, and for helping to shape this manuscript by commenting on several drafts in various states of completion. I was only one of the dozens of overworked, underpaid, and unheralded research assistants who endured 14-hour days and four months of desolation to help with John's data collection. For their extraordinary efforts, I thank John's 40-plus Dog Squad members during 1995–2005. They are too numerous to name here, but they know who they are.

Sylvester Allred (Northern Arizona University) and John L. Koprowski (University of Arizona) graciously accepted the considerable responsibility of reviewing this manuscript. Their comments helped me improve the book, and I thank them for their willingness and professionalism.

Participants in Utah prairie dog management and conservation initiatives were helpful to me during this project. Bill Branham, coordinator of the Utah Prairie Dog Recovery Implementation Program (UPDRIP); Keith Day, wildlife biologist with the Utah Division of Wildlife Resources (UDWR); and Laura Romin of the United States Fish and Wildlife Service (USFWS) offered helpful and astute comments on drafts that improved this book. Taylor Jones of WildEarth Guardians provided information and commentary on Utah prairie dog conservation. And Erica Wightman, coordinator of the Utah Prairie Dog Habitat Credits Exchange Program (HCEP), offered updates regarding the program's progress.

For the use of photographs and other materials, I thank Dennis Baresco, Bill Branham, Keith Day, Ruthanne Johnson, Martin Richter, Brian Slobe, Erica Wightman, the Humane Society of the United States, the Utah Prairie Dog HCEP, and the World Wildlife Fund. For information on locating documents, I thank Leif Milliken and Barre Toelken. The helpfulness and flexibility of these professionals and organizations allowed me to add character to the text, report additional information, and provide important visuals for readers.

Officials and personnel at Bryce Canyon National Park (BCNP) allowed John and his Dog Squad to conduct research there during 1995–2005. Sarah Haas and Jan Stock also provided me with information on the history of Utah prairie dogs in the park.

For financial support of John's research, I recognize the National Fish and Wildlife Foundation, National Science Foundation, University of Maryland Center for Environmental Science (UMCES), and the USFWS. And for minimizing John's teaching responsibilities so that he could pursue his research during the preparation of this book, I thank the three directors of the Appalachian Laboratory at UMCES: Kent Fuller, Robert Gardner, and Louis Pitelka. Without the help of these supporters, I would never have had the opportunity to become a member of the Dog Squad.

For being the original "Ace Photographer," Elaine Miller Bond and I would like to thank Alan M. Bond. His guidance and unshakable desire to look at hundreds of Utah prairie dog photos made Elaine's work possible and shaped the presentation of this book. We also thank John Greenleigh for assistance with the color inset photos.

Lili DeBarbieri assisted with the Dog Squad's field research in 2005 and observed many of the predations described in the following pages. Perhaps because she is also a writer, Lili responded to this project in a manner that many fiancées would not: she patiently tolerated my moodiness, unavailability, reclusiveness, and malaise during preparation of the manuscript.

Most of all, I acknowledge the prairie dogs of southern Utah who unwittingly devoted their lives to science. I thank them for being my study animals and enriching my life. I enjoyed their company, and my memories of them will last a lifetime.

Prairie Dog Town

I'm moving to a Prairie Dog Town.
I'm going where a kiss is a handshake
And mother's milk feeds growing pups
Born in a hole in the ground.
Community,
Made of grasses and buttercups
And bravery
To face the fox
To trace red-rock shadows
To take the western winds into your throat
Throw back your head
And bark.

Ground, grounded, groundling
The dirt is my retreat
With its roots and agates and arrowheads
Its wagging tails.
For you don't have to be a prairie dog
To move to Prairie Dog Town.
You only need to have your dreams
And dig your tunnels
Toward any one of the four directions
That helps you stay
Connected.

—ELAINE MILLER BOND

The Utah Prairie Dog

1

Life in the Big City

In this plain and from one to nine miles from the river or any water, we saw the
largest collection of the burrowing or barking squirrels that we had ever yet seen;
we passed through a skirt of the territory of this community for about seven miles.
—MERIWETHER LEWIS, 1805[1]

This interesting little animal . . . never fails to attract the attention of every
traveler on the western prairies; and an approach to one of their settlements
after long and dreary marches is always hailed with delight.
—C. B. R. KENNERLY, quoted in *Mammals of the Boundary*, 1859[2]

☾

*Watching the sunrise over a Utah meadow, I prepare to spend the day observing a colony
of small, auburn-colored, burrowing critters. As they arise for the morning, a few put
their mouths together as if to "kiss." Others sniff the undersides of their family members.
Eventually, most are busy with digging, grooming, running, eating, playing, fighting,
or scanning for predators. Vocalizations ring out from every corner of the field, offering
messages I will never truly understand.*

Prairie dogs are American icons. Over 200 years ago, explorer Meriwether Lewis described their presence as "infinite" because massive sprawls of burrows sometimes contained millions of residents and extended for miles across the pre-settlement frontier landscape.[3] Today, the coloniality of prairie dogs continues to make them striking to professional and amateur naturalists. The charismatic behavior of prairie dogs, including their social interaction, fighting, chasing, and the upright, humanlike posture they use to watch for predators, is one reason that few other animals are better able to capture our hearts. Prairie dog colony sites also attract other fauna such as American badgers (*Taxidea*

taxus), bison (*Bison bison*), black-footed ferrets (*Mustela nigripes*), coyotes (*Canis latrans*), and prairie falcons (*Falco mexicanus*), making these areas centers of ecological interaction.[4]

Scientists and nature lovers are fervent in one direction about prairie dogs. Many ranchers, developers, and gun enthusiasts are fervent in the other direction. The latter assert that prairie dogs reproduce unabated and destroy forage for livestock. Another complaint is that cattle (*Bos primigenius*) break legs in prairie dog burrows. Prairie dogs have therefore been exterminated in myriad ways, including shooting, poisoning, and drowning.[5] Most of their colony sites, once vibrant

FIGURE 1.1. *Larger than life*. Our study animal, the Utah prairie dog.

FIGURE 1.2. *Still standing*. The Utah prairie dog has been eliminated from the majority of its historical range, but protections under the Endangered Species Act (ESA) have saved the species from extinction.

with activity, are now ghost towns. Formerly distributed across the Great Plains and Intermountain West with an estimated population of over five billion, prairie dogs now occupy less than 5 percent of their former range.[6]

The Utah prairie dog (*Cynomys parvidens*) is one of the five species of prairie dog, and the only mammal living in Utah and nowhere else (fig. 1.1).[7] Residing in south-central and southwestern Utah,[8] it has the smallest geographical range of any of the five prairie dog species. This confined range is largely a result of the precipitous decline of Utah prairie dog populations following the initiation of control programs in the 1920s. Utah prairie dogs are thought to have numbered around 95,000 individuals before these programs started.[9]

Eventually, Utah prairie dogs were eliminated from major portions of their historical range while falling to an estimated population of 2,160 in the 1970s.[10] Declining numbers made the Utah prairie dog one of the original species offered "endangered" status (that is, at risk of extinction throughout all or a significant portion of its range) by the Endangered Species Act (ESA) in 1973.[11] Since 1984, the Utah prairie dog has remained a species at risk, with a "threatened" listing (that is, likely to become endangered within the foreseeable future) from the United States Fish and Wildlife Service (USFWS), making it illegal to kill Utah prairie dogs unless excepted by the USFWS.[12] The federal government stopped poisoning programs in 1963, but not until the ESA was extermination forbidden for private individuals (figs. 1.2 and 1.3).[13]

The situation for Utah prairie dogs and their allies is not hopeless, and opportunities

FIGURE 1.3. *Brought to the brink*. Utah prairie dogs, like this one marked by John Hoogland in Bryce Canyon National Park (BCNP) with a unique marker for study, are currently listed as threatened under the ESA.

remain to address the conflicts surrounding them. Reasons for optimism include the occasional positive press that can benefit all five species (fig. 1.4). Prairie dogs have entered popular culture through a phenomenon called "prairie dogging," where office workers stand and peer over the walls of their cubicles to hear the latest gossip, much like prairie dogs look out from their burrows for predators (fig. 1.5).[14] With no fewer than 60 geographical locations or landscape features named for them,[15] prairie dogs are beloved by many tourists (figs. 1.6 and 1.7), and their likeness appears on countless greeting cards and souvenirs. They have appeared in commercials for hamburgers and sport-utility vehicles and have even been seen in Super Bowl advertisements. In circles with high admiration for prairie dogs, the rodents are honored with their own holiday. Prairie Dog Day,

on February 2, is observed in several western states and coincides with the traditional holiday of Groundhog Day, which was started by German settlers in Pennsylvania to mark the day a groundhog (*Marmota monax*) is aroused from hibernation to predict the weather.[16]

From 2004 to 2005, I assisted with John Hoogland's research on Utah prairie dogs en route to receiving my PhD. Our goal was to provide information on Utah prairie dog biology so that management policies could be data driven. To achieve this objective, we practically lived with a colony of Utah prairie dogs throughout their entire reproductive cycle, being with them almost every waking hour. John was with the study animals from dawn to dusk, seven days per week, for an entire four-month field season each year for a decade.

We learned a lot about Utah prairie dogs from our efforts, but we generated more

FIGURE 1.4. *Lovebirds*. Although they are reviled by many ranchers, Utah prairie dogs sometimes receive positive press and are loved by animal enthusiasts because of their "cuddly factor." For instance, these two female relatives are grooming—or sharing a secret.

FIGURE 1.5. *Spread the word*. "Gossip" on a Utah prairie dog colony spreads fast and usually contains information on the whereabouts of a predator.

FIGURE 1.6. *Sightseeing*. Utah prairie dogs are beloved by many tourists and are therefore an icon of some places frequented by travelers, such as the Prairie Dog Gift Shop on Route 63 in Utah.

FIGURE 1.7. *Close encounter*. All four species of prairie dog have popularity and allure with the public. At this roadside attraction in South Dakota, for instance, tourists are charged a nominal fee to feed peanuts to black-tailed prairie dogs. Photo by Theodore G. Manno.

questions than answers. Among many puzzles, we are not sure why individuals benefit from emitting an alarm call when a predator arrives, or why the callers are almost always female. Nor do we know why females sometimes move their unweaned juveniles aboveground from one nursery burrow to another. Or why some litters contain healthy, heavy offspring, while others have sickly juveniles of low body mass. Or why certain females mate with as many as five different males in rapid succession on their single day of sexual receptivity, while others mate with only a single male. And we are totally baffled as to why male Utah prairie dogs sometimes kill the unweaned pups of females with whom they have mated—their own potential offspring.

The Utah prairie dogs at our study colony suffered many trials and tribulations during our time together. We witnessed their daily difficulties of surviving in the wild and followed their lives as though we were watching a soap opera. We knew the genealogy of almost every individual in the colony, along with his or her mating partners and territory boundaries. We knew when almost all the study subjects emerged from hibernation, when they were born, and when they died. We even knew when they sneezed—yes, Utah prairie dogs do occasionally sneeze.

While I hope to communicate that Utah prairie dogs are fascinating, puzzling, and social animals, I will also write about the adventure of studying them. I will recount our challenges such as frigid conditions, desolate locations, struggles to remain alert while watching for behaviors, and long summer days spent trying to capture elusive pups. Another theme will be that it's tough being a prairie dog. I will describe the many difficulties through the life of a representative female. I will explain when she mated, how her first offspring fared, what challenges she faced in maintaining her family's territory, how she barely escaped predation on numerous occasions, and her eventual fate.

Finally, I will pursue the theme of "Let's give 'em a chance." I will explain why Utah prairie dogs are rare, describe the methods humans have used to eradicate them, and discuss the realization that the illegality of killing Utah prairie dogs is difficult to enforce. Then I will turn to more upbeat topics such as improving the survivorship of Utah prairie dogs that are translocated to minimize conflict with humans, and the importance of large sanctuaries where Utah prairie dogs can roam unmolested. I will emphasize that Utah prairie dogs are amazingly resilient, and that they will persist for our grandchildren if we just give them an opportunity.

This is the story of the Utah prairie dogs that were my faithful research animals during some of the best years of my life. My book is the culmination of years of thought, research, and personal and professional relationships. It is the story of never-say-die rodents that roam the valleys of southern Utah and practice the same mating rituals every year, maintaining a presence in small parts of their historical range unaware that many of their ancestors have been slaughtered.

Years of observations have allowed John, me, and others to chronicle the behavior of Utah prairie dogs, but the final chapters of the conservation efforts have yet to be written. As the USFWS continues to label the Utah prairie dog as a threatened species, I can only hope that our efforts to know and understand the animals will promote better conservation.

FIGURE 1.8. *Portrait*. Utah prairie dogs have eyes near the top of their head to spot aerial predators, and a rounded nose that they use like a shovel while digging their burrows.

☾

Utah prairie dogs are not dogs! They are burrowing rodents of the squirrel family (Sciuridae). Squirrels have small furry bodies and two large front teeth that grow constantly. Although prairie dogs are related to other tunneling rodents (order Rodentia) like marmots (genus *Marmota*) and ground squirrels (genera *Urocitellus* and *Ammospermophilus*, for example), scientists place them into a distinct genus called *Cynomys* that contains five species—one being Utah prairie dogs. Fossil records indicate that all five species of prairie dog have a common ancestor with ground squirrels going back about two to three million years ago. The larger body size, higher-crowned teeth, and broader skulls of prairie dogs differentiate them from their ground squirrel relatives.[17]

FIGURE 1.9. *Run for safety*. When Utah prairie dogs spot a predator, they run for cover. If they do not spot a predator before an attack, they must rely on camouflage to allow them enough time for escape. Unfortunately for Utah prairie dogs, this is impossible when the Utah landscape is covered with snow in March and April.

Utah prairie dogs are pear-shaped, portly rodents that are about 10–15 inches (25–40 cm) long (excluding the tail). They have brown or yellowish fur and tails that are about half an inch (1 cm) long with a white tip. Males are 10–20 percent larger than females, and body mass for both sexes depends on the time of year. Following winter into spring, when Utah prairie dogs emerge from their burrows after several months of scarce food, females sometimes weigh less than two-thirds of a pound (around 300 g). But in the summer, after a season of eating premium vegetation, some male Utah prairie dogs can bulk up to over two pounds (more than 1 kg).[18]

Many other physical features of Utah prairie dogs, most of which are also present in the other four species, play a role in their ability to survive a harsh environment. A few stand out in importance. First, Utah prairie dogs have keen vision and eyes at the top of their head, allowing them to accurately spot aerial predators like golden eagles (*Aquila chrysaetos*) and prairie falcons (fig. 1.8). When the ground is free of snow, camouflage also protects Utah prairie dogs if they do not see a predator soon enough to thwart an attack (fig. 1.9). Second, Utah prairie dogs have rounded noses, which they use to shovel and pat down dirt while shaping mounds at the entrances to their burrows. They also have long claws on their front and back paws that they use for digging. Finally, they have excellent hearing, which probably helps them stay aware of predators and colony mates while underground.[19]

The Utah prairie dog is one of three species of prairie dog with a white-tipped tail, the others being white-tailed prairie dogs (*Cynomys leucurus*), their closest relatives, and Gunnison's prairie dogs (*Cynomys gunnisoni*).[20]

The other two species, black-tailed (*Cyno-mys ludovicianus*) and Mexican prairie dogs (*Cynomys mexicanus*), have black-tipped tails that are longer than the tails of the white-tailed species, among other differences (table 1.1).[21] When people talk about "prairie dogs," they usually mean black-tailed prairie dogs because those are the most common in the wild, and the most likely to be seen by tourists or visitors to North American zoos (fig. 1.10a–b). However, this convention is obviously different for residents of Utah, because the state has populations of Utah, Gunnison's, and white-tailed prairie dogs, but no black-tailed prairie dogs.

Early Accounts and Folklore

So how did prairie dogs get their name? The "prairie" part of the name is a reference to the habitat of most prairie dog species, particularly the prototypical black-tailed variety, which lives in the prairies of North America. The "prairie" namesake for Utah prairie dogs is not as obvious as it is for black-tailed prairie dogs, but the mixed-grass valleys between southern Utah's mountain ranges that Utah prairie dogs inhabit are nonetheless clearly distinct from the nearby woodlands.

But why do we call them "dogs"? The reason is probably that the alarm calls of prairie dogs reminded early European settlers of a domestic dog's bark. Early French explorers knew the black-tailed prairie dog as *petit chien*, or "little dog," which was the name they submitted to Meriwether Lewis when he explored the territory of the Louisiana Purchase. Lewis described the *petit chien* in his 1804 expedition journals:

As we descended from this dome, we arrived at a spot, on the gradual descent of the hill, nearly four acres in extent, and covered with small holes: these are the residence of a little animal, called by the French petit chien *(little dog), who sit erect near*

the mouth, and make a whistling noise, but when alarmed take refuge in their holes.[22]

Lewis also used the name "barking squirrel," but he and his party continued to write of the "prairie dog," again referring to black-tailed prairie dogs. From an incident they observed on September 7, 1804, Lewis wrote the following:

After digging down another of the holes for six feet [about 2 m], we found, on running a pole into it, that we had not yet dug half way to the bottom: we discovered, however, two frogs in the hole, and near it we killed a dark rattlesnake, which had swallowed a small prairie dog . . . the petit chien *are justly named, as they resemble a small dog in some particulars, though they have also some points of similarity to the squirrel.*[23]

So compelling were the black-tailed prairie dogs that Lewis sent two live specimens east to President Thomas Jefferson, who exhibited one of them in a museum at Independence Hall in Philadelphia.[24]

Although used by early-nineteenth-century icons such as Washington Irving and Josiah Gregg, the term "prairie dog" was just one of many monikers for the colonial rodent during that time, along with burrowing squirrel, barking squirrel, mound yapper, prairie squirrel, prairie marmot, prairie barker, and yaprat.[25] The name "prairie dog" seems to have achieved uniformity and permanency after it was used by the famed French American ornithologist John James Audubon in his 1846 natural descriptions of the Louisiana Territory.[26] In fact, the name of that territory is used in the scientific name of the Utah prairie dog's cousin, the black-tailed prairie dog, *Cynomys ludovicianus* (translated as "doglike mouse of the Louisiana Territory"). Likewise, the complete Latin name for Utah prairie dogs, *Cynomys parvidens*, literally translates as "doglike mouse with small teeth," but the second part of the name is puzzling. While Utah prairie dogs have

TABLE 1.1. Comparison of the Five Species of Prairie Dog

	Black-tailed prairie dog	Mexican prairie dog	White-tailed prairie dog	Gunnison's prairie dog	Utah prairie dog
Range	Extreme southern Saskatchewan to northern Mexico, and approx. 98th meridian west to the Rocky Mountains	Nuevo León, Coahuila, and San Luis Potosí, Mexico	Western and central Wyoming, northwestern Colorado, southern Montana, and northeastern Utah	The "Four Corners" area of Arizona, Colorado, New Mexico, and Utah	Southwestern Utah
Altitude	2,300–6,000 feet (700–1830 m)	5,250–7,220 feet (1600–2200 m)	5,500–9,500 feet (1700–3000 m)	5,500–9,500 feet (1700–3000 m)	5,500–9,500 feet (1700–3000 m)
Tail	Black tip, 2.5–4 inches (65–100 mm)	Black tip, 3.5–4.5 inches (90–115 mm)	White tip, 1–2.5 inches (25–65 mm)	White tip, 1–2.5 inches (25–65 mm)	White tip, 1–2.5 inches (25–65 mm)
Black spot above eye	No	No	Yes	No	Yes
Burrows	Sometimes have rim craters, usually 1–2 entrances	Sometimes have rim craters, no information on number of entrances	Do not have rim craters, often have ≥6 entrances	Do not have rim craters, often have 3–4 entrances	Do not have rim craters, often have ≥6 entrances
Hibernation	No	No	Yes	Yes	Yes
Number of chromosomes	50	50	50	40	50
Gestation (days)	34–35	Unknown, probably around 1 month	28–30	29–30	28–31
Lactation (days)	37–51	41–50	35–42	35–44	37–42
Alarm calls	"Chirks" by males and females	"Chirks" by males and females	"Clicking" mostly by females	"Chee-Chee-Chee" by males and females	"Clicking" mostly by females

TABLE 1.1. Comparison of the Five Species of Prairie Dog (*continued*)

	Black-tailed prairie dog	Mexican prairie dog	White-tailed prairie dog	Gunnison's prairie dog	Utah prairie dog
Jump-yips ("all clear" calls)	Yes	Yes	No	No	No
Mating call by males	Yes	Yes	Yes	Yes	Yes
Laughing (territorial) bark by males	No	Probably same as black-tailed	Yes	No	Yes
Number of teats	8	8	10	10	10
Social system	Coterie—rarely changing common territories defended by related females over generations	Probably same as black-tailed	Clan—common territories defended by related females over generations; territorial boundaries that fluctuate with time	Clan—common territories defended by related females over generations; territorial boundaries that fluctuate with time	Clan—common territories defended by related females over generations; territorial boundaries that fluctuate with time
Usual age of first copulation	2	1 for females, 1 or 2 for males	1 for females, 1 or 2 for males	1 for females, 1 or 2 for males	1 for females, 1 or 2 for males
Infanticide	Common in both sexes, including females killing lactating offspring of close kin	Unknown	Rare or absent	Rare or absent	Common, and only adult or yearling males kill
Communal Nursing	Common	Unknown	Rare or absent	Common	Common
Status of species	Unlisted	Endangered	Unlisted	Unlisted	Threatened

TABLE I.I. Comparison of the Five Species of Prairie Dog (continued)

	Black-tailed prairie dog	Mexican prairie dog	White-tailed prairie dog	Gunnison's prairie dog	Utah prairie dog
Major public viewing areas*	North Dakota: Lewis and Clark State Park, Theodore Roosevelt National Park South Dakota: Badlands National Park, Buffalo Gap National Grassland, Conata Basin National Grassland, Wind Cave National Park Wyoming: Devils Tower National Monument	Mexico: El Tokio Grasslands	Colorado: Arapaho National Wildlife Refuge, Dinosaur National Monument Utah: Ouray National Wildlife Refuge	New Mexico: Valles Caldera National Preserve	Utah: Bryce Canyon National Park, various colonies along State Highways 12 and 63

Sources: Most data for this table come from Hoogland, *Black-Tailed Social Life*, 1–562. See also Clark, "Ecology and Ethology," 1–97; Ceballos and Wilson, "*Cynomys mexicanus*," 1–3; Egoscue and Frank, "Burrowing and Denming Habits," 495–498; Goodwin, "Pliocene-Pleistocene Biogeographic History," 407–411; Harrison et al., "Phylogeny," 249–276; Haynie, et al., "Parentage, Multiple Paternity," 1244–1253; Hollister, "Systematic Account," 1–37; Hoogland, "Alarm Calling," 438–449; Hoogland, "Black-Tailed, Gunnison's," 917–927; Hoogland, "Sexual Dimorphism," 1254–1266; Hoogland, "Evolution of Coloniality," 252–272; Hoogland, "Why Do Gunnison's," 871–880; Hoogland, "Duration of Gestation," 173–180; Hoogland, "Why Do Female Gunnison's," 351–359; Hoogland, "Estrus and Copulation," 887–897; Hoogland, "Philopatry, Dispersal," 243–251; King, "Social Behavior"; Lehmer and Biggins, "Variation in Torpor Patterns," 15–21; Manno, "Utah Prairie Dogs Vigilant," 555–563; Merriam, "Prairie Dog," 257–270; Pizzimenti, "Evolution of the Prairie Dog," 1–73; Pizzimenti and McClenaghan, "Reproduction," 130–145; Pizzimenti and Collier, "*Cynomys parvidens*," 1–3; Rioja-Paradela, et al., "Reproduction and Behavior," 147–154; Scott-Morales, et al., "Continued Decline," 1095–1101; Treviño-Villarreal, "Annual Cycle," 1–27.

*The list of major public viewing areas is not meant to be comprehensive.

FIGURE 1.10. *Black and white.* In contrast to Utah prairie dogs, black-tailed prairie dogs, like these at the San Francisco Zoo, have black-tipped tails *(top)* and live in very structured family groups called coteries *(bottom).* See table 1 for the differences between a black-tailed prairie dog coterie and a Utah prairie dog clan.

FIGURE 1.11. *Zuni fetishes.* Native American tribes, like the Zuni in New Mexico, revere prairie dogs and reflect their ecological roles in oral tradition and artwork, such as these fetishes. Left (standing) carved by Sedrick Banteah from serpentine, 1.75 inches (about 4.5 cm) tall; right (all fours) carved by Dane Malani from Picasso marble, 0.625 inches (about 1.6 cm) tall. From Gathering Tribes Gallery, Albany, California.

the smallest teeth of any of the five species, the characteristic is neither prominent nor vital to their ability to survive. In addition, their teeth are no smaller in proportion to their skull than those of the other prairie dog species.[27]

Regardless of how the term "prairie dog" became ubiquitous among Western pioneers, homage should be paid to Native American tribes of the plains such as the Cheyenne, Comanche, Crow, Navajo, Pawnee, Paiute, Sioux, Ute, and Wichita, who knew about the interrelationships of various prairie dog species and their ecosystem long before European settlers came to North America.[28] Though not as entrenched in Native American mythology as animals like coyotes and foxes, prairie dogs were routinely revered in oral tradition, as several tribes sang to them or told legends with prairie dogs as characters (fig. 1.11).

The Navajo, whose reservation encompasses parts of eastern Utah, associated prairie dogs (or *ni'ch'osh*) with water. They told stories with coyotes, skunks (family Mephitidae), and other animals that cast prairie dogs as providers, and believed that prairie dog burrows helped connect to underground sources of water or that their vocalizations were a "cry for the rain."[29] Members of the Havasupai Tribe in present-day Arizona believed that women could conceive more easily if they consumed prairie dog meat, perhaps assuming that the rodents were prolific breeders.[30] The Ute people, who are the namesake of the state of Utah, had traditional music involving prairie dogs (or *tûn-uck*). In one of their songs

the prairie dogs and wildcats were all white. There was a prairie-dog [sic] man who wanted a wildcat

*woman to run away with him. At first she did not
like him, but afterwards she ran away with him.
Her mother did not want her to marry the prairie
dog because he did not hunt. Her mother wanted
her to marry the magpie, who hunted and got
rabbits from other animals. So the mother went and
took her daughter away from the prairie dog and
gave her to the magpie, who gave his mother-in-law
everything that he got in the hunt. They lived up in
the mountain. The mother-in-law told the prairie
dog that he was of no use because he lived in the
ground.*[31]

Certain Native American cultures also
hunted prairie dogs for food using bow and
arrow. Excavations of some ancient ruins,
most notably those of the Anasazi, have
yielded piles of prairie dog bones. Ethnolo-
gists hypothesize that prairie dogs, because
they were abundant and rich in protein, may
have provided secondary nutrition for certain
tribes during times of the year when primary
sources of nourishment, like bison, were
scarce. The roaming nature of game animals
like bison and deer (family Cervidae) may have
occasionally rendered stationary colonies of
prairie dogs as the only omnipresent source
of meat.[32]

Although these traditions had existed
for hundreds of years before, the first formal
scientific description of a prairie dog was not
written until 1815, when American naturalist
George Ord borrowed the Latin name for
marmots at the time and designated black-
tailed prairie dogs with the name *Arctomys
ludoviciana*.[33] Two years later, French zoologist
Constantine Samuel Rafinesque, who had
moved to Philadelphia at age 19, examined the
black-tailed prairie dog specimens brought
there by Lewis and Clark and coined the name
Cynomys, finding that prairie dog morphology
was distinct enough to delineate a separate
genus and species (*Cynomys socialis*, a now
defunct name) that differentiated prairie dogs
from marmots.[34] Meanwhile, as naturalist
Spencer F. Baird settled the conflict over these

two designations for black-tailed prairie dogs
by providing their current Latin name in 1858
(*Cynomys ludovicianus*),[35] Utah prairie dogs
waited for recognition. Despite an awareness
of prairie dogs in southern Utah by Paiutes
and by Mormons who settled there during
the nineteenth century, the Utah prairie dog
was not officially recorded as a distinct species
until described as *Cynomys parvidens* by mam-
malogist Joel Asaph Allen in 1905.[36]

Where Do Utah Prairie Dogs Live?

Historically, the range of the five species of
prairie dog collectively encompassed the entire
Intermountain West, starting in western
Canada and continuing south through twelve
states into northern Mexico.[37] Utah prairie
dogs, however, are specifically adapted to
the mixed-grass valleys of south-central and
southwestern Utah. As recently as 1920, they
inhabited the Pine and Buckskin Valleys in
Beaver and Iron Counties and were found as
far north as Nephi, south to Bryce Canyon, and
east to the Escalante and Aquarius Plateaus.[38]
Currently, substantial populations of Utah
prairie dogs are found only on the Awapa Plateau, along the East Fork of the Sevier River,
and in eastern Iron County (fig. 1.12). These
populations occur at elevations anywhere
between 5,500 and 9,500 feet (1700–3000 m).
Their presence in some of these locations is a
result of translocations into their historical
range. For instance, when Utah prairie dogs
were listed as threatened under the ESA, one
conservation strategy was to reintroduce
them to Bryce Canyon National Park (BCNP).
Then in 1992, Utah prairie dogs were trapped
within the park and transported to the Awapa
Plateau to establish another viable colony.[39]
Geographic ranges of the five prairie dog
species do not overlap. Consequently, anyone
can use the top row of table 1.1 to determine
the species of prairie dog that he or she is
observing from locality alone.[40]

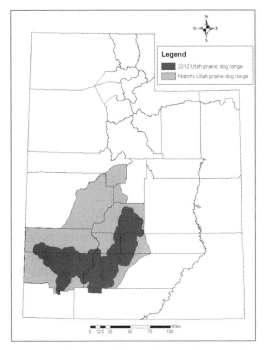

FIGURE 1.12. *Current and historical geographic range of the Utah prairie dog.* Utah prairie dogs are endemic to south-central and southwest Utah. Because of events over the last 150 years, Utah prairie dogs now inhabit only a small fraction of their former range. This map shows approximations for the current and historical ranges of the species. Data were obtained through a request under Utah's Government Records Access and Management Act. Artwork by Keith Day, courtesy of the Utah Division of Wildlife Resources (UDWR).

Life Underground

For all five species of prairie dog, burrows are among the most conspicuous features of a colony site. Many nineteenth-century survey-ors of the West were amazed by expanses of holes in the ground. Naturalist Josiah Gregg, for example, wrote about prairie dog burrows in *Commerce of the Prairies* (1844), an account of his time spent as a trader on the Santa Fe Trail from 1831 to 1840. Gregg compared the burrow-laden colonies of prairie dogs to human-built cities:

Of all the prairie animals, by far the most curious, and by no means the least celebrated, is the little

prairie dog . . . it was denominated the "barking squirrel," the "prairie ground-squirrel," etc., by early explorers, with much more apparent propriety than the present established name . . . a collection of their burrows has been termed by travelers a "dog town," which comprises from a dozen or so, to some thousands in the same vicinity; often covering an area of several square miles . . . approaching a "vil-lage," the little dogs may be observed frisking about the "streets"—passing from dwelling to dwelling apparently on visits—sometimes a few clustered together as though in council—here feeding upon the tender herbage—there cleansing their "houses," or brushing the little hillock about the door—yet all quiet. Upon seeing a stranger, however, each streaks it to its home, but is apt to stop at the entrance, and spread the general alarm by a succession of shrill yelps, usually sitting erect. Yet at the report of a gun or the too near approach of the visitor, they dart down and are seen no more till the cause of alarm seems to have disappeared.[41]

Burrows are integral to everyday life, and prairie dogs spend over half of their time underground. Some of the importance of bur-rows stems from their use as a rodent subway system. Burrows interconnect to create large systems of underground tunnels, with large burrows usually having several entrances. Many people assume that each prairie dog has his or her own personal burrow, but this is not the case.[42]

Almost all burrows can provide escape from a predatory attack or bad weather. But while they might look similar, burrows can have different purposes. Some burrows are nurseries that females use for rearing pups, and other burrows are used specifically for spending the night. When bad weather comes, most prairie dogs submerge in a nursery burrow, but any nearby burrow becomes a hideaway when a predator strikes.[43]

Both sexes assist in the construction and maintenance of burrows throughout the entire year. Most burrows have some sort of mound at the aboveground entrance,

FIGURE 1.13. *Digging in the dirt*. A Utah prairie dog burrow with a mound at the entrance.

FIGURE 1.14. *Low to the ground*. A Utah prairie dog burrow without a mound at the entrance.

although Utah prairie dog burrows are never surrounded by the "rim craters" that black-tailed prairie dogs and Mexican prairie dogs sometimes assemble (table 1.1). A dome-shaped mound of dirt helps prevent flooding after a rainstorm and improves ventilation underground. Prairie dogs also run to the high mounds to scan for predators. Some burrows do not have a mound, but prairie dogs can still use them to escape a sudden attack (figs. 1.13 and 1.14).[44]

Especially after a rainstorm, when the soil is moist, prairie dogs of all species will reshape the mounds on top of burrows by digging inside the hole, shoveling the soil to the outside with their front and rear paws, and pounding the soil with their noses (fig. 1.15a–b). Humans who observe prairie

FIGURE 1.15. *Construction work*. Utah prairie dogs construct burrows by using their front *(top)* or rear *(bottom)* legs for digging and shoveling soil.

FIGURE 1.16. *Prairie pancake*. Sunbathing Utah prairie dogs are amusing to both scientists and tourists.

dogs working on their mounds are often amused, as the animals seem so intent on conducting the task and get dirty faces and feet.

Utah prairie dogs also use burrows for hibernation, a state of deep sleep that they enter during winter to conserve energy. Reproductive males and nonreproductive individuals of both sexes begin to hibernate first. Females that have weaned a litter and have been busy taking care of their pups take the much-needed opportunity to feed on lush grasses before entering hibernation later than other adults. Juveniles enter hibernation last. Although the three species of prairie dog with white-tipped tails hibernate during the coldest months of the year,[45] black-tailed prairie dogs and their closest relatives, Mexican prairie dogs, sleep often and eat little during these months but do not enter full hibernation (table 1.1).[46]

The amount of aboveground activity exhibited by Utah prairie dogs is affected by day length, season, and temperature. When the weather is cool, they appear aboveground for the day later and submerge for the night earlier. When the weather is warm, Utah prairie dogs spend more time aboveground, emerging earlier in the morning and submerging later in the evening. They seem to enjoy warmth but not excessive heat, typically retreating to a burrow to cool down if it becomes hot during midday. Balmy weather sometimes gives Utah prairie dogs a chance to sunbathe while lying flat on top of their burrow mounds. A "prairie pancake" is amusing in every way (fig. 1.16).

What's for Lunch?

Utah prairie dogs feed on grasses and grasslike plants. Most foraging occurs in or near the colony site once the snow has melted, around mid-April (fig. 1.17). They walk purposefully and bob their heads up and down to look for predators while chewing.[47] After Utah prairie dogs emerge from their burrows in the

FIGURE 1.17. *Eat up.* When the warmth of spring and summer arrives, Utah prairie dogs munch on grasses.

morning, they often range farther away from the area as the day goes on.

Favorite foods of Utah prairie dogs during the spring and summer include buffalo grass (*Bouteloua dactyloides*), rabbitbrush (genus *Chrysothamnus*, *Ericameria*, or *Lorandersonia*), and sagebrush (*Artemisia tridentata*). In addition to grasses, Utah prairie dogs occasionally eat insects, flowers, seeds, fruit, or carrion.[48] They also seem to enjoy the grass-containing scats or "patties" of animals like horses (*Equus ferus caballus*) and cattle. Although it is rare, we have seen Utah prairie dogs killing and eating smaller ground squirrels, or cannibalizing other Utah prairie dogs after roadkills or infanticides. Utah prairie dogs probably acquire most of the water they need from their food, or from dew on plants at dawn, because usually no obvious source of water is present at a colony site.

During the summer, Utah prairie dogs begin the process of improving their general physical condition and accumulating fat reserves, both of which are crucial for over-winter survival. Winters in Utah are brutal, so Utah prairie dogs prepare by becoming quite pudgy just before the onset of hibernation.[49] Upon emergence from hibernation the following March, Utah prairie dogs often awake to a bleak, snow-covered, unforgiving landscape with limited foraging opportunities in which to find mates (fig. 1.18).

Biology and Conservation

The steady annihilation of prairie dogs after Western settlement nearly wiped out all five species. But prairie dogs continue to grace America's valleys, oblivious to the controversy that surrounds them. Ernest Thompson Seton said it best in his 1913 work *Wild Animals at Home*:

Poor helpless little [prairie dog], he has no friends; his enemies and his list of burdens increase. The prey of everything that preys, he yet seems incapable of any measure of retaliation. The only visible joy in his life is his daily hasty meal of unsucculent grass, gathered between cautious looks around for any new approaching trouble . . .

Could any simpler, smaller pleasure than his be discovered? Yet he is fat and merry; undoubtedly he enjoys his every day on earth, and is as unwilling as any of us to end the tale. We can explain him only if we credit him with a philosophic power to discover happiness within in spite of all the cold unfriendly world about him.[50]

Because many people have regarded them as pests, prairie dogs of all species have been killed using every method imaginable over the last 150 years.[51] By 1900, Texas had become the first state to organize prairie dog annihilation efforts, and by the 1920s, federal poisoning programs were operational in every state with

FIGURE 1.18. *Closed for the winter.* Utah prairie dogs emerge from hibernation in March but often awake to a barren, snow-covered meadow with little opportunity to feed.

prairie dogs.[52] Although fewer are present to eliminate nowadays, prairie dogs that are not protected by the ESA are still exterminated legally via recreational shooting; poisons like Kaput-D, Rozol, and zinc phosphide; various fumigants and gases; explosive devices; and other tactics.[53] Such exterminations of Utah prairie dogs, now listed as threatened by the USFWS, are illegal and have been since the species was federally listed as endangered in 1973.[54]

Current threats to Utah prairie dogs include habitat destruction and modification, development and urbanization, geological exploration, vehicles, and poaching (namely, illegal shooting or poisoning).[55] Bubonic plague (*Yersinia pestis*), which can be carried by fleas (order Siphonaptera) living in the depths of a prairie dog's pelage, is also a significant threat to the long-term persistence of all five species of prairie dog. Because fleas are

mobile, plague can threaten even Utah prairie dogs that enjoy the protection offered by a national park. Because its virulence is usually exacerbated by the constant physical contact of socializing prairie dogs, plague can wipe out large colonies quickly, with death rates of up to 95–100 percent.[56]

Declaring the Utah prairie dog a keystone species will likely be crucial for efforts to spare it from these threats. A keystone species has a unique, significant, and disproportionately large impact on its ecosystem, meaning that ecological interactions in an area might collapse if the species were to disappear.[57] The term was originally applied to black-tailed prairie dogs, but an increasing number of scientists, including the author, think that the Utah prairie dog is also a keystone species.[58]

Consider that Utah prairie dogs are prey for animals such as northern goshawks

(*Accipiter gentilis*), red foxes (*Vulpes vulpes*), and red-tailed hawks (*Buteo jamaicensis*). Like those of their black-tailed counterparts, Utah prairie dog burrows and colony sites provide shelter and nesting habitat for myriad other animals such as American badgers, long-tailed weasels (*Mustela frenata*), and hundreds of insect and arachnid species (fig. 1.19a–b). And, Utah prairie dogs likely offer many of the same benefits to plant communities that black-tailed prairie dogs do, such as aerating the soil, controlling noxious weeds or native invaders, and mixing nutrients between subsoil and topsoil through burrowing.[59]

Because of their ecological importance, efforts to save Utah prairie dogs from extinction are numerous and varied. These efforts range from translocating colonies, to killing fleas by applying powder to individuals and their burrows, to restoring appropriate habitat, to controversial arrangements that allow ranchers and developers to kill Utah prairie dogs on their property if mitigated with contributions that help Utah prairie dogs elsewhere.[60]

Continued progress in the management and conservation of Utah prairie dogs and their grassland ecosystem will require thorough knowledge of their biology. But despite the central role of biology in conservation, it was years following the ESA listing of Utah prairie dogs as threatened in 1984 before we knew much about their ecology and social behavior.

For example, it was only a dozen years ago when many assumed that Utah prairie dogs were prolific breeders with rapidly expanding colonies. That way of thinking is slowly changing, because John Hoogland has documented that only about two-thirds of females wean a litter each year, that the most common litter sizes at weaning are only four or five pups, and that less than half of those juveniles will survive until the next year. Even under ideal natural conditions, a female Utah prairie dog can carry and wean only one litter per year.[61] Furthermore, colonies do not necessarily become larger each year, and under natural conditions, population crashes often follow population explosions.[62]

This new framework of slow reproduction reveals other particulars of the breeding system. Within colonies, Utah prairie dogs live in family groups called clans that consist of closely related females who defend a common territory that persists across many generations. Each clan is usually dominated by a different reproductive male every year. This "resident" male usually mates with the females as they become sexually receptive (fig. 1.20).[63]

Males usually change territories shortly after emerging from hibernation in early March. Establishing residence in a territory with females during this time is crucial to male reproductive success. Thus, despite the bitter cold in March, males are driven to battle for glory in five-foot (1.5 m) snowdrifts with no dependable supply of grasses on which to feed. Fights between males and a flurry of courtship behaviors during this period result in a spectacle called "mating season," which lasts for two to three weeks and was the highlight of our year while we were studying them.[64]

Once the last female has copulated, mating season is over, and subsequent portions of the reproductive cycle are based on female behaviors such as gestation (pregnancy), lactation (nursing), and weaning. Because all of the days of sexual receptivity in the colony are scattered across a two- to three-week period, these intervals overlap among females. Some females are pregnant while others have not yet copulated, for example.[65] But for the most part, from early April through the beginning of May, females have a period of gestation that usually lasts 28, 29, or 30 days.[66]

In early to mid-May, pups are born underground and females start nursing, which will last about five weeks. It is during this time that, for reasons that remain unclear, pups are sometimes victims of infanticide by marauding males from the home or adjacent territories.[67] If they survive the risk of infanticide,

FIGURE 1.19. *Allies of a keystone species*. Utah prairie dog colonies provide homes for many other animals, including this chipmunk *(top)* that lived at our study colony in 2005. Grazing animals such as pronghorn *(bottom)* are also spotted as they enjoy grasses that are maintained by the digging activities of Utah prairie dogs.

FIGURE 1.20. *All in the family*. Utah prairie dogs live in clans of related females that interact amicably and are associated with a different reproductive male each year. These four female clan mates are close relatives and have just emerged from hibernation out of the same burrow.

pups begin to emerge from their natal burrows in mid-June, and they are weaned about one to two weeks afterward. By the end of June or the first week of July, the yearly reproductive cycle has ended. Facing a dangerous trifecta of extreme weather, predation, and competition for food and resources, young Utah prairie dogs are lucky to survive until their first mating season.

Utah prairie dogs eat grass fervently while they have the opportunity during the summer. Nature waits for no one, and when winter comes to a mile-and-a-half-high meadow, there is no turning back. Activity ceases dramatically, and soon it becomes hard to believe that the area used to be a big city of around one hundred busy rodents. One day, they are everywhere. The next, a few dozen remain, and the next, only a few. Another winter passes, and in March, the meadow is once again teeming with Utah prairie dogs.

While Utah prairie dogs were in their burrows hibernating, John Hoogland was recruiting field assistants who would help him study the rodents upon their emergence in March. After responding to an advertisement for the 2004 Prairie Dog Squad he sent me in December 2003, I received an e-mail containing a description of his field research and information on prairie dog behavior. At first glance, Utah prairie dogs seemed to live peacefully in utopian family groups. But then came accounts of their shocking "misconduct."

Cuckoldry. Deceit. Promiscuity. Infanticide. Burglary.

Murder.

Also enclosed was a file containing what John callously refers to as "The Scare Letter." Because of the rigors of field research, John made his expectations clear early in the recruitment process:

December 20, 2003

Hi Theo:[68]

I thank you for your interest in serving as an assistant for my 2004 research on Utah prairie dogs. Our most important objectives will be to decipher (a) why females that mate with two or more males wean larger litters than females that mate with only one male, (b) why males kill and cannibalize offspring of females with whom they mated, (c) which individuals give alarm calls in response to real and simulated predators, and (d) why mothers nurse the offspring of other mothers.

Below I discuss various critical issues that might influence your decision to join the Prairie Dog Squad.

1) There is no salary for research assistants. Students therefore should consider helping me for reasons other than financial. Research assistants usually are undergraduates or recent graduates who are considering M.S. or Ph.D. research. Unless a research assistant is fervent about behavioral ecology, he or she will not be properly motivated. If the adventure is not worthwhile for you, then it is not worthwhile for me either.

2) While helping with my research, you and three other students will stay in a mobile home about 7 miles [11 km] from our study colony and about 100 yards [91 m] from my wife's and my mobile home. Your food expenses will depend on how you eat, but should average about $30–$35 per week.

3) In 2004, I will be at Bryce from March 3rd through July 20th. I am especially interested in research assistants who can stay for this entire time, but might consider students who can stay for only part of the field season.

4) Since I started my study of prairie dogs 35 years ago, I have had 160 different research assistants. Upon departure, most students have echoed the same theme: "I never worked so hard in my life." Another common theme in March and April is "I have never been so cold in all my life." Occasionally we will work 15-hour days, and

sometimes we will work for 30 or 40 consecutive days. The physical labor on any particular day usually is not overwhelming, but the string of 30–40 consecutive days greatly tests one's endurance and commitment.

5) One lazy or whining research assistant is worse than no helper at all. I am running neither a reformatory nor a babysitting service, and therefore will dismiss indolent, shiftless, contumacious, or complaining research assistants.

6) While working with me, a student might learn that he or she never again wants to do field research. But this can be a valuable lesson, indeed, for an undergraduate or recent graduate. Alternatively, a student might learn, as several of my previous students have learned, that field research is exactly the type of work that he or she wants to pursue.

7) I do not consider research assistants to be slaves. I will involve you with the research as much as I can, and will give you as much responsibility as you can handle. Usually you will be doing the same things that I also am doing or already have done.

8) Students will start working at a colony of approximately 100 prairie dogs of known ages and genealogies. All techniques for marking and handling the prairie dogs have already been worked out, and the hypotheses to be tested are clearly defined. For the appropriate person, assisting on the Dog Squad is a unique and superlative opportunity that you will never forget. Just ask some of my former research assistants, several of whom have recently co-authored publications with me.

9) One of my research assistants once remarked: "Ya know, John, one thing that I like about your style is that you never let any of your students work harder than you." My style has not changed: if you come to Utah, you will never work harder or longer than I do. The reason is simple: I love what I do.

10) In approximately one-half of my field seasons, one of my research assistants has been on the verge of departure because the work was too demanding. When I asked

the indecisive students to reread the letter similar to this one, each agreed that all of the conditions of the research had been clearly and fairly explained. Some of the wavering assistants went home, others stayed. Thus, please read this letter carefully! More than anything else, studying prairie dogs will involve hard work—often in freezing weather. Note especially that we, like the prairie dogs, will work every day regardless of conditions.

The purpose of this letter is to encourage students who are passionate about behavioral ecology, and to dissuade everybody else. I want you to know exactly what to expect. If you have a good reason for wanting to do field research, and are fully aware of what lies ahead, then I encourage you to contact me soon.

Enclosed also are e-mail addresses of several of my recent research assistants. I strongly encourage you to communicate with some of them before making a final decision. That's the best way to get answers to your questions about me, my research, and the Prairie Dog Squad.

Are you up to the challenge of prairie dogs in Utah next spring? I hope so. If you are, or if you have any remaining questions before making a decision, please contact me at your first convenience.

Cordially,

John L. Hoogland
University of Maryland Appalachian Laboratory

"Prairie dog research. It's not a job—it's an ADVENTURE."

Was I up to the challenge of the Dog Squad?
Of course I was. It was time for an ADVENTURE.

2

Dog Squad

Teamwork divides the task and multiplies the success.
—Author unknown

☾

*The central feature of Bryce Canyon National Park (BCNP) is the so-called canyon,
which is technically a misnomer because it was not initiated from a stream. Instead,
horseshoe-shaped amphitheaters have been carved by frost and rainwater, creating a
landscape of colorful mazes.*

*The hallmarks of these labyrinths are hoodoos, which are spires composed of soft
sedimentary rock (figs. 2.1 and 2.2).[1] BCNP has one of the highest concentrations of
hoodoos anywhere, and these red rocks are so salient that the Paiute Indians have a
mythology surrounding them. They believe that the hoodoos (or* Anka-ku-was-a-wits,
*a Paiute phrase meaning "red painted faces") are a group of ancient inhabitants called
Legend People whom Coyote turned to stone.[2]*

*White people did not explore the area until late in the eighteenth century. One of the
pioneers was Ebenezer Bryce, a Scottish immigrant and Mormon convert, who came to
the nearby Paria Valley with his wife, Mary. The Latter-day Saints encouraged Bryce's
residence there because of his useful carpentry skills, and as infrastructure developed,
other Mormon settlers came to the valley and used the area for cattle grazing. Bryce and
his compatriots completed a seven-mile-long (over 11 km) irrigation ditch, and when a
water shortage limited irrigation, settlers diverted water from the nearby Sevier River.
The resulting canal provided the foundation for a new town site, Tropic, which became
the most notable Utah settlement east of present-day Bryce Canyon.[3]*

*Despite Bryce's best efforts, the area around the canyon remains relatively uninhab-
ited because it is surrounded by federal or state land. In the distance, visitors can observe
the Kaibab Plateau in Arizona, and occasionally, the Black Mesas in western New Mexico over 200 miles (320 km) away. When the sun sets, the transparent sky is among the
clearest in North America, allowing stargazers to observe heavenly bodies that they never
knew existed. Thousands of people attend the annual Bryce Canyon Astronomy Festival,
and full-moon hikes and astronomy-related events continue throughout most of the year.[4]*

*While the American Southwest has experienced a population boom during the last
150 years, southern Utah's scarcity of water and three-to-one ratio of public to private
land continue to restrict human development. Consequently, the environment has not
changed much compared to areas like Cedar City, Saint George, and Salt Lake City.[5] For
years, the lowest areas of BCNP have been dominated by small trees like aspen (Populus*

tremuloides), desert bitterbrush (Purshia glandulosa), cottonwood (genus Populus, section Aigeiros), water birch (Betula occidentalis), and willow (genus Salix), and higher areas have larger trees such as ponderosa pine (Pinus ponderosa) and Great Basin bristlecone (Pinus longaeva). Some of these latter trees are ecological treasures, thought to be over 1,600 years old.[6]

Portions of BCNP are over 8,000 feet (2438 m) in elevation, resulting in cooler weather with more precipitation than in nearby regions. Summers are short and mild, while winters are long, snowy, and cold. Frozen precipitation can occur during any month of the year. Massive snowdrifts, some as deep as five feet (1.5 m), remain on the ground from December until spring in some years.[7] *In March, Utah prairie dogs emerge from hibernation and usually step into a barren, snow-covered landscape that has little food.*

They are not the only mammals to venture into these frozen conditions. On the frigid first day of the 2004 field season, John Hoogland bounces out of his trailer in tattered, ink-stained blue jeans with a banana in one hand and several clipboards in the other. He is wearing several layers of shirts and socks that are covered in black stains. He begins handing out data sheets and tower assignments.

"Mornin', everyone," he says. "It's a cold one out there. Welcome to the Dog Squad."

FIGURE 2.1. *Red rocks.* Bryce Canyon features an amphitheater, a spectacular site carved over the course of millions of years by frost and rainwater.

FIGURE 2.2. *Standing tall*. Bryce Canyon is known far and wide for its pointed rock structures known as hoodoos.

Near the red rocks of Bryce Canyon lies the study colony, one of the few protected prairie dog colonies in Utah. It contained about 100 individuals during our research and was complemented with excellent wildlife viewing and nearby grasslands (fig. 2.3). The Utah prairie dog is my favorite mammal at BCNP, of course, but almost five dozen others, including the American badger, coyote, elk (*Cervus canadensis*), mule deer (*Odocoileus hemionus*), pronghorn (*Antilocapra americana*), and red fox, call BCNP home. I also enjoy BCNP's 170 bird species, most of which visit during the spring and summer months—especially the mountain bluebird (*Sialia currucoides*) and the western tanager (*Piranga ludoviciana*; fig. 2.4).[8]

Utah prairie dogs were a fun animal to study. Besides their scientific interest and their need for biologists to tell their story, their diurnality and adherence to a schedule that vaguely resembled orthodox working hours were convenient. Further, their coloniality allowed us to hunker down and watch them once we knew their location, rather than expend energy trying to find them each morning before we observed their behavior.

So that we could reference areas of the study colony quickly, John delineated sections named for the person observing from the tower in that area (e.g., John's tower, Theo's tower). Other named areas included the North Pole and South Pole, at the extreme northern and southern ends of the colony, respectively. Whatever area was assigned to a Dog Squad member became his or her home for the next four months.

Living among Them

From the beginning of March to the end of June, the Dog Squad occupied two mobile homes in a complex at the junction of Utah State Routes 12 and 63. One was for research assistants, and the other was for John and his family (his wife and four children). The mobile homes each had a small kitchen, living room, two bedrooms, and a bathroom. Running water and electricity were available, and we could even set up internet access and television. But because field research was so demanding, assistants typically opted for the former but not the latter. Dog Squad members usually had about five days off during the four and a half months of study.

John jokingly called the area "metropolitan Bryce," but the town, or what passed for it, had a population of only a few hundred people. It was a great jumping-off point to see classic southwestern scenery like Arches National Park, or to travel to Las Vegas, Salt Lake City, or Arizona, but overall we were quite isolated during the dog days of field season. Most "going out" during our paltry

FIGURE 2.3. *Grasslands*. Rock formations are popular with visitors to southern Utah, but the area's grasslands are just as scenic.

FIGURE 2.4. *Bird on a wire*. Mountain bluebirds are among my favorite animals at BCNP.

free time revolved around the nearby hotel a mile down the road, which offered limited services for locals, such as post office boxes, gasoline, a small grocery store, a gift shop and bookstore, a few community events, and most importantly, a Western-style buffet with discounts for area residents.

A special treat came every so often when hotel personnel placed a television in the lobby and broadcast basketball games played by the University of Utah Utes. The nearest towns with other services like barbers, chain restaurants, electronics, libraries, and mechanics were Panguitch (a 30-minute drive) and Cedar City (a 90-minute drive that John's wife, Judy, made weekly to pick up bulk groceries for the team). Cell phone reception at the field site and in the mobile home was sporadic, but luckily we could receive some radio stations from our observation towers. This nominal entertainment sometimes helped us get through a long day of waiting to see whether an infanticide would occur.

Our daily routine included bumbling down a single-lane highway to the park in the aptly named "Squad Car," which barely started each morning and transported us to and from the site. We then assumed our positions in nine-foot-high (3 m) observation towers before the study subjects appeared aboveground in the early morning. The towers were like little wooden offices, but without amenities like furniture and internet access (fig. 2.5a–b).

Attributes of the towers included a make-shift ledge on which to put pens and mementos, large Plexiglas windows that allowed us to see Utah prairie dogs while protecting us against wind and other bad weather, and a public school–type desk-chair. The ledge also held our walkie-talkies, which enabled us to communicate between towers. Climbing up into the tower could be a hassle, especially with cold-weather gear and other materials secured on one's back (fig. 2.6).

We remained at the colony holding vigil until the last Utah prairie dog submerged for the night.[9] The exact timing of our arrival and departure varied with many factors. For instance, on cold days in March, the first Utah prairie dog sometimes did not emerge from its burrow until 9–10 a.m., but in the middle of June, Utah prairie dogs often appeared aboveground before 6:30 a.m.

At least three people were at the colony from dawn to dusk every day from early March until we captured the last juvenile in early July. This schedule meant that we practically lived with Utah prairie dogs and thought of hardly anything else for four months. Dog Squad members had little life outside of watching Utah prairie dogs.

FIGURE 2.5. *Before and after*. John's tower at the field site under a six-foot snowdrift in March *(top)* and after the snow melted in May *(bottom)*.

Keeping Records

When people hear of my involvement with the Dog Squad, they understandably have questions, which usually go something like this:

Why in the world would you sit in freezing weather for twelve hours consecutively to follow the sex lives of rodents? You seem like an otherwise rational, normal person. How are you not bored into submission? Don't you get cold?

These are legitimate questions, but what many laypeople do not realize is that the

FIGURE 2.6. *Tree house*. Climbing into the observation towers was not an easy task.

antics of Utah prairie dogs are so remarkable that we were almost never fed up with surveying them. We also had a tremendous amount of data to record, which kept us busy.[10]

The first and last pieces of data we took every day identified the burrow from which each individual emerged in the morning and into which it submerged at night. These seemingly trivial details were actually important. One of the best ways to verify that Utah prairie dogs belonged to the same family group was to see whether they used the same burrow system at night. We could link mothers with offspring by verifying that females consistently spent the night in a burrow from which juveniles later emerged (fig. 2.7). Similarly, a change in the maternal pattern of burrow usage usually indicated that the mother had lost her litter to infanticide, spontaneous abortion, or predation.

Burrow submergences during the day were also important to record. Copulations occasionally occurred before a male and female emerged from the same burrow in the morning or after they submerged together for the night, and the only way to document these copulations was to record first emergences and final submergences. An unusually early final submergence at the end of the day by a male and female together was a good indicator of underground copulation, as was an abnormally late first emergence in the morning of a male and female together. And 28–30 days after a female copulated, an unusually early final submergence often meant she would give birth in her burrow the next day, while an unusually late first emergence often meant that she had just given birth.

In addition to daily emergences and submergences, one of our most important tools was the "missing male list" (MML). The list, contrary to its name, actually listed all males and females near our observation towers. Every 20 minutes, we marked off each

FIGURE 2.7. *Taking notes.* An assistant records the linkage of a captured Utah prairie dog pup to its mother as the pup is initiated into the study. The mother had been sleeping for weeks in the burrow from which the pup subsequently emerged.

individual as we located him or her during our check. Because Utah prairie dogs almost never submerge into a burrow after "waking up" except during inclement or hot weather, or when a predator enters the colony, or when they are taking nest material underground, an individual's absence during a check made us suspicious that an underground mating was occurring.

On the way back home in the Squad Car, we analyzed the results of our MMLs and discussed which females had already experienced their single annual day of estrus (sexual receptivity) and which ones were still "hot"—in other words, which ones had not yet mated. The nightly process was essentially detective work. MMLs combined with our other notes

allowed us to determine when a missing pair might have been mating underground. In the same manner, MMLs also helped us determine the whereabouts of all individuals when an infanticide took place by providing a list of possible suspects.

When we were not completing MMLs, our objective was simple—to be "dogged" observers of everything else. We recorded every social interaction that we observed, such as a kiss, sniff, chase, or territorial dispute. To study all calls and predations by enemies such as American badgers, northern goshawks, red foxes, and golden eagles, we recorded the time and place that any potential predator entered the colony. We also conducted experiments to obtain data on antipredator alarm calls and other reactions in response to American badgers stuffed in lifelike poses.

Don't Badger Me

"Chubs," one of our mounted American badgers, took pleasure in scaring Utah prairie dogs.[11] His services allowed us to obtain larger sample sizes for our study of antipredator calls than we would have obtained from natural predators alone, and to improve the scientific meaning of our data by controlling the level of (simulated) danger to Utah prairie dogs (figure 2.8a–b).

Chubs started his "attacks" covered by a black plastic bag beyond the outermost peripheral burrow mounds in the colony, attached to a fishing wire wound around a garden hose reel in an observation tower. When an assistant pulled Chubs through the colony at a rate of eight inches (20 cm) per second, some Utah prairie dogs ran and stood atop their burrow mounds to look for danger; some ran to their burrows and submerged; others emitted an alarm call that sounded like a series of "clicks" to warn nearby Utah prairie dogs; and a small number looked up briefly and went back to foraging.

FIGURE 2.8. *Mad as a badger*. Our aptly named colleague, "Chubs," in all his glory *(left)*. When attached to a long wire and rolled from an inconspicuous area outside a clan of Utah prairie dogs *(right)*, Chubs launched a simulated attack that helped us acquire data on antipredator behavior.

We carefully recorded whatever each Utah prairie dog did when Chubs moved through the home territory of its clan. Specifically, we recorded the identity of individuals that called or did not call, where each individual was located, and how long each call lasted. With this protocol, we were able to generate large sample sizes for our study of alarm calling.

Trapping, Marking, and Handling

John's motto was "Trap 'em, mark 'em, watch 'em." Almost every day, we livetrapped Utah prairie dogs that needed to be marked, weighed, have their reproductive status established, or have blood taken. We often started our day by setting hundreds of live traps, and our objective was to capture every individual in the colony at least twice per

year. Utah prairie dogs liked whole oats, so we would place a live trap containing that bait around a burrow entrance, which was marked with a jumbo yellow cattle ear tag mounted on 16 inches (40 cm) of clothesline wire. All we needed to do was open the trap, toss in a few oats, and away we went (fig. 2.9).

Most individuals obliged within about half an hour of seeing one or two of these arrangements and were rewarded handsomely with the oats. But some uncooperative members of the colony needed extra convincing. When that was the case, one of us walked toward the individual, noted the burrow where it submerged, and surrounded it with traps while stuffing nearby burrows with orange construction cones. This cat-and-prairie-dog game could continue for hours, and sometimes days, if the runaway dug under the traps instead of entering them, climbed over the surrounding

FIGURE 2.9. *Casting a wide net*. Our days often started by setting hundred of traps.

traps, or simply stayed in the surrounded burrow to avoid the traps.

Juvenile Utah prairie dogs, called pups, which John named with their mother's number followed by an X (e.g., 75X, 98X), were also "squirrelly" when it came to livetrapping. To ensure that we recorded them with the appropriate mother, we had the additional hassle of capturing pups at the nursery burrow before they moved to another location. Pups did not care for oats, so without bait, we completely surrounded the natal burrow with dozens of traps on the same day or the day after the pups first emerged. Again, we also stuffed or surrounded all burrow entrances we knew were connected to that natal burrow, so the pups had no place to go aboveground except into one of the traps— at least in theory (fig. 2.10).[12]

Sometimes it was as if mothers had explained to their pups what the traps were

and how to avoid them. I could just imagine a mother talking to her pups in the burrow: "When you go aboveground, you'll see these metal rectangle things—don't go in them." It was not unusual to endure long sequences of walking toward an errant pup and resurrounding and restuffing again and again until the furry escapee was mercifully captured.

It was also commonplace for a mother to serve as an accomplice to a juvenile's escape from our trapping matrix. On many occasions a mother climbed over the surrounding traps, grabbed the pup by the scruff of its neck, and dragged it over the surrounding traps to apparent freedom. We even saw mothers transfer their pups into a burrow that contained other pups we had not yet trapped, thereby ruining our efforts to identify them as their mother's offspring.

When a furry fugitive was finally captured, we always followed John's cardinal

FIGURE 2.10. *Surrounded*. Utah prairie dog pups were quite elusive, so we surrounded them with traps not long after they emerged from their natal burrow to ensure their capture.

FIGURE 2.11. *Cardinal rule*. The cardinal rule of trapping is to always place a label with the location of capture on the handle before moving the trap elsewhere.

rule of livetrapping: before picking up or moving a live trap with a Utah prairie dog inside, we would label the trap with a flag that indicated the site of capture. This tedious but important task ensured that an adult was returned to its clan territory, or a pup was returned to its natal burrow (fig. 2.11).

The proclivity of individuals to enter live traps varied widely and was a common topic of

discussion among the Dog Squad. Most individuals were easier to livetrap after they had experienced traps a few times. In fact, every year some became so trap-happy that they would exit their home clan territories in search of oats, interfering with our trapping setups in other territories. On the other hand, some individuals became more difficult to trap over time. Either way, we kept oats in a bucket that was elevated on a hook attached to the tower. Oataholics tended to jump into the buffet of tasty treats if we kept the bucket on the ground, almost like a child jumping into a bathtub full of candy.

It was exasperating to witness uncooperative individuals escaping from surroundings, jumping on traps and closing them, and digging under cones used for stuffing burrows. The exploits of these emboldened rapscallions could wreak havoc on our trapping strategies. It was a routine occurrence, for instance, for us to set traps every morning for a week or more in an effort to capture a "shy" individual. While we waited for our target individual, trap-happy oat lovers repeatedly became ensnared, occupying our matrix until it was apparent that the individual we hoped to trap would not appear. At this point, we were forced to emancipate those who were caught and shut down the traps. We would return to our towers, and then, as if to taunt us, the untrapped bugger would emerge, take a look around, and be on its way. Unbelievable!

What makes one individual bold and another shy we will never know. Likewise, we will never determine why some absconders escaped nine surroundings, only to be captured shortly thereafter by the tenth. Or, why the same scofflaw was caught easily sometimes but was unrepentantly elusive at other times. But somehow, some way, we captured every individual at least once, and usually at least twice, per year.

Once we trapped a Utah prairie dog, we moved it to the infamous Dog Squad Van, an ancient artifact with an archaic vanity license plate appropriately labeled *Cynomys*—the Latin genus of prairie dogs (fig. 2.12). The van was only vaguely drivable but was nevertheless handily equipped for the data-taking process. This confiscation allowed us to mark Utah prairie dogs in a laboratory setup without disturbing other trapping efforts, and also to sequester the trapee in the confines of the van. Without this system, individuals might not find their way back home if they escaped during handling, an accident that occurred once or twice per year.

Capture was followed by a line of Dog Squad spoken code that delineated the location, the identity of the caught individual, and the logistics of when or where to handle and mark the detainee (figs. 2.13 and 2.14).

"Got the baby?" asks Theo.

"Roger that, I've got the baby at Y21 from Female-69. Someone meet me at the van to mark, please."

"10-4, John, I'll help mark the 69X."

In the van "laboratory," we prodded adults out of the trap and into a conical canvas bag that could be unzipped from either end. Some captives remained in the trap, probably averse to enduring a complicated 10-minute procedure. John would explain to these uncooperative individuals that the marker would make them look pretty as well as make them famous. After hearing this rationale and being nudged repeatedly with a paintbrush, tentative subjects usually became resigned to getting it over with. We then unzipped the wide end of the bag to reveal the rear legs and body. From this position, we were able to count the number of fleas the animal harbored as well as the number of scars it had (fig. 2.15). The canvas bag was not necessary for pups, which we held with gloves and placed into a plastic sandwich bag with a few cut-out breathing holes for weighing (fig. 2.16a–b).

While handling each adult or juvenile, John collected six or seven capillary tubes of blood for genetic analysis so that the complete genealogy of the colony could be determined. This procedure involved clipping the tip of a toenail of our study subject, a procedure that

FIGURE 2.12. *Cynomys*. A vanity license plate like no other.

FIGURE 2.13. *Success*. Some days of trapping were more productive than others. On occasion, six Utah prairie dogs would be taken back to the Squad Van at one time.

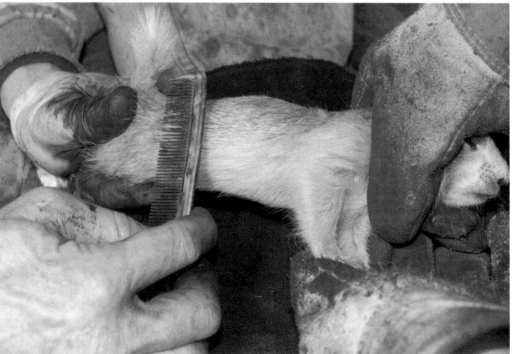

FIGURE 2.14. *Two by two*. Every so often, Utah prairie dogs pulled a "Noah's Ark" by becoming ensnared in the same trap.

FIGURE 2.15. *Flea bath*. A yearling is brushed to determine the number of fleas in its fur.

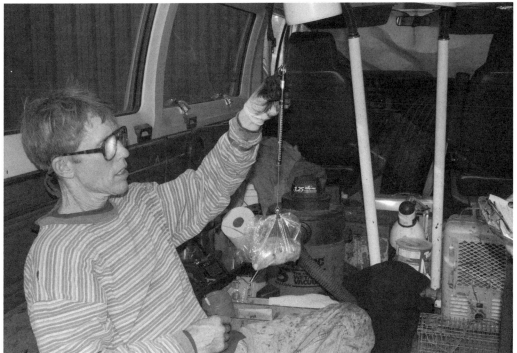

FIGURE 2.16. *Weigh-in*. A pup is placed into a plastic bag, attached to a spring balance *(top)*, and weighed *(bottom)*.

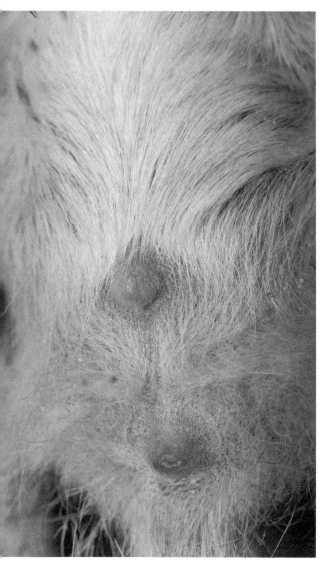

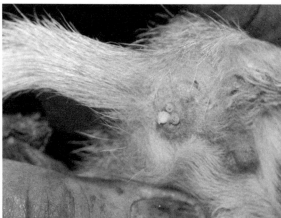

FIGURE 2.17. *Private parts.* Male genitalia with the penis and anus farther apart *(far left)* than female genitalia *(top)*. Utah prairie dogs also had three glands on their underside that expanded when they were handled, probably from the tension brought on by our handling and marking *(bottom)*.

caused little or no discomfort. We kept the van warm with a space heater so as to facilitate faster bleeding. John simply placed a capillary tube up to the drop of blood, filled it, and blew the blood into a bigger tube with his mouth. This cavalier technique expedited the procedure at the cost of putting John at risk if the Utah prairie dogs happened to carry any diseases. Rationalizing this risk by reminding himself that he had never contracted anything harmful, he mostly just refused to ponder that negative possibility.[13]

While the rear portion of the bag for adults was open, we also obtained the sex and reproductive state of the study animal. We distinguished males by their noncontiguous penis and anus; the female vulva and anus have very little space between them (fig. 2.17a–c). Males that were ready to reproduce that year (all those two years of age or older and about half of the yearlings) exhibited a pigmented scrotum with descended testes. If they were pups or yearlings and were not ready to reproduce, they had unpigmented scrotums and undescended testes.

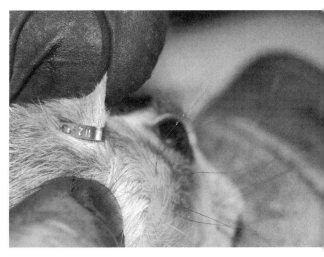

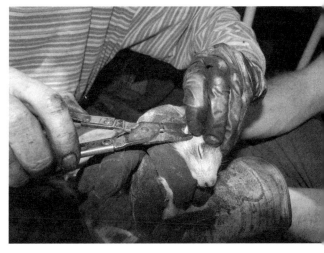

FIGURE 2.18. *Tag along*. An assistant reads ear tags on a veteran of the study colony by moving his ears with a paintbrush.

FIGURE 2.19. *Positive ID*. The ear tags on this captive Utah prairie dog are confirmed while John has it in a canvas bag.

FIGURE 2.20. *Branded*. John applies ear tags to a Utah prairie dog pup by squeezing a tag through the leathery part of its ear.

For females, we determined how close they were to estrus by examining the vulva. A closed, swollen vulva meant that estrus was imminent. An open vulva meant that the female had already mated. We could also tell that a female was pregnant or nursing if she had long, turgid nipples. When a female lost her litter to predation, infanticide, or some other cause, her nipples became flat within a few days.

Before we took these data, however, we gave the adult or juvenile ear tags. If the individual had been studied before, we checked the ear tags already present against our records to confirm its identity (figs. 2.18 and 2.19). For a previously uncaptured Utah prairie dog, we closed the back of the bag and opened the other end just enough for its head to protrude. We then inserted an ear tag with a three-digit number into each ear, which the individual usually carried for its entire life, barring loss in a vicious fight. Probably because the outer ears of a Utah prairie dog are tough and leathery, individuals seemed oblivious to the ear tags, even while we were inserting them. For juveniles, who were all previously uncaptured by definition, we simply inserted the ear tags while they were in our grasp following their short stay in the sandwich bag (fig. 2.20).

FIGURE 2.21. *New member*. Female-51 receives her marker with Nyanzol-D black fur dye and a paintbrush.

we changed their marker to any number under 50. Adult and yearling females were assigned any two-digit number of 50 or more. Females also received unique combinations of other marks, like rings, stripes, black butts, or black collars, combined with any number.

Juveniles of both sexes, like yearling males, had to survive for at least eight months to be assigned their own marker. Each juvenile got its own ear tags, but John's research objectives dictated that we know which juveniles belonged to each mother, not necessarily the differences between juveniles in the same litter. For this reason, we simply marked juveniles with the same marker as their mother and added a black "cap" on top of the head if the pup was a male (figs. 2.21 and 2.22a–b).

Amazingly, Utah prairie dogs seemed oblivious to their own marks and the marks of others. Recognition cues appeared to be mostly through scent, as they treated clan members just the same immediately after marking, even with radical markers with all sorts of combinations of numbers, stripes, and so forth. Nor did we notice that any predators seemed to target Utah prairie dogs with more or less pelage covered by fur dye, even when the markers stood out to us as distinctive.

We made the markers with a product called Nyanzol-D black fur dye, which John ordered as a powder and dissolved in water. Just before applying a marker, we mixed a small volume of this solution with an equal volume of 6 percent hydrogen peroxide (H_2O_2). The dye worked best at warm temperatures, so we sometimes placed it next to a heater in the van, even though this infringed on our own comfort. All told, this technique, which did not incur the dangers of anesthesia and was safe for both scientist and rodent, allowed us to provide each Utah prairie dog with a distinctive marker that remained for several months. When Utah prairie dogs molted in May, they lost their markers along with their fur—so we repeated this whole

Ear tags cannot be seen from a distance, so after we read the ear tags, we matched the numbers with the fur marker assigned to that Utah prairie dog in our records. For each pup or new individual, we embedded tags in the ear and then decided on its fur marker. We marked adult males with any number under 50 (with one number on each side, like a football helmet), and we marked yearling males with black rear legs plus a two-digit number under 50; when they reached their second year,

FIGURE 2.22. *Getting his stripes*. John applies a "cap" to a pup, distinguishing him as a male *(top)*. In the bottom photo, John brushes Nyanzol-D black fur dye onto a Utah prairie dog as an assistant looks on.

FIGURE 2.23. *Take it back home*. Utah prairie dog females are markedly sedentary. Many of them spend their entire lifetimes in a small clan territory. Returning them to that home base is crucial to their survival. John has just marked Female-Triple-Stripe (TS) and is returning her to the exact burrow entrance where she was livetrapped. Those three stripes will stay with TS until she molts in late spring.

FIGURE 2.24. *With kid gloves*. Dog Squad members hold Utah prairie dogs with thick gloves to prevent injuries.

process to re-mark our subjects for experiments with the stuffed badgers.

Only after all of these procedures did we return a study animal to the trap and put it in a shady spot until its release at the spot of capture (fig. 2.23). The entire protocol was so strict and straightforward that injuries to us

or the rodents almost never occurred. Our main issues came when we trapped in May or June, because of the possibility of Utah prairie dogs overheating. To reduce that possibility, we checked live traps frequently on hot days (over 80°F, 27°C)—sometimes as often as every 20–30 minutes.

The release of the detainee seemed fraught with danger to us but was really just the opposite. Utah prairie dogs escaped the traps like schoolboys saved by the bell and were so focused on freedom that they had no interest in taking revenge on their captors by ricocheting backward to bite them. We just had to tell them to "get along, little doggie," and that was all. To further reduce our chance of injury, we usually wore leather gloves to protect our hands from errant Utah prairie dogs, cuts from metal traps, splinters from the wooden towers, and other minor risks (fig. 2.24). This was despite the fact that John never wore gloves during his first 15 years of field research.

Individuality

Despite the stuffy atmosphere of the van, where the temperature could soar to over 90°F (32°C), marking Utah prairie dogs was one of the most enjoyable parts of field research. Individuals with unique markers suddenly came alive and revealed different behaviors, dispositions, habits, idiosyncrasies, preferences, and proclivities. Varying levels of boldness when dealing with humans or traps, deviant sexual habits, diverse vocalizations, unusual nest-building behavior, bizarre social interactions, dominance and subordination, myriad levels of violence or social activity— these are the qualities that, when combined with a distinctive marker, allowed us to detect the unique personality of each individual Utah prairie dog within our study colony each year (fig. 2.25).

In 2004–2005, we observed over 100 different Utah prairie dogs and saw the same number of personas. The first component of an individual's aura was its name, which came about in several ways. Most names were derived or corrupted from the pattern of the unique dye marker that we provided after trapping. A female whose rear end we painted black with the number 2, for instance, was called Black-Butt 2, or BB2 for short. Another female with one horizontal stripe across each

FIGURE 2.25. *One of a kind*. Utah prairie dogs, like this bold male observing us walking back to our towers, have individual "personalities" that shine through once the animals are marked with a unique number or design.

side of her body was called Racing-Stripe. Some other classics included Bisbee (for BSBB, Back-Stripe-Black-Butt); 49er (from the number 49); Wide-Apart-5 (from Wide Apart Stripes and the number 5); Deucey (from the number 2); R21 (from Rear-Legs-21); Ought-4 (from the number 04); Risrab (from RSRAB, Racing-Stripe-Ring-Around-Belly); Conine (Collar and the number 9); and, perhaps my favorite, Wetsuit (black marker everywhere except the head).

Sometimes, names developed that were based loosely on the dye marker but did not mention it explicitly. Notables included Tic-Tac-Toe (a.k.a. WARS, from Wide-Apart-Racing-Stripe, which created a Tic-Tac-Toe pattern on her back); Skunky (from RSBS or Racing-Stripe-Back-Stripe, which created a striped pattern that resembled a skunk); Junior (marked with Rear-Legs-15 or R15 after Male-15 was killed by a badger); and Bicentennial (from the number 76).

Names also emerged after we observed individual behaviors. I-15, the original Male-15 (from Interstate-15, the main thoroughfare through southern Utah), was named after he covered a record amount of acreage during his search for receptive females. Tumbleweed was dubbed as such because she seemed to roll through her home territory as she engaged in an inordinate amount of dust bathing.

Even with all of these amazing individuals, we were unable to top a bizarre tale from John's study of Gunnison's prairie dogs in Arizona during the 1980s. Gunnison's Female-BS (Back-Stripe) jockeyed for territory like a male, seemed to defend the clan with which she was associated like a male, failed to sire offspring year after year, and offered no parental support to the offspring of her female relatives. In almost four decades of research, John has never spent so much time looking in between the legs of an animal as he did with Female-BS.

Some Utah prairie dogs engaged in scores of social interactions per day (53, Collar-3). Others, by contrast, were loners that lived on the edge of the colony, where they had few interactions with their conspecifics (Black-Butt-9, Head-Wide-Apart, Rear-Legs-10). We observed that some individuals were easily excitable by real or potential danger (Racing-Stripe, 98), while others, usually males, merely looked up and then continued feeding (22, Ought-4). Some Utah prairie dogs were often trap-happy (35, Black-Butt-2, Double-Z), but others were reticent and shunned traps (71, Black-Butt-9).

We monitored Utah prairie dogs with oddities, like Triple-Stripe (TS), whom we considered aggressive because she killed a golden-mantled ground squirrel (*Spermophilus lateralis*) for no apparent purpose in 2005

(fig. 2.26); 51, who secured her nurturing reputation by filling her burrow with an inordinate amount of nest material in spring 2004; and 69er, whom we nicknamed the "Nervous One," because every day she would face the woods and make a chittering sound for no particular reason that we could determine.

Was it a problem for us to be objective scientists while perceiving the Utah prairie dogs to have personalities? Absolutely! We tried to refrain from attributing truly anthropomorphic qualities such as empathy to the Utah prairie dogs but usually failed. While we were careful to treat them as wild animals, we often noted that watching the Utah prairie dogs was like watching little people. We even had an acronym for the phenomenon—"JLP," for "Just Like People."

Trials and Tribulations

Sometimes, it takes a little failure to succeed. A case in point is the beginning of John's 42-year research career studying animal behavior, which started with experiments on bank swallows (*Riparia riparia*). Starting with some fundamental questions about why animals live in colonies, John worked with another graduate student named Paul Sherman, who is now a professor at Cornell University. John and Paul published an article titled "Advantages and Disadvantages of Bank Swallow (*Riparia riparia*) Coloniality," which is still their most cited publication, even though neither author ever studied swallows again.[14] Instead, John sought a mammalian species for follow-up research. Not wanting to be typecast as a "bird guy," he traveled the American West looking for a mammal and found black-tailed prairie dogs.

John began studying these cousins of Utah prairie dogs near a pig farm in Colorado. He wanted to compare the large, densely populated colonies of black-tailed prairie dogs with the smaller, less densely populated colonies of

FIGURE 2.26. *Carnivore*. Female-Triple-Stripe (TS) eats a golden-mantled ground squirrel she just killed as Female-81 sniffs her, probably hoping for a bite of the victim.

white-tailed prairie dogs in his effort to determine why prairie dogs live in colonies. After a series of experiments led by Chubs the badger, lower predation emerged as the most likely reason prairie dogs live in groups.[15]

With a newfound interest in antipredator behavior, John wanted to see whether prairie dogs that submerged when Chubs approached always chose burrows with at least two entrances, to give themselves more options if the (simulated) predator tried to dig them out. To determine the number of entrances per escape burrow, John planned to use smoke bombs, which other papers reported to be nontoxic.[16] After blowing smoke out the escape burrow with an air blower, John counted entrances to each burrow by simply watching for smoke at nearby burrow entrances.

The morning after placing the smoke bombs at his colony of black-tailed prairie

dogs, John showed up at the colony as he did every morning to watch the black-tailed prairie dogs emerge. The usual time for prairie dogs to wake up passed, but he thought that perhaps an overnight predation or a weather event had occurred that was keeping the prairie dogs submerged for a little extra time. He continued waiting patiently, but after a few hours, only a few prairie dogs had emerged.

And then it hit him. He had killed almost all of them.

It was not a good start to John's research career. Devastated, he wept for days afterward, mourning the loss of his beloved field animals and worried that his career as a biologist was over almost as soon as it had started. Thankfully, he had the resiliency to channel his frustration productively. That week, he began to scour for colonies of protected black-tailed prairie dogs and found one in Wind Cave National Park (WCNP),

South Dakota, where he would live among the prairie dogs every spring and summer for the next 15 years.[17]

It did not seem like it at the time, but the event now referred to as "The Incident" turned out to be a blessing in disguise from a research standpoint. The small colony of black-tailed prairie dogs at the pig farm never would have yielded the large sample sizes and data that he eventually collected at WCNP. And it was what John learned about the social behavior of black-tailed prairie dogs that led him to seek comparisons with other species of prairie dog, including Gunnison's prairie dogs in Arizona, Utah prairie dogs in Bryce Canyon, and during two separate periods, white-tailed prairie dogs in Colorado.[18]

Since "The Incident," John has missed only one day of field research in over 40 years, the lone absence due to an incapacitating 24-hour illness. He compares his family's leaving Maryland every March for prairie dog season to living "like gypsies," and his wife, Judy, has homeschooled their children in adjustment to the demanding lifestyle. Meanwhile, John has missed weddings, funerals, and professional conferences because of his insistence that the prairie dogs be monitored during all of their waking hours from before the start of each mating season until the capture of the last juvenile each year. Key events John has missed because of his regimented field schedule include various prairie dog conservation events in Denver, national conferences on animal behavior, the retirement party for his doctoral adviser, and an invitation to speak at an international conference on infanticide in Sicily.

Likewise, the timing of Utah prairie dog field season often precluded Dog Squad members from participating in the culture of their educational institutions. After failing to get tenure following six years as an assistant professor at Princeton University, largely because his boundless desire for fieldwork was anathema to the on-campus demands of

the position, John was lucky enough to find a tenure-track job in Maryland that did not involve classroom teaching and allowed him to stop everything and watch prairie dogs for four months of the year. Assistants were usually in their twenties and needed some sort of waiver or arrangement with the college they were attending, unless they were in between college and graduate school. Even then, the Utah prairie dog field season of March–July did not fit with most college semester schedules and wreaked havoc on bureaucratic paperwork and day-to-day life by creating problematic periods of unemployment or absence from class. I experienced some of these issues and asked the Utah prairie dogs about possibly moving their mating season to accommodate a typical academic semester, but they never acquiesced.

John's experience with the smoke bombs at the beginning of his career is a microcosm of the adjustments that new Dog Squad members made to the rigors of prairie dog research. New recruits could be quite unsettled in the first weeks of their experience. For example, I drove the wrong way into a snowdrift upon my first arrival at the trailer park, putting myself at the mercy of locals with snow shovels.

The enormous snowdrifts at the colony in BCNP, sometimes as high as five to six feet, required us to borrow snowshoes from park staff as our first order of business. We used them well into April, giving us quite a workout as we trudged about the colony—so much that I lost 17 pounds (8 kg) during my first field season. Because we set up our equipment before beginning field observations, we became familiar with snowshoes fairly quickly out of necessity. Within days, assistants were flying around the colony on the tennis-racket-shaped footwear while carrying three double-door Tomahawk live traps in each hand (fig. 2.27).

Even though the ground was covered with snow and the weather was freezing, the sun could still be absolutely oppressive at BCNP. After my first two days in the field

FIGURE 2.27. *Snowed under*. Sometimes, the Utah prairie dogs enjoyed helping us with our snowshoes.

made me look like a lobster, I was almost never seen at the colony again without my frequently applied sunblock and my lucky orange hat.

John learned the harder way. Back in the 1980s some growths began to appear on his hands. When he sought medical help, the doctor discovered what he did for a living and offered some sound advice. To paraphrase, if John expected to continue watching prairie dogs from a tower much longer, he would need to change the way he did business immediately. After that, John not only wore lightweight long-sleeved shirts even during the summer but also designed a makeshift sun-protecting hat by attaching a long, wide piece of material to the back of a baseball cap. Between the unorthodox headwear, the 11 layers of tattered clothing, and blackened fingernails from the fur dye used to mark the Utah prairie dogs, the "Caped Crusader"

looked unusual from head to toe but got the job done (fig. 2.28).

Along with style of dress, eating habits also changed when one joined the Dog Squad, as meals tended to become simpler. Preparing food was a drag when work started at dawn and lasted until dusk every day, and the situation was exacerbated by the lack of both income and proximity to a town with typical services. My trademark was eating generic-brand boxed macaroni and cheese—sometimes doing so for breakfast, lunch, and dinner while consuming nothing else, keeping my food bill under a dollar for that day. Another assistant was known for an even more pathetic behavior—eating two packs of dry quickie-noodles for lunch in her tower every day. The Dog Squad also took to lime gelatin, an inexpensive and easy-to-prepare Utah staple, after the influence of community members.[19] For me and some other assistants,

FIGURE 2.28. *Covered up.* The "Caped Crusader" in all his glory.

Wyoming, to arrive at 6 a.m. to watch wake-ups at a site in Colorado, he was drinking powdered milk to reduce costs wherever possible. One night, he vowed that when he got his PhD and landed his first assistant professorship, he would never drink the stuff again. In 1977 he received his PhD and has been consuming a gallon of whole milk every day since.

When no food was available, or at least no prepared or healthy food, Dog Squad members turned to coffee (and if they brought it outside the trailer, they occasionally endured long looks from devout Mormons during consumption).[20] No percolator was provided with the trailer, and new assistants usually did not think to bring one, so we often stirred ground coffee together with hot water as if it were a packet of instant cocoa. The alertness-providing elixir was makeshift but became an integral part of Dog Squad life for everyone except John, who never succumbed to the lure of caffeine. Another distraction he managed to ignore was the luxury of being able to check e-mail from his cell phone in the tower.

The lack of free time, amenities, and socially acceptable eating habits had a way of putting us in a position to learn about ourselves and helped us handle new challenges. No trial seemed insurmountable after enduring a grueling field season. In addition, many Dog Squad members came to Utah looking for prairie dogs but found themselves instead. Former "Squaddies" often report returning to their college or hometown with a better understanding of ultimate goals, increased self-discipline, and higher motivation. And after the seclusion of living among the Utah prairie dogs, Dog Squad members usually changed their outlook on life, being forever reminded of a world that is bigger than their career, possessions, or subdivided neighborhood. For many members of the Dog Squad, the oneness with nature they experienced during field research changed their lives forever.

the weekly hot meals prepared by John's wife, a biologist who studied prairie dogs with John when he was starting out, were the only healthy, balanced meals we consumed.

An exception to this rule was John, who does not eat much anyhow. John's breakfast at 5:30 a.m. before going out to see the Utah prairie dogs consisted of two bananas with hazelnut-cocoa butter, a seemingly inadequate source for his constant energy in the field, especially because he ate no lunch. A voracious milk drinker, John arranged for six gallons of bottled milk to be delivered to his trailer by truck every week.

The special delivery was quite a step up from the days when John started as a graduate student. Back then, at one point commuting an hour and a half one way from Laramie,

Recipe from the Field

Dog-a-roni and cheese

Ingredients:

One box of generic brand "Mac 'n' Cheese"

One generic brand "prairie dog" (hot dog)

1. Open box of macaroni.

2. Pour macaroni into a large pot of boiling water. Place hot dog in pot. Wait 10 minutes.

3. Remove water from macaroni and hot dog with a colander.

4. Open cheesy powder packet.

5. Pour cheesy powder packet in pot. Stir.

6. Serves up to 4.

3

Staying Connected

To live gregariously is to become a fibre in a vast sentient web overspreading
many acres . . . it is also to become the occupier of every bit of vantage
ground whence the approach of a lurking enemy might be overlooked.
—SIR FRANCIS GALTON, *Gregariousness in Cattle and Men*, 1871[1]

☾

*For a few years, the largest clan of females in the colony has lived just below John's
tower, providing a prize for any male who can gain control of the area before mating season. In 2003, the main victor was Male-Rear-Legs-13 (R13), who, despite being only one
year old, managed to capture the clan's territory after jousting with his opponents. But
his clan governance was constantly challenged, as yearling counterparts Rear-Legs-22
and Rear-Legs-37 also copulated with some of the females and resided in the clan territory for portions of the mating season.*

*One year later the clan is up for grabs again, and the annual musical chairs of males
is set to begin. We are eagerly awaiting the emergence of the clan members, the moment
when they will surge through snowdrifts and emerge from their burrows. In particular,
we are waiting for a female named Wetsuit.*

*Wetsuit, so named because she is marked with black dye everywhere except her head
so that she resembles a prairie dog wearing a wetsuit, has been the clan's icon. Wetsuit
earned this distinction through her central location, proclivity for social activity, and
heavyset figure. I called her the "big dog." Every day in the summer, before she and her
associates would embark toward the woods to forage on the tall grasses, she would awake
and start to kiss, sniff, and groom her clan mates. And in the evening, when the females
returned from the woods as the bright Utah sky turned to dusk, it was time for the clan's
nightly happy hour. At least that was how I thought of it. That's right—it's as though
prairie dogs like to relax with their friends after a tough day in the grass (fig. 3.1a–b).*

*We have been observing from our towers for a week, and we are officially concerned.
Where is Wetsuit? Is she still with us, or did she perish over the long winter? Will she
emerge in a few minutes, or was she sustenance for a hawk or fox?*

*"If she's still around, Wetsuit should get into online social networking," a Dog Squad
member proclaims. The comment is right on. Every individual in a clan, or even the
entire colony, is linked by a complicated series of social interactions. This network helps
Utah prairie dogs stay connected with their families.*

*Psychologist Stanley Milgram once said that humans live in a "small world," a vast
network where random people can be connected by an average of six handshakes,*

or degrees of separation.[2] Whether the number of connective links is more or less for Utah prairie dogs is anyone's guess. Some pariahs, like loner Black-Butt-9, have only a few "friends" in the network—several partners for social interaction. Wetsuit was much more popular last year. She had at least a dozen friends.[3]

But as we wait impatiently to see whether Wetsuit and last year's clan mates are still alive and whether they will arouse from hibernation, we remember that the clan was not always such a party. Life in the big city presents some challenges, after all. In 2003 alone, Wetsuit's clan featured fearsome territoriality, battles among females for nest burrows, violent competition among males for mates, and other atrocities by human standards. Why, with all the unpleasantness, would Utah prairie dogs live in such close quarters? And why would they be lovey-dovey at some times but come to blows at others?

Another hour and a half of silence passes on the meadow. All of a sudden, words are spoken.

"Prairie dog up at burrow E8!" John exclaims, "Looks like some of her marker stayed on over the winter. Almost never happens."

"It's probably Wetsuit."

Utah prairie dogs are communal animals, and their social structure is fascinating. The typical clan of Utah prairie dogs contains three or four reproductive females who are related to each other (e.g., aunts, mothers, daughters, sisters, half-sisters), a few nonreproductive yearling male offspring of those females, and an older male who is at least one year old and sexually mature. Female Utah prairie dogs always mate as yearlings, but only about 50 percent of males do the same. Clans sometimes contain two or three sexually mature males or have a single male that resides there during the mating season and then moves to a different territory.[4]

Clans have as few as 1 female, or as many as 15. Most clan territories are defended and passed down through generations. Communal defense of their home clan territory helps females maintain foraging grounds and burrows.

By contrast, the reproductive resident males in a clan are almost always the offspring of females from other clans, and males usually remain in the same territory for only one year before moving to a different territory. When a male is ready to reproduce, he will disperse from his natal clan and journey to find his own clan of females, all the while jockeying for position with other males. This sort of "musical chairs" with the males every year is a way in which Utah prairie dogs prevent incestuous copulations (fig. 3.2).[5]

The typical Utah prairie dog female remains in the territory where she was born for her entire life. But exceptions to this rule sometimes occur. A female might move to an adjacent territory, for example, or a large territory might contain one or two females from other clans.

Another form of change in clan territory and membership occurs when Utah prairie dog clans split up into two or three new clans or fuse together into one conglomerate. Clan splitting is called fission and typically occurs when a clan is very large. Fusing clans are rarer but not extraordinary. For instance, when a clan experiences significant mortality and only a few females are left to reside in a clan territory, the females of two formerly separate clans might start to interact amicably.[6]

FIGURE 3.1. *Happy hour*. Utah prairie dog clans are especially ripe with social interaction just after dawn *(above)* and a few hours before dusk *(upper right)*.

FIGURE 3.2. *(right) Moving out*. Yearling males remain in the clan of their birth if not reproductive but disperse to another clan if they will mate that year. Such was the case for Male-Rear-Legs-17 (R17), who in 2005 moved several dozen yards to conquer a clan of females despite being wet and cold.

Most Utah prairie dogs live in a clan, but in rare cases, individuals reside alone on the edge of a colony. Males like Rear-Legs-10 (R10) and Rear-Legs-19 (R19) were loner yearling males who were unable or unwilling to compete with older, more experienced males and left the natal territory to wait and establish position for next year's mating season. Some males, such as two-year-old Male-29, were sporadically present in a clan territory during the mating season and even grabbed a few copulations, but for the most part they were unable to secure and maintain their own clan of females and therefore lived at the periphery of the study colony.

Getting to Know You

Western settlers who came upon prairie dog towns were captivated by the social behaviors they witnessed. For instance, George Wilkins Kendall wrote about the complexity of black-tailed prairie dog society in 1846 following his experience on the Texan Santa Fe Expedition:

In their habits, they are clannish, social, and extremely convivial, never living alone like other animals, but, on the contrary, always found in villages or large settlements. They are a wild, frolicsome, madcap set of fellows when undisturbed, uneasy and ever on the move, and appear to take special delight in chattering away the time, and visiting from hole to hole to gossip and talk over each other's affairs . . . I particularly noticed a very large dog, sitting in front of the door or entrance to his burrow, and by his own actions and those of his neighbors it really seemed as though he was the president, mayor, or chief—at all events, he was the "big dog" of the place . . . during that time [he] received at least a dozen visits from his fellow-dogs, which would stop and chat with him a few moments, and then run off to their domiciles. All this while he never left his post for a moment, and I thought I could discover a gravity in his deportment not discernible in those by which he was surrounded. Far is it from me to say that the visits he received were upon business, or had anything to do with the local government of the village; but it certainly appeared so. If any animal has a system of laws regulating the body politic, it is certainly the prairie dog.[7]

In his 1835 narrative *A Tour on the Prairies*, essayist Washington Irving documented his fascination with prairie dog social interaction at an even higher level, with amateur naturalists attributing an almost humanlike quality to the behavior:

The prairie dog is, in fact, one of the curiosities of the Far West, about which travelers delight to tell marvelous tales, endowing him at times with something of the politic and social habits of a rational being, and giving him systems of civil government and domestic economy, almost equal to what they used to bestow upon the beaver.[8]

Social interactions were the first thing that I noticed about Utah prairie dogs, too. The Dog Squad sometimes recorded over 200 interactions per person in a single day, meaning that we were constantly writing on our pads. Interactions occurred during the entire field season but were especially frequent during the mating season of late March and early April.

Amicable interactions allow Utah prairie dogs to identify each other, and occur among members of the same clan. The most common amicable interaction is a "kiss," when two individuals touch mouthparts. This amicable social greeting is likely a rodent equivalent of "hello" and probably helps confirm by scent that the other individual belongs to the same clan. Kisses are frequent at dawn and dusk, and are endearing gestures that remind us of ourselves (fig. 3.3a–b).[9]

A Utah prairie dog often touches the derriere of a conspecific with its nose. We called this interaction a "sniff" and presumed that the first Utah prairie dog was smelling

FIGURE 3.3. *A kiss is just a kiss*. Utah prairie dogs kiss to identify each other. Kissing involves mouth-to-mouth contact, while sniffing involves mouth contact with any other part of another Utah prairie dog's body (often the anal area).

FIGURE 3.4. *Get that flea, please.* Utah prairie dogs allogroom members of their clan. Allogrooming helps remove irritating, disease-carrying parasites such as fleas, lice, ticks, and mites.

FIGURE 3.5. *Start the morning right.* There's nothing like a good allogrooming session on a warm summer's day.

the second. Sniffing is often preceded or followed by kissing and can also serve as a "get-to-know-you" for females of the same clan, or for a male who is pursuing a sexually receptive female.[10] Allogrooming is another, less common amicable interaction that helps the participants rid themselves of fleas, ticks, and other disease-causing parasites (figs. 3.4 and 3.5).

Hostile interactions occur between females of different clans, between females of the same clan who are defending burrows in which to raise offspring, and between males that are warring over a territory with potential mates during mating season. In general, interactions involving members of the same clan are more likely to be amicable than those involving members of different clans.[11]

If Utah prairie dogs from different clans encounter each other at the border of their adjacent clan territories, they usually engage in a territorial dispute. This activity is particularly common when resident males meet near a territorial boundary during mating season. When two Utah prairie dogs have a territorial dispute, they will stare at each other, puff out their bodies, and crouch close to the ground to appear larger (fig. 3.6a–d). Disputes can also escalate into individuals flaring their tails, chattering their teeth, curving their bodies into defensive positions, or chasing and fighting (fig. 3.7a–b).

Fights are especially prevalent among males before and during mating season, although less vicious kerfuffles can also occur between two females near the boundary of a clan territory (fig. 3.8).[12] Fights among males can lead to bloody facial injuries, loss of fur, and leg wounds. Some are riveting, prolonged battles for glory, with opponents clashing in

FIGURE 3.6. *This means war*. Male Utah prairie dogs often battle for territory during mating season and sometimes maintain their animosity into summer. When two rivals meet at the boundary of a clan territory, they square off *(top left)* and size each other up with oral contact that is much different than an amicable kiss *(top right)*. Adversaries might also skip the pretense of squaring off and move directly into hostile oral contact *(bottom left)*, concluding the interaction by jumping away from each other *(bottom right)*.

midair and then rolling in the dirt or snow (fig. 3.9a–b). Rarely, fights result in the death and cannibalistic consumption of the loser.

Despite the ferocity of some hostile interactions, Utah prairie dogs are not fervently territorial for the entire year. Males are brutally territorial during mating season (figs. 3.10 and 3.11), and that aggressiveness wanes after all the females have mated. But females collectively defend the clan territory all year against females of other clans, and within the home territory, pregnant and lactating females also

defend nursery burrows that contain (or will soon contain) their offspring.[13]

Utah prairie dogs sometimes seem to "rank" themselves on the basis of body mass and reproductive status. During mating season, heavy males are dominant over females of lower body mass and initiate almost every male-female social interaction in the clan. Heavy reproductive males regularly initiate and win aggressive encounters with nonreproductive males of lower body mass. And heavy females, who consistently copulate earlier

FIGURE 3.7. *Duel*. Hostile interactions between male Utah prairie dogs occur during mating season. These duels can involve oral contact, vocalization *(above)*, or positioning in which rivals size each other up by forming a *C* with their bodies to line up their mouths and anuses *(top right)*. The resulting sniff is hostile.

FIGURE 3.8 *(right) Cattiness*. Female Utah prairie dogs from different clans engage in hostile interactions, just like males. Female-66, (Route 66), a particularly catty female, rebuffs Female-95, a female from a nearby area, as 95 ventures too close to Route 66's clan.

FIGURE 3.9. *Backyard brawl*. Males fight for females during a three-week mating season in late March through early April. Fights sometimes lead to serious injuries, or even death. Pictured is an all-time classic romp in 2005 between Male-16 (Sweet-16) and unassuming yearling Male-Rear-Legs-33 (R33), who was clobbered *(above left)*. But the upstart R33 landed some blows of his own during contests with other rivals *(above right)* before he finally settled into a small territory of females.

FIGURE 3.10. *Catch me if you can*. After territorial displays, the victor chases the loser from the clan. Two-year-old Male-16 (Sweet-16) is shown here winning hostile interactions against inexperienced yearling male Rear-Legs-12 (R12).

FIGURE 3.11. *Border war*. Sweet-16 chases, and eventually pummels, his younger archrival Rear-Legs-33 (R33).

than females of lower body mass, typically win hostile encounters.[14]

Homeland Security

Few animal behaviors are more endearing to humans than the upright, anthropomorphic posture of Utah prairie dog vigilance. But the standing is certainly not an effort on the part of the rodent to be cute. Because Utah prairie dogs are prey animals, they must maintain an almost constant "neighborhood watch" for predatory attacks, from both the ground and the air.[15] Utah prairie dogs are watchful by bobbing their heads up and down while foraging, by standing atop a burrow mound on all fours to gain a vantage point, or by standing tall on only their rear legs (figs. 3.12 and 3.13).[16]

Probably because vigilance behavior is so visible, compelling, and easy to observe, John and I both wrote about it in our first few published papers, even though our careers started 30 years apart. During my routine checks of activity in the colony, I recorded whether Utah prairie dogs in my sight were vigilant, and if so, what posture they exhibited.[17] Because of our MMLs and knowledge of when individuals emerged from and submerged in their burrows, I was able to compare different levels of vigilance with the number of individuals aboveground, both within the clan and across the entire colony. My results were interesting for several reasons.[18]

I found, for example, that Utah prairie dogs of both sexes are less vigilant when there are more Utah prairie dogs aboveground in the clan and the colony. In addition, Utah prairie dogs living on the edge of the colony are more vigilant than those living in the center.

These results are classic examples of "selfish herd" effects.[19] The rationale is as follows: an individual living in a central clan territory surrounded by other territories has

FIGURE 3.12. *Guard dogs*. Utah prairie dogs often watch for predators while upright on their hind legs.

FIGURE 3.13. *On your guard*. Even if they are not upright, Utah prairie dogs can detect predators while scanning the colony on all fours.

many vigilant, alarm-calling conspecifics and numerous burrow entrances between itself and a predator that approaches from outside the colony site. An individual in a peripheral territory, by contrast, has fewer conspecifics and burrow entrances between itself and the predator and therefore should be more susceptible to capture. The same logic applies to Utah prairie dogs during times when there are either more or fewer other individuals aboveground.[20]

Vigilance clearly reduces the risk of predation. But Utah prairie dogs are also vigilant for another reason—to monitor the activities of competing conspecifics.[21] During mating season, for instance, a male must watch for estrous females or other males who might try to invade his territory. And after the pups are born, females must protect their burrows from marauders who are attempting to commit infanticide.[22] Most Utah prairie dogs spend about a third of their time in vigilant

postures, but males and females significantly increase the time they spend vigilant under certain circumstances. Sexually mature males during the mating season, for example, often spend more than 50 percent of their time watching for invading males—more time than they spend feeding.[23]

Sound the Alarm

Utah prairie dogs are vocal creatures. The functions of their vocalizations include warning others of predatory attacks, defending a mate or territory, and communicating aggression. Their repertoire contains variations in tone, volume, and repetition. These variations might indicate a different meaning for each call and allow other Utah prairie dogs to hear the calls over grassy or steppe terrain.[24]

The function of many Utah prairie dog vocalizations remains unclear. Not so for the

FIGURE 3.14. *(above) The scream*. Utah prairie dogs emit alarm calls to warn siblings and offspring of predators such as American badgers, northern goshawks, and red foxes.

FIGURE 3.15. *(right) Overprotected*. Alarm calls can occur a few feet away *(top)* or directly in the vicinity *(bottom)* of offspring.

most important and noticeable vocalization—the alarm call. When a vigilant Utah prairie dog spots a predator, it frequently runs to a burrow and sounds the alarm call, a high-pitched "Click! Click! Click!" When another individual hears the call, it stops all activity and sits upright to scan the area for predators. If that Utah prairie dog detects a predator also, then it too runs to a burrow mound, where it might initiate its own call.[25]

Contrary to popular belief, Utah prairie dogs do not automatically submerge into a burrow upon spotting a predator or hearing an antipredator call. They prefer to keep track of the predator's location and remain able to return immediately to foraging after it departs. Submergence is therefore reserved for situations with clear, immediate danger, generally for individuals that are closest to the predator.[26]

Emitting a loud sound would seem to attract attention to the caller and make it easier for a predator to locate potential prey. So why do Utah prairie dogs give an alarm call after spotting a predator? Two factors are probably at work. First, Utah prairie dogs benefit from selfish herd effects as a direct result of the call.[27] The individual closest to the potential predator is more likely to call than other individuals. When members of the home clan and other clans run to their burrow mounds after hearing the call, those other Utah prairie dogs are suddenly more visible to the predator, and therefore more likely to be pursued by it. The caller gets lost "in the crowd" and can be safer from the predator. Further, additional Utah prairie dogs standing on their burrow mounds mean that the predator is monitored more closely and is therefore less likely to be successful during an attack.[28]

Second, the alarm call warns kin in the clan. Indeed, Utah prairie dogs with kin present in the home clan territory are more likely to call than Utah prairie dogs without nearby kin.[29] The reason involves a concept called "kin selection."[30] Family members such as aunts, brothers, cousins, offspring, sisters, and uncles carry many of the same genes as the caller, so Utah prairie dogs that warn nearby associates with an alarm call are essentially protecting their own genes from danger.[31] While an alarm call is altruistic in the sense that it benefits other members of the species, the caller nonetheless benefits, because his or her shared genes are being protected (figs. 3.14 and 3.15a–b).[32]

Not all alarm calls are created equal. Some calls contain a few clicks and are over in a few seconds, while others contain hundreds of clicks and last over an hour. While the fundamental sound of the call seems the same each time, Utah prairie dogs seem to emit a few short, hard clicks for an aerial predator, and

FIGURE 3.16. *Sound the alarm.* Utah prairie dogs usually respond to the alarm calls of clan mates with vigilance.

repeated, more prolonged, softer chirks for a terrestrial predator. This difference probably reflects the increased urgency of an aerial predator attack and dictates the amount of vigilance other Utah prairie dogs demonstrate in response (fig. 3.16). The level of urgency is also clear when Utah prairie dogs call at a faster rate for other imminent danger, such as a red fox that suddenly appears within the clan territory.[33]

Because of their variability, John and I have an interest in alarm calls that is never ending. Among our remaining questions is why Utah prairie dog males and pups hardly ever give alarm calls, even though they typically share genes with many members of the home clan.[34] Another puzzle is that immigrants who have no close kin anywhere in the home or adjacent colony sometimes give alarm calls. Finally, we continue to wonder about the calls that appear to be false alarms or "cries of wolf." Frequently we were flummoxed when

FIGURE 3.17. *False alarm*. Every so often, Utah prairie dogs from all over the colony would stand vigilant and emit alarm calls for no apparent reason. Perhaps a predator lurked in the woods unbeknown to us.

almost every Utah prairie dog in the colony was standing alert and vigilant, and 10 to 20 of them were alarm calling, but we never saw a predator (fig. 3.17a–b).

Mortality and Dispersal

As noted above, most females remain in the territory of their birth for life, and almost all males disperse to other territories within the colony when they become sexually mature at one to two years of age.[35] So when an individual went missing from the colony completely, the Dog Squad tried to ascertain the reason why. Did the study animal attempt long-distance dispersal and emigrate to another colony, or was he or she captured by a sneaky predator?

An individual that we looked forward to seeing during all of the off-season sometimes did not return when the others emerged from hibernation. And every so often, a study animal was recorded as missing in action (MIA) after we realized that we had not seen him or her for two to three days. Deciphering what happened in these situations was complicated by the fact that Utah prairie dogs usually die underground. Often, disappearance was the only diagnostic signal of death, even though the same signal would apply to Utah prairie dogs that attempted long-distance dispersal.[36]

Predations, however, were usually a different story. The Dog Squad always watched carefully for signs that Utah prairie dogs had become prey, and we found a tremendous amount of variation in predation from year to year. In 2004, we saw no predations, but in 2005, we observed a whopping 26. Including pups, almost 10 percent of the colony was eaten by red foxes or northern goshawks![37]

Because we lived among the Utah prairie dogs during their entire breeding cycle, we saw almost all daytime predations and could confirm death in those cases. For nighttime predations by American badgers, we usually noticed evidence on the following morning in combination with the absence of a marked resident. In these instances, some burrows were expanded, with fresh subsoil on their mounds. Surviving individuals in those areas emerged for the morning late, and the surrounding once-open burrows were clogged with soil, apparently placed strategically by the badger to cut off the escape routes of its prey. Aerial predations left little evidence, if any, but because Utah prairie dogs submerge for the night and are not seen again until morning, we never considered the possibility of aerial predation during the night.[38]

In other cases of disappearance, a Utah prairie dog showed a gradual decline in health followed by a sudden vanishing, so we inferred that the individual had died underground.[39] Such was the case in 2004 for Female-53, who lived under my tower and emerged from hibernation underweight after a tough winter with five feet (1.5 m) of snow still on the ground. After a few days, she stopped feeding, her attentiveness during alarm calls ceased, and she stopped interacting with her family. One evening, she quietly slipped into a burrow well before other clan members submerged for the night, and I never saw her again.

Our best chance to detect long-distance dispersal was simply to eartag and mark all individuals in our study colony. This simple but effective demonstration of study colony membership occasionally allowed us to confirm a case of dispersal when a marked individual appeared in another colony, or when an unmarked individual arrived in the study colony.[40]

Some immigrants came from an assemblage of a dozen or so Utah prairie dogs about half a mile (just under 1 km) from our study colony. We did not observe these individuals, but John trapped, eartagged, and marked them after mating season for several years.

FIGURE 3.18. *Hunting season.* The journey of an immigrant Utah prairie dog is fraught with danger from predators like northern goshawks *(top)*. Male-Rear-Legs-44 (R44), an immigrant from another colony, was among the victims in 2005 *(bottom)*.

He made this exception of tagging outside the study colony because he knew that the proximity of the other colony offered an outstanding opportunity to observe immigration and emigration. Not habituated to biologists and with a wilder personality all their own, these dogs were a trick to capture, handle, and tag, but the evidence we gained was worth it.

When an immigrant arrived at the study colony, it was usually chased out of one clan territory, then out of another, and so forth, until it either established itself in a clan territory or disappeared—presumably to search for another colony with better possibilities for invasion. Some immigrants, like Male-Rear-Legs-21, became entrenched at the study colony after invading an occupied clan territory and killing some of the current offspring. And in 2004, immigrant Male-39 did something John had never observed before and has not seen since. He arrived in a territory in the study colony from elsewhere in the park, mated with two females over several days, and then left the study colony for the rest of the year.

But for every immigrant that instituted a stronghold, another fared poorly. The journey of an immigrant from his or her colony of origin was fraught with potential difficulties, most notably bad weather, prolonged exposure, and predation. Succumbing to a predator was particularly likely for dispersing Utah prairie dogs because traveling from the home colony in search of another colony meant that there were few nearby burrows for retreat.

In 2005, Male-Rear-Legs-44 (R44), a yearling immigrant to the study colony, became a classic example of the plight of immigrants when he attempted to invade the territory of another reproductive yearling male, Rear-Legs-15 (also known as "Junior"). Over a two-day period, R44 waged coordinated attacks against Junior to obtain his clan territory with five females but was ousted each

time and probably returned to another colony in the park at the end of those days. On the third day, R44 mustered one final challenge, battling with Junior during an epic siege that led to R44's demise. Having lost an opportunity to establish residency in the study colony for good, R44 began to retreat once again. At one point, when R44 was at the edge of our study colony, he was captured by a northern goshawk (fig. 3.18a–b).[41]

Not all incidents of long-distance dispersal were from colony to colony. An intriguing episode of within-colony dispersal involved the indecision of Female-Racing-Stripe, who in 2005 disappeared from a small clan territory around my tower where she had lived for two years. Like magic, she reappeared a few days later at the easternmost limits of the colony, gathering nest material and apparently preparing to give birth. A few weeks later she did just that, raising a litter of four pups that were all still alive when we ceased research at the end of 2005. The reasons for Racing-Stripe's relocation remain unclear, but her move likely resulted from the death of her close relatives. Indeed, John has discovered that females typically disperse from their natal clan territory when all close kin have disappeared. This pattern is surprising, as scientists originally theorized the opposite trend—that the presence of close kin would induce competition among them and cause their dispersal.[42] But, probably because cooperation among kin is more important than competition for Utah prairie dogs, we often observed females like Racing-Stripe move elsewhere rather than stay in a territory with no close relatives.[43]

Whether they die or disperse, losing animals that you have studied for years is sad. But such was life for members of the Dog Squad. I frequently reminded myself that good researchers accept the ways of Mother Nature and simply continue their work.

Doggin' It

Observing Utah prairie dogs feeding, watching for predators, or engaging in social interaction is fascinating. The rodents are easily startled, and individuals will run to their burrows and freeze while emitting alarm calls if you are walking near or into their colony site. Thus, the best way to experience Utah prairie dogs is from a distance with a good pair of binoculars.

Social interactions of Utah prairie dogs are most common during the mating season of late winter and early spring, but the weather is much colder then. Late May or June, when the weather is warm and pups have appeared aboveground, is perhaps the most convenient time to watch Utah prairie dogs. On hot days, the best time to watch is early in the morning and one to two hours before sunset.

Please remember that Utah prairie dogs are wild animals and should be treated as such. Wildlife enthusiasts traveling through Bryce Canyon National Park should inquire at the Visitor Center upon arrival to learn the location of the best areas to observe Utah prairie dogs.

For a more intense experience, you can acquire the proper permits and copy the methods of John Hoogland's Dog Squad. For 11 years, the University of Maryland Prairie Dog Squad sat in towers every day during March through June from dawn until dusk, often in freezing weather, thinking about and discussing nothing but Utah prairie dogs during every waking hour. This endeavor took effort, patience, stamina, and lots of coffee. You can do this too! Here's how[44]—

Step 1.   Wake up. Think about prairie dogs. Curse the 5 a.m. wake-up time and lack of heat in the trailer. Press "snooze" and mentally prepare to sit still in subzero weather waiting alertly and endlessly for specific behaviors that will surely occur.

Step 2.   Bundle up. Bring earmuffs, hats, gloves, mittens, handwarmers, and toewarmers. Wear 7 pairs of pants, 3 pairs of socks, and 11 shirts. Cover your face with anything that will fit. Stock socks in your cabin and your observation tower as if the apocalypse is imminent. Despite the ferocious cold, wear sunscreen, and reapply all day.

Step 3.   Fill two gallon-sized jugs with water—no water is available at the field site. Ignore John's example and hydrate throughout the day.

Step 4.   Deal with every problem in your life before the onset of mating season. Time is hard to come by, and phone and internet access is sparse. Need a root canal? That's a problem.

Step 5.   Ignore passersby or scientists who study other animals and do not appreciate that watching Utah prairie dog mating season is an all-day affair.

Step 6.   Climb into a slightly tilted tower with gear on your back. Sit. Pray that the tower does not topple to the ground, resulting in your fiery death.

Step 7.   Wait for Utah prairie dogs to come out of the ground. Drink coffee.

Step 8.   The critters will wake up and emerge from their burrows. Write this down. Drink more coffee.

Step 9.   The study animals will kiss and sniff each other. Write this down. Drink coffee again.

Step 10.   Utah prairie dogs will participate in other discreet, subtle behaviors that occur in a split second. Definitely write these down, and drink some more coffee . . . why not?

Step 11.   Coffee is all gone. Lament your lack of coffee.

Step 12.   Return to your trailer. Discuss Utah prairie dogs with your colleagues. Eat one of those boxes of macaroni and cheese with the powdery cheese packet (if you have the energy to make it) and go to bed.

Step 13.   Fall into bed. Ignore the mice rummaging around the trailer. Dream about prairie dogs.

4

Out on the Town

I should premise that I use the term Struggle for Existence in a large and
metaphorical sense, including dependence of one being on another, and
including (which is more important) success in leaving progeny.
—CHARLES DARWIN, *Origin of Species*, 1869[1]

☾

*Anticipation fills the air on this frigid March morning. The long winter wait is almost
over. Any day now, the first copulation of the year will occur.*

*Those Utah prairie dogs that are lucky enough to have survived the assaults of
winter and predation have already begun to appear aboveground for the first time after
five months of hibernation. The ground is exploding, and the males are carving out the
borders of their territories with carefully placed hostile interactions. Their mission is
clear—to find females and mate with them.*

*At 7:30 a.m., Male-2 (a.k.a. "Deucey"), a veteran of the colony, emerges to a lonely
meadow. Unaware that he is among the last of his species, he continues unfettered, moving step by step from the burrow before making small forays a few feet from where he
awoke. Pickings are lean during the winter, and the grass on which he subsists is covered
in colossal snowdrifts. He is surviving solely on the fat he accumulated last summer.
After the snow clears in late April and early May, grasses will be abundant, and he will
spend his days foraging.*

*Deucey struggles to move across the snow, but he will stop at nothing in his quest
for a mate. He runs all the way from his burrow toward the line of trees on the meadow's boundary, popping his head into burrows that might contain receptive females. For
now, this is his domain, but he is the not the sole occupant of the area for long. A tough,
up-and-coming yearling challenger named Rear-Legs-33 emerges a few hours later,
and he climbs onto one of our live traps, emits a territorial call, and stands to scan the
meadow. Soon, each male is aware of the other. For what seems like forever, they remain
like statues in the snow, standing rigidly in a light snowfall and subtle wind.*

*The males want sex, plain and simple, and they are out on the town looking for
females. Last year's territories are in the past, and the contenders are starting fresh as
they jockey for new territory. Soon they begin a clichéd Wild West face-off, with their
proverbial guns drawn. Finally, after 10 minutes of posturing and braggadocio, one runs
toward the other to begin the duel. They come together violently as an airborne ball of
fur, rolling across the snow like a tumbleweed. The younger contestant tries to gain an
advantage by landing on top of Deucey, beating and kicking his rival into the snow.*

Deep in the woods, a red fox has prairie-dogs-to-go on his mind for lunch. He does not attack now, but the quarreling males know of the necessary compromise between finding mates and survival. A moment's inattention could be the difference between life and death.

The casus belli is Female-75, who has been active for a few days following her emergence from hibernation. Today might be her "special" day. If it is, then many more titanic battles between her possible suitors will occur. With the first mating comes the highest likelihood of siring offspring,[2] but if a male does not win the first copulation with her, he will fight to be her second or third mate. Rear-Legs-33 looks like the real deal this year, and with some luck, he will maintain residency with a clan of females and be the first to mate with all of them. But along the way he probably will need to defeat the indefatigable Deucey, who is pummeling any male that comes close to him (fig. 4.1a–b).

The imperiled situation of Utah prairie dogs makes the upcoming mating season crucial. How they go through this yearly ritual in such brutal conditions is truly awesome.

Mating season for Utah prairie dogs runs from the last week in March to the second week in April, almost like clockwork. Males are especially attracted to females that have not yet copulated, and each female is sexually receptive for only several hours of a single day each year. Some females mate with as many as five different males during this special day.[3]

As they jockey for position around females, sexually mature males will run distances of over a mile (almost 2 km) per day in the hope of securing as much ground as possible. During this time, males frequently emit a vocalization we have deemed the "territorial call." Also called a "laughing bark," the call advertises male presence in the area and tells rivals to bring it on (fig. 4.2). All it takes is a few males to emerge for the spring, and the meadow resonates with cacophony.

Disputes over real estate commence soon after the first few males emerge from hibernation and are frequent before and during the mating season. During a dispute at the boundary between two clan territories, males will size up their opponents by touching their mouths together and making their bodies

FIGURE 4.1. *Deuces wild.* As the resident male of his clan, Deucey (Male-2) chases away contenders like Rear-Legs-12 (R12) *(left)* and Rear-Legs-33 (R33) *(right).*

appear as large as possible, often chattering
their teeth in disapproval of the perceived
invader. Adversaries will then curve their
bodies into a *C* shape, again trying to establish
position. Several similar encounters can lead
to all-out rumbles, with the winner gaining
new or larger territory (fig. 4.3).[4]

For well-established males that have
maintained their weight, it might not take
much to deter an invader. Males of this ilk,
like Ought-4, 25, and 46, were a bit "in your
face" about defending territory. Less adept
males usually preferred not to repeat a costly
melee when they (and Dog Squad members)
knew the inevitable result. One look from the
big boys usually did the job and thwarted such
tomfoolery from upstarts. In a constant battle
to enter genes into the next generation, only
the most savvy were able to mate and produce
offspring.

Dating and Mating

So how do males know when a female will
become sexually receptive? The probable
answer is that no male ever knows for sure.
Perhaps females leave a scent through their
urine or by contacting the ground or vegetation with their genitals. Establishing the
sequence of behaviors prior to intercourse was
difficult, and the Dog Squad never investigated the possibility of a scent from females
before and during estrus (sexual receptivity).

A male will usually closely follow a female
that is approaching estrus and will frequently
interact with her. The vulva of a female near-
ing estrus is sealed shut or just beginning to
open, and she will present her anal area to a
male for sniffing (fig. 4.4). Anal sniffing might
also be preceded by kissing or other oral and
bodily sniffing (fig. 4.5). Females just before
estrus are receptive to this action, but females
that have just emerged from hibernation
and are not in the mood will usually flee an
advancing male (fig. 4.6a–b).[5]

FIGURE 4.2. *No laughing matter.* Male Utah prairie
dogs emit a laughing bark to claim territory during
mating season.

FIGURE 4.3. *Comes with the territory.* Territorial
displays between males may occur during any time
of year but are most prevalent just before and during
mating season.

Males frequently check unmated females for
estrus, sometimes minute to minute. The male
proceeds with his activities according to what
he finds during these interactions. If a female
stays away after a male attempts to kiss or sniff
her, the male will work on overtures to other
females until he returns to her and finds that
she is receptive to social and sexual interaction.

Sequences of interactions can therefore
become quite complicated before and during

FIGURE 4.4. *Asking her out*. Male-Rear-Legs-33 (R33) invades the territory of Male-16 (Sweet-16) to check the sexual receptivity of Female-77 during mating season 2005.

FIGURE 4.5. *First kiss*. Sweet-16 courts Female-72 with a kiss.

estrus. For instance, a male might monitor a female's receptivity through anal sniffing, attempt to mount her, and eventually be rebuffed. A minute later, he might sniff another female in that home territory and be rebuffed once again. Meanwhile, another male invades the home territory, and the resident chases the invader until he departs. He again monitors the first female through oral sniffing, and the female runs away from

him, causing him to shift to interactions with another female. The new couple enjoys a mutual roll around in the dust, and the male tries to mount the female, even though she is still not quite ready to copulate. On and on, the fun continues.

The nearly continuous series of interactions, challenging and exhausting but also riveting and exciting for Dog Squad members to record on paper, spans about three weeks each year. A female can have her single interval of sexual receptivity during any day over the three-week mating season, and females within a clan sometimes seem to time their days of sexual receptivity so that they command as much attention from males for themselves as possible.[6] But, it is not unusual for females of the same clan to be estrous on the same day.[7] Whether females in a clan determine their order of estrus remains a mystery, but if they do, the frequent anal sniffing that occurs among the females could somehow be involved.

A similar rotation applies to emergence from hibernation, as some females appear aboveground earlier in March than others. For those that arouse late, estrus usually comes just two to three days later—as opposed to early birds, who can wait up to a week to be sexually receptive.[8] Female-Racing-Stripe, for instance, aroused early in 2004 and waited almost a week before coming into estrus. Female-Tic-Tac-Toe, by contrast, aroused from hibernation late that year and came into estrus within the first few days after she first appeared aboveground.

Copulation

After all of the conspicuous aboveground interactions that precede it, copulation usually occurs underground. This is both frustrating and challenging for behavioral ecologists, as we spent the majority of our time trying to determine which duos mated.[9] John still fields questions about how one can be certain that Utah prairie dogs are copulating when the behavior is occurring underground. Luckily, a host of aboveground behaviors can be diagnostic for underground copulation.

As interactions increased with a female that seemed to be coming into estrus, we watched carefully as dusk approached to see which male would submerge for the night with her. When a female with a closed vulva submerged with a male for the night after numerous interactions, that male was usually the first to mate with her early the next day. The following morning, we waited intently to observe whether the pair emerged from the same burrow, or whether the female emerged for the morning with a different male.[10]

Beds and wake-ups were often a good indicator of which male was controlling an area but were not a guarantee of copulation. Nor did they necessarily dictate the pattern of copulations that would occur during the female's day of estrus. But when copulation did occur as the result of spending all or part of the night together, the couple would wake up from the same burrow later than the rest of the colony, at around 9 to 10 a.m., rather than the usual 8 or 8:30. In most cases, after a male and an unmated female spent the night together, the female came into estrus the next day.

Certain females were really secretive with their matings. And that was when our MMLs were crucial. The MMLs helped us keep track of as many as 15 sexually mature males in the area of one of our observation towers. If a male was aboveground and visible, then he obviously was not consorting with a female. But if he was missing, then he might have been mating underground, and so we then attempted to locate all of the unmated females in the area. If one of them was also missing, then we suspected that copulation was taking place underground.[11]

In typical matings, the female preceded the male underground—scored on our data sheets as a "BD," for "both down." Most mating

FIGURE 4.6. *Rejected advances.* Females not close to estrus often respond negatively to potential suitors. Here, Female-52 is rather testy toward Male-26 because she will not be sexually receptive for another few days—not to mention that 26 has invaded the clan of resident Male-Rear-Legs-41 (R41) to check her estrus status *(top).* Another female (unmarked at the time of the photo) shows the same behavior as the reproductive but small and inexperienced Male-Rear-Legs-12 (R12) attempts to court her *(bottom).*

sequences involved many BDs, and as with every other aspect of matings, BDs showed marked variation. Some pairs remained underground for as little as one minute, but other pairs stayed underground for as long as four hours. How much of each BD was devoted to intercourse remains unknown.[12]

FIGURE 4.7. *Mating call.* A yearling reproductive male emits a mating call after copulating with a female (pictured center, marker unclear) who is upright and perhaps looking for additional mates. Meanwhile, another female (far right) is in the area for reasons that are unclear, also upright and apparently making the rarely seen mistake of misinterpreting a mating call for an alarm call.

Other Behaviors Associated with Copulation

Utah prairie dogs exhibit various behaviors in concert with copulation that occur at no other time. Among the most salient is a vocalization emitted by males before or after copulation that we have called the "mating call."[13] This repetitive vocalization sounds very much like an alarm call but is softer and slower and can be distinguished by its occurrence just before or just after a BD. Indeed, Utah prairie dogs seem to differentiate between utterances based on the context. Nearby individuals run to a burrow mound in response to an alarm call but often do not respond in any way to a mating call (fig. 4.7).[14]

No one knows why male Utah prairie dogs give a mating call. Just distinguishing whether the mating call is directed at an estrous female or male adversaries is difficult because of massive variance in the vocalization.[15] Some males always call in response to an estrous female. Some never call. Some females elicit one mating call during estrus, but others elicit scores of mating calls. And, for extra fun, some males call for certain females but not for others! Mating calls can last a few seconds or an hour, and the same male can discharge frequent, long mating calls in response to some estrous females but short calls for others. I have also observed males calling during courtship, after copulation, or both, although most call before sex.[16] One would think that a call that clearly broadcasts the presence of an estrous female to competing males would be unwise for the announcer, but mating calls nonetheless occur for about 50 percent of estrous females each spring.

In one sense, the mating call seems to assert a male's competitive status to a rival so as to make him less vulnerable to take-over. Because the call occasionally comes after copulation, it is unlikely that the call is given to increase the sexual receptivity of the female—why would the male bother, having already copulated? Another possibility is that the mating call serves to advertise the male to females who will come into estrus in the future by showing that he is virile, or to allow other females to copy the current estrous female by choosing him.[17]

Other behaviors helped us identify BDs. For instance, within minutes after emergence from a BD, the male sometimes licked his penis or the female licked her vulva (fig. 4.8). Self-licking of genitals is a difficult maneuver for Utah prairie dogs, and they often amused us by falling over in the process. These behaviors might thwart certain genital infections or sexually transmitted diseases, or otherwise clean the area of irritation associated with copulation. Dust bathing also occurs after some BDs. Being a "dusty dog" appears to be equivalent to having a postcoitus prairie dog shower.[18]

More evidence that these interesting aboveground behaviors were diagnostic of underground copulation came later in the field season. The dates that juveniles emerged from their natal burrows correlated almost exactly with the dates of copulation we inferred from aboveground behaviors. This is good evidence that BDs really do involve copulation.[19]

Ready for More

When compared to females with only one mate, polyandrous Utah prairie dog females

FIGURE 4.8. *Postcoitus.* Sweet-16 licks his penis after copulating with a female.

(i.e., females that copulate with two or more males) are more likely to conceive, wean large litters, and produce pups that survive to become yearlings and beyond.[20] The exact mechanism for these advantages remains unknown, but mating with more than one male makes good sense. Perhaps this is why females can mate with up to five males during their single annual day of sexual receptivity.[21]

If a female mates with only one male, then that male will inevitably sire all of her offspring. But if she mates with two or more males, the first male might sire some, none, or all of the female's offspring. In fact, data show that while the first male is the most likely progenitor, over 50 percent of litters might be sired by more than one male.[22]

We could tell that an estrous female was seeking additional mates because of the abrupt change in her behavior after copulation. Before insemination, a reproductive male initiates behavioral interactions with the estrous female, who reciprocates his interest. But after the last BD with that male, the estrous female no longer allows anal sniffing, runs away from him, and usually ambushes him if he comes too close for her comfort.[23]

FIGURE 4.9. *Close to the vest*. Sweet-16 guards Female-72 near the burrow where they just copulated *(left)*. After staying in her vicinity for a few minutes, he emits a mating call *(right)*.

A male's behavior also changes drastically after mating with a female. When copulation has occurred late in the day, a male can usually incarcerate a female until the end of the day and then submerge with her for the night. But when the copulation occurs in the morning, the male can usually maintain control only for several hours (fig. 4.9a–b). Males often have to stop their guarding when they lose a crucial fight with another male, or when the female escapes the area. Males also shorten their guarding when a second female in the home clan territory is estrous on the same day, making it a better investment for the male to mate with her before she can leave the area temporarily and be monopolized by another male.

When a female copulates with a second, third, or fourth male, the chance of paternity for each male becomes lower and lower. This means that the first mate has proportionately more to lose than the second and third mates when a female copulates with an additional male. Accordingly, first-mating males guard females longer and more assiduously than other males.[24]

For males who are not the biggest of the bunch, the propensity of Utah prairie dog females to have multiple mates is good news.

In many animals, males almost always win the right to copulate with females simply by being the largest and the strongest. With Utah prairie dog males, larger size certainly helps win a fight and access a female, but bigger is not always better.[25] Home-field advantage is also important, as a male must invade a territory and thrash the resident convincingly to gain entry. Also important is the ability to win hostile interactions, and smaller males are sometimes more adept than large males at the nuances of combat.[26] With all reproductive males in on the action, and several estrous females per day in different areas of the colony, the Utah prairie dog mating season is a festival of laughing barks, mating calls, sniffing, kissing, BDs, territorial displays, chasing, and fighting that epitomizes the arduous fight to reproduce.

Till Death Do Us Part

Reproductive males search for mating opportunities at a substantial cost. They increase the overall time they spend vigilant during mating season in order to watch their rivals and possible mates. This means less time for foraging

FIGURE 4.10. *Foxhunt.* Red foxes are stealthy hunters of Utah prairie dogs, especially reproductive males that are preoccupied with looking for mates.

and searching for predators. In 2005, the latter were the downfall of a dozen sexually mature males, even though they were heavyset and in excellent condition for reproduction (figs. 4.10 and 4.11a–c). Among the victims was Male-Zero, taken by a red fox shortly after long bouts of vigilance geared toward seeking the company of an estrous female. Male-21 was also among the victims of a red fox, but at least he died happy—he had copulated earlier with a female and was aiming for more action with another. And Male-17 suffered the same fate when he strayed too close to the edge of the colony to emit territorial barks (fig. 4.12).

Reproductive males are therefore much more likely than random members of the population to be taken by predators during mating season. Indeed, we never witnessed a predation of a reproductive male during any other time.[27] This is an expected result, perhaps, but is inconsistent with conventional views of predation. When predators chase prey, adult victims are often the old and

FIGURE 4.11. *Sneak attack.* It takes only a split second for a red fox to explode out of the woods around a Utah prairie dog colony *(top)*, chase down an unassuming victim such as Male-Rear-Legs-12 (R12) *(middle)*, and capture it *(bottom)*.

FIGURE 4.12. *Too little, too late.* Male-17, consumed with the festivities of mating season, failed to spot a lurking red fox in time to save his life.

the weak. But nonjuvenile Utah prairie dog victims of predation are commonly young and middle-aged individuals that are in excellent condition rather than feeble.[28] These results also demonstrate the importance of long-term research with marked individuals for understanding the effects of rare events and unusual years. Had John terminated his research in 2004 rather than 2005, we would not have discovered this selective predation of Utah prairie dogs. And had the Dog Squad not marked every individual, or had we chosen to watch Utah prairie dogs at certain times but not others, we would have missed this pattern along with a host of other compelling behaviors.

Exceptions to the Rules

The fanfare of mating calls, laughing barks, and territorial displays was always thrilling.

But the rarest treat of any mating season was an aboveground copulation.[29] About three to four times a year, we saw a male mount an estrous female from the rear and immediately begin pelvic thrusting, while the pair lay on their sides. It was a bizarre sight, and sometimes an uncomfortable one for new assistants, who kidded that they were infringing on the privacy of the couple. For some females, all copulations occurred aboveground, and some males, like Male-16 (Sweet-16), seemed to exhibit a proclivity for aboveground copulation that surpassed that of their conspecifics (fig. 4.13a–d). A few females copulated with some males aboveground, and with other males underground. Go figure!

One disadvantage of copulating aboveground is the risk of disruption by competitors.[30] Males commonly invade an adjacent clan territory while the resident male is copulating with an estrous female aboveground.

FIGURE 4.13. *Exploits of Sweet-16.* The outgoing Sweet-16 sniffs the anal area of estrous Female-61 *(upper left)* and seems to be rebuffed *(upper right)* but is persistent and begins copulating with her. Inexplicably, the copulation occurs aboveground *(lower left)*. Afterward, he emits a mating call as Female-61 flees the area to search for additional mates *(lower right)*.

Stopping an aboveground copulation of a competing male sometimes allows the marauding male to sequester the female for himself, or, if he has already copulated with the female, to protect his reproductive investment. Another likely disadvantage of copulating aboveground is that the mating pair is more vulnerable to predation. Perhaps that applies to Utah prairie dogs, but we never observed a predation on either partner of a copulation that occurred aboveground.

Other events that occurred during mating season were completely bizarre. One afternoon in late March 2004 was especially unusual. Male-15, who started my fieldwork career by being the first animal I livetrapped, was one of the first individuals in the entire study colony to emerge from hibernation in 2004. For several days after, I watched Male-15 run unabated across a snow-covered wonderland, winning one territorial dispute after another. I gave him the nickname "I-15," after the interstate highway in southern Utah, because his efforts at one point enveloped several clans. His domain during this time was an area from the center of the colony all

FIGURE 4.14. *Taking the interstate*. The legendary I-15 was not the biggest Utah prairie dog in the colony, but in 2004 he emerged earlier from hibernation than all other males in the area around my tower. Resourcefulness helped him copulate many times that year. Photo by Theodore G. Manno.

the way back to the South Pole, the largest range of any Utah prairie dog John had ever seen, even though I-15 was neither the largest nor the most experienced male in the colony (fig. 4.14).

But no male could continue at that pace, and I-15 would eventually relinquish some of his territory as he focused on a large clan of females behind my tower. One day, warfare between males was particularly frequent, with I-15 fighting off three males (23, Ought-4, and Rear-Legs-25) who challenged the dominance of his clan the entire afternoon. The day ended with I-15 and Ought-4 coming to blows over the prize, a battle in which I-15 prevailed yet again.

The prize was a beauty and contained fertile females like 53, 69er, 98, Bicentennial, Black-Butt-2 (BB2), Collar-3 (C3), and Wide-Apart-5 (WA5). I-15 had won not only the opportunity to remain as the resident male of that clan territory, but also the right to sleep with BB2. I-15's intentions were

obvious. Even though BB2 was only a yearling female, I knew she would come into estrus the next day because of her swollen, closed vulva, observed during trapping.

The night got even more interesting as Wide-Apart-5 (WA5), an older female well known among Dog Squad members because of her stout figure and calm demeanor, entered the same area of connected burrows with I-15 and BB2 for the night, thus creating the possibility of a kinky threesome the next morning. Looking forward to the show but shivering with the beginning stages of hypothermia, I returned to metropolitan Bryce to eat some boxed macaroni and cheese, sleep, and do it all again the next day.

I-15, BB2, and WA5 awoke in the same area the next morning, interacted vibrantly for a few hours, and then went back down together. Apparently, both females were sexually receptive at the same time, and the ménage à trois was no longer speculation. With two females to monopolize instead of the usual one, the polygamist I-15 started his mating call directly after emerging from the copulatory burrow—"Hey! Get away from my females!" Ultimately, both of I-15's mates were able to leave the area and copulate with other males. But as their first mate, I-15 probably sired most of their offspring.

Issues with Weather

Inclement weather was the Dog Squad's worst enemy when it came to behavioral observations.[31] A thick layer of snow on the colony was evident during March and April, but the snow did not hinder our observations. Actually, Utah prairie dogs were easier to observe in the snow than when they blended in with the brown soil while no snow was present. But extremely cold days or periods of heavy snowfall created several problems. On cold days and during or just after heavy snowfall, Utah prairie dogs emerged for the day late, submerged for the night early, and submerged periodically throughout the day for protection from snow or to warm up from the cold temperatures. When they did, estrous females could copulate inconspicuously, and our system of doing 20-minute checks and watching for unusual emergences or submergences was less valuable than usual.

It became even harder to infer copulation if heavy snowfall continued for the majority of the day, because Utah prairie dogs stayed underground for most of the time and did not exhibit the aboveground diagnostic behaviors normally associated with copulation. Females can sometimes delay their estrus until a good weather day so as to have access to the full gamut of males, but such delays are unusual.[32]

Our ambitious goal was to witness all copulations every year, but unfortunately, that accomplishment was usually unattainable. A particularly exasperating situation occurred in March 2004, as I waited intently for the females in a small clan just east of my tower to become estrous. The clan was governed by the portly and experienced Male-Ought-4. Females Ring-Around-Rump-4 (RR4) and Racing-Stripe (RS) emerged for the morning every day for a week and kissed Ought-4 but showed no signs of looming estrus. Meanwhile, most of the females in the two adjacent clan territories under my tower had mated and were preparing for parturition.

Both RR4 and RS continued to interact with Ought-4, but with little vigor. I wondered about these unusual circumstances until we remembered a day the prior week when we had woken up to a heavy snow and could not venture out to the colony until about 9:30 a.m. When we did, only several individuals had emerged. We sat in the towers for the rest of the day, saw very few Utah prairie dogs, and witnessed no diagnostic behaviors of copulation. Discouraged, I figured that RR4 and RS must have mated with Ought-4 on this day, and perhaps with other males as well. I was not surprised to find that when

RR4 and RS finally did venture into a trap in mid-April, they had gained weight and showed protruding nipples, a sure sign that they were pregnant.[33]

Another day that week had been tough on me in other ways. Extreme cold had penetrated my dozen layers of clothing over about 11 hours of observing from the towers and 2 more of marking the few Utah prairie dogs we had trapped. I had returned home not just cold but actually shaking from the inside, numb in a few extremities, and probably in the beginning stages of hypothermia. Another assistant eventually developed bronchitis, which seemed to be traceable back to that ordeal. To suffer through a frigid day and not come out with a copulatory sequence was intensely disappointing. The only saving grace was that Elaine attained several one-of-a-kind pictures of Utah prairie dog behaviors in the snow.

When snow or rain began while traps were set, our preparedness was key (fig. 4.15). John always kept a master list of traps and when inclement weather came, we sprang into action and checked every single trapping station, ensuring that Utah prairie dogs were either released or taken to the van for processing. We did not want to find out what would happen to our study animals if we left them in a rain-soaked trap.

During an incident in May 2004, thunder and lightning arrived in concert with heavy rain. Dog Squad members, after a few months of doing fieldwork, seemed to consider staying in the towers to be a badge of honor and would often remain even when the situation became unreasonable. As the lightning came closer and the thunder gained volume, we pontificated through our walkie-talkies about the lack of need to abandon the towers and take cover, saying that we would wait out the storm in the towers until the prairie dogs emerged afterward. I was irrationally stubborn about leaving the tower, stating that the event was "just a little thunderstorm . . . no big deal."

FIGURE 4.15. *Calm before the storm*. Skies above the study colony often offered an empty threat of rain. On the rare occasions when precipitation occurred, we were prepared with lists so that we would not leave a trapped Utah prairie dog out in bad weather.

About 20 seconds later, a lightning bolt struck directly behind me, within a few yards of my tower. By then, of course, I was anxious to jump ship. "Yeah," I said, in the understatement of the month, "I guess maybe we should go into the van."

Why was I so low-key after nearly being killed by a lightning bolt? Perhaps it was because I was told that lightning had struck a tower before. In 1999, John's tower was struck by lightning at BCNP. John always told assistants it was the second closest he had come to death while studying prairie dogs, the first being the encounter with a charging bison in South Dakota while he was studying black-tailed prairie dogs in 1976.

Another disconcerting presence at the study colony was the occasional dust devil. Resembling a small tornado, these bundles of swirling wind would usually just liven up our day, but sometimes they were frightening. The worst dust devil we ever observed lifted a huge tarp from the park facilities, made it airborne, and threw it like a rag doll over a territory dominated by Male-23—over 100 yards (about 91 m) from its original location. A tower started to creak as it barely held together, and another lost part of a wall when a piece of plywood unhinged and flew off, bumbling across the colony as if it had made a great escape. One dust devil developed and started darting about the area as I was in the open field during a trap check, almost putting me down for the count. After that incident, I fretted each time the wind became strong, concerned that a dust devil would uproot my tower.[34]

At mating season's end I began to fight dehydration, even though temperatures at BCNP seldom climb above 90°F (32°C), even in summer.[35] I succeeded by drinking a few gallons of water a day. Typical practice was to freeze half a dozen jugs of water the night before and pass them out among the assistants upon arrival at the site, with emergency water always on hand in the Squad Van.

But bad weather and all, nothing stopped the Dog Squad from observing what was to come at the study colony. Following mating season, females were pregnant and faced all sorts of hardships on their way to giving birth underground. The onset of maternal behaviors from early-mating females arrived even before the end of the mating season. For those that were lucky enough to survive, a difficult road lay ahead for weaning a litter. Main problems included predators and competition with other Utah prairie dogs.

When the hustle and bustle of mating season passed, the number and quality of offspring was determined by the events of the next two and a half months, when females were pregnant and lactating. The weather slowly became warmer, the snow gradually melted, and so much more awaited the Dog Squad.

5

A Dog's Life

My mother groan'd, my father wept,
Into the dangerous world I leapt.
Helpless, naked, piping loud,
Like a fiend hid in a cloud.

Struggling in my father's hands,
Striving against my swaddling bands,
Bound and weary I thought best,
To sulk upon my mother's breast.
—WILLIAM BLAKE, "Infant Sorrow," 1794[1]

☾

Few events are more exciting than the year's first appearance of a Utah prairie dog pup aboveground. Dog Squad members scrutinize the colony with their binoculars, hoping to discover the precocious pup, waiting to tell the others like a lucky player at bingo night. By this time in early to mid-June, most of the snow has been gone for about six weeks, and the fresh grasses that will supply the young ones with nutrition are here to stay for the rest of spring and summer.

What follows over the next three weeks is an uprising of sorts. Litters from every mother in the colony will spring up all over. We will place hundreds of traps per day in an effort to capture the newcomers, assign them to their mothers, and initiate them into the long-term study with ear tags and dye markers. The first emergences of scores of new litters over a period of only five or six days cause chaos and pandemonium.

The transition of a barren, snowdrift-covered meadow to a grassy, warm field teeming with baby Utah prairie dogs in June is what Dog Squad members live for. The quantity of pups might seem to suggest that Utah prairie dogs are reproductively prolific, but unfortunately, the arrival of the pups is bittersweet. By the time the Dog Squad returns in March of the following year, almost half of the pups will have succumbed to starvation, predation, infanticide, or some other mishap. Even before the emergence of the first pup, some youngsters have been conceived but not weaned because of miscarriage, genetic defect, or the death of their mother.[2]

For the first pup of the year, victory results from surviving its mother's pregnancy, being born naked and blind in a natal burrow, and spending around five weeks underground during lactation. It's a dog's life for a new pup, and emerging from the natal burrow to warm weather and plentiful food is a milestone for each surviving baby.

FIGURE 5.1. *Ageless wonder*. The only known photo of Female-Black-Butt-9 (BB9, pictured right), the longest-lived Utah prairie dog on record. BB9 was mostly spared from the rigors of pregnancy and lactation, as she weaned only one litter during her eight years of life (she might have lived longer, but records do not extend beyond 2005). Perhaps this limited-stress lifestyle accounts in part for her longevity.

Utah prairie dog clans are cooperative breeding groups.[3] While reproductive individuals of both sexes live in a clan, yearling males and females often do not produce offspring. In addition, older females that have mated can sometimes lose their litter during pregnancy or lactation, making them nonreproductive as well. But everyone in the clan except the resident reproductive male is usually related to other clan members, so nonreproductive Utah prairie dogs of both sexes can still perpetuate their genes indirectly by helping the females in the clan that are raising litters.[4] This is where the cooperation comes in, and alarm calling or helping with burrow excavations and territorial defense are examples of how nonreproductive Utah prairie dogs can enhance the reproduction and survivorship of close kin.[5]

Barring captivity, where Utah prairie dogs do not experience the difficulties of surviving in a natural environment and therefore live longer, Male-25 holds the Utah prairie dog longevity record for his sex at seven years old. The record for a female, and overall, is held by Black-Butt-9 (BB9) at eight years old (fig. 5.1).[6] But these life spans are highly unusual. Just achieving sexual maturity or adulthood alone is an accomplishment for most Utah prairie dogs, and for those that do, females usually live about three to four years, and males about two to three years. With only a one- to two-year window for reproduction, and the capacity to produce only one litter per year, every postcopulatory behavior is crucial for the reproductive success of a pregnant female and her sexual partners.[7]

Competition among females is also a component of Utah prairie dog clans, and the delicate balance between competition and cooperation is precarious throughout the year.

Before and during the mating season, interactions among females of the same clan are usually amicable. But after females get their sperm and become pregnant, amicability turns to hostility (fig. 5.3). Fights between pregnant females are common, and the onset of maternal behaviors is obvious one or two days after sex. A female that has copulated will stop showing interest in males and will start competing for nursery burrows. And so the long road of pregnancy begins.

Filling an Empty Nest

Females claim their prospective nursery burrows by spending every night alone there and chasing all others away from the immediate area.[9] The most entertaining component of pregnancy involves a female taking nest material (NM) into her nursery burrow (figs. 5.4 and 5.5). Sometimes the nest building is sporadic, with a few mouthfuls of NM here and there over a few days. In other instances, females take dozens of clumps of NM to the nursery burrow on the same day. And some females take only four or five loads of NM to their burrow during a measly half-hour period.[10]

Females treat the collection of NM with great importance no matter how many mouthfuls they collect. Dedicated females often travel as far as 100 yards (91 m) to find dry grass that is acceptable for NM. Upon arrival at her nursery burrow with a bundle of grasses, a female will stop for a few seconds to arrange it in her mouth before diving in.

Some females take an easier route. They burglarize from another female while she is in the woods by sneaking into her burrow and stealing NM.[11] Over 50 percent of the NM for some nests consists of stolen property. This was just as well for the Dog Squad, because documenting the stealing of NM was often great fun. In one case from a territory south of my tower in 2004, Female-76 (Bicentennial)

FIGURE 5.2. *Fattening up*. Heavy females, like this one, typically mate early and have first dibs on child-rearing resources like nesting burrows.

FIGURE 5.3. *First weeks of pregnancy*. While fights between males are common during mating season, fights between females increase in frequency as pregnancies begin.

The fun begins during the summer, when females are fattening up to prepare for hibernation. If a female becomes heavy, she has an opportunity to emerge early in the mating season instead of continuing to hibernate for an extra few days to save energy. This typically yields a reproductive advantage, because females that mate early have first claims on resources in the home territory (fig. 5.2).[8]

FIGURE 5.4. *Feathering the nest*. Female-71 stuffs tough grasses into her mouth for transportation to her natal burrow.

FIGURE 5.5. *Homemaker*. Males like Sweet-16 sometimes help females gather nesting material.

stole from Female-98 while 98 was stealing from Bicentennial. And then an hour later, Bicentennial stole from BB2 while BB2 stole from 69. This charade grew to involve the entire clan and went on for days.

Pregnancy and Birth

As with most other Utah prairie dog behaviors, documenting that a female gave birth usually involved doing some detective work and spending almost every waking hour in the field. One possible shortcut was to livetrap the female just before birth and then immediately afterward. But usually we could not implement this strategy because it was disruptive to the mother and impractical for us. Besides, many females carefully avoided traps on the days just before and just after giving birth, having no interest in a whole-oat treat because they were preoccupied with parturition and neonatal care.[12]

Every so often a pregnant female would happen to walk into a trap. Those that did exhibited a white vagina before parturition, which turned pink (or in extreme cases, red, with bloodstains on the fur) within a day after giving birth. On the same day that the vagina changed color, a precipitous drop in the female's body mass—usually 1.8–3.5 ounces (50–100 g)—also occurred (fig. 5.6).[13]

Because regular livetrapping of females to verify parturition was not feasible, the other method for determining most parturitions, though a bit less exciting, was to simply observe diagnostic aboveground behaviors. Once again, we had our MMLs to thank. Originally designed to help us find couples that were copulating underground, MMLs that were revised to include females in April and May also helped us determine when females gave birth. Any striking change in routine made us suspicious.[14]

Pregnant females usually emerge early in the morning. They spend the entire day

FIGURE 5.6. *Losing the baby weight.* Pregnant females have round stomachs but show a precipitous weight loss after they give birth.

foraging aboveground or in the woods collecting nest material and consistently submerge for the night just before sunset. But on the night before parturition, a mother usually goes to bed two to three hours earlier than usual, either to give birth that night or to prepare for parturition the following morning. A female that has just given birth sometimes does not emerge for the morning until three to four hours after other Utah prairie dogs, or she does not appear aboveground at all. Later that day, the female also makes one or more long visits to her nursery burrow or is among the first in the colony to submerge for the night.[15]

This difference in routine indicated that the female had given birth underground and was retiring early to her nursery burrow to nurse her litter. We therefore inferred that

the date of birth was the first day of the pink vagina, or the day of a precipitous weight loss, or an unusually late first emergence by the mother in the morning, or an unusually early final submergence by the mother at night, or some combination thereof. Subtracting this date from the female's date of mating that we observed, John determined that the length of pregnancy was usually 29 or 30 days but was occasionally as short as 28 days or as long as 31 days.[16]

It would be a simpler story if every female that copulated gave birth, but that was not the case. About 20 percent of females that copulate never exhibit parturition.[17] Despite having sex, some of these females probably never actually conceive. Other nonbirthing females probably conceive but abort all embryos at some point during pregnancy.[18] In particular, yearling females have a lower rate of parturition than adult females.[19] Picking the proper nest materials, establishing a mini territory around an appropriate nursery burrow, gaining sufficient body mass during the preceding winter, having the physical maturity necessary to stay pregnant and give birth—these are all areas in which older Utah prairie dog females probably have an advantage over yearling females.

One issue the Dog Squad did not investigate is whether the number of pups in the litter just after conception is the same as it is when the female gives birth. Is it possible that some females resorb certain embryos and later give birth to the others? Can a female give birth underground to a litter of four, even though five embryos existed at some point during the pregnancy? And what about after birth? Do some pups perish in a way not visible to scientists, so that the number of emergent pups is different from the number at birth?[20] These are the types of questions that remain, along with determining the intention of a few females that took their helpless young aboveground and moved them to another natal burrow just after parturition (fig. 5.7).

FIGURE 5.7. *Making a move.* Female-Front-Legs (F) inexplicably transfers her preemergent pup to another natal burrow. Perhaps the behavior results from predation or infanticide risk near the original natal burrow.

These cases involved either the transfer of entire litters from one burrow to another, or in a few cases, movement of one or two pups from a litter of several followed by abandonment of the relocated pups.

A serious risk to pregnant Utah prairie dog females is a higher probability of predation. During 2005, we observed four pregnant females succumb to predation by red foxes and northern goshawks (fig. 5.8). From females like Bicentennial, who was victimized when a red fox surprised her while making some finishing touches on her burrow mound, to 5-Stripe-Racing-Stripe (5SRS), who could not easily retreat to the colony center when a red fox made a strike in the woods, pregnant females were evidently at a major disadvantage because of their inability to run fast. Future researchers may discover that pregnant females of other mammalian species may be similarly vulnerable.[21]

Don't Be a Loser

Some female Utah prairie dogs can lose their litter during pregnancy, but others lose litters during the period of lactation. Either way, Dog Squad members could easily identify a "loser" because we lived with the Utah prairie dogs every day. Changes in routine, as usual, were pivotal. A pregnant or lactating female spends most of her time in the vicinity of her nursery burrow. She vigorously defends the nursery burrow from other Utah prairie dogs, frequently rearranges the soil at its entrance, and sleeps in it each night.[22] Toward the end of pregnancy and through lactation, Dog Squad members with adequate binoculars and good eyesight could detect enlarged teats on the chest of the mother from the observation tower (fig. 5.9).

But when a female became a loser, these standard practices went by the wayside and

FIGURE 5.8. *Looking for lunch*. Northern goshawks feasted on slow-moving pregnant females in 2005.

FIGURE 5.9. *With child*. Pregnant females have visible teats on their underside. Dog Squad members could see them during fights.

she began to exhibit behaviors that were consistent with those of nonreproductive females. Usually we became suspicious when we saw a female wake up in a burrow other than the one she had reserved for her nursery burrow. At that point, we tried to livetrap the female to look for other signs to determine whether the unusual wake-up was an anomaly or a diagnostic indicator of a lost litter. Females that are late in their pregnancy or that have given birth and are nursing offspring have long, turgid nipples. Flat and dry nipples indicate a loser.[23]

Infanticide

It was a routine afternoon for the Dog Squad in late May 2005, as we drank coffee and waited for litters to emerge. By our side were our trusty MMLs, with all individuals in the area listed, although they were not particularly useful at that moment because our study animals had left for their usual late afternoon foraging in the woods. Many individuals had therefore not shown up for the 20-minute check, but we had little concern that anything unusual was taking place as we continued with the lazy afternoon.

Suddenly, our peace was disturbed. Yearling Male-Rear-Legs-17 (R17) emerged from a nursery burrow behind John's tower with a small pink animal in his mouth, twirling it with his paws. Could it be? Was it?

It was.

R17 was killing, and apparently devouring, the unweaned offspring of Female-Ring-Around-Rump-5 (RR5X). Mother RR5 was in the woods foraging, none the wiser.

Infanticide undermines any pretense of Utah prairie dogs being "cute little furry critters." Nature is tough, sometimes cruel, and Utah prairie dogs are wild animals.

R17 would go on to kill another pup that day (Collar-Back-Stripe-X, or CBSX). During

both of R17's maraudings, the mother was away foraging in the woods, and R17 simply submerged into the nursery burrow and emerged a few minutes later with a pup in his mouth (fig. 5.10a–b). Later, the mothers returned and spent an inordinate amount of time examining the inside of their burrow, as if they knew one of their offspring was missing.

Other cases of infanticide that occurred the year before were just as macabre, as the actions of Male-Rear-Legs-21 (R21) made the colony literally a dog-eat-dog world. Female-Racing-Stripe-Back-Stripe (RSBS, whom we called "Skunky" because the pattern of these stripes on her back resembled those of a skunk) left her clan territory in midafternoon to take a foraging trip, and after her clan mates did the same, the territory was void of defenders. Once Skunky was about half a football field from her nursery burrow, Male-Rear-Legs-21 (R21), who had already killed two 55Xs on different days, spotted the opportunity. R21 invaded Skunky's territory and submerged into her nursery burrow.

He emerged several minutes later with a squirming youngster, which he slammed onto the ground and hit with his paw. Seeming like she was somehow vaguely aware of the situation, Skunky moved closer to the burrow halfheartedly, causing R21 to drop the pup and go back to his adjacent home territory. About half an hour later, R21 returned to munch on Skunky's daughter—and so did Skunky. This bizarre episode was among the most puzzling and ghoulish we ever observed.

Infanticide—the killing of juvenile animals by a member of the same species[24]—is the ultimate exception to cooperative breeding in Utah prairie dogs, and it is yet another behavior for which we have ten times as many questions as answers. Our fascination with the morbid behavior motivated us to generate the dedication necessary to document it. An infanticide occurred only once about every 400 human-hours of dawn-to-dusk watching,

FIGURE 5.10. *Marauder*. Male-Rear-Legs-17 (R17) killed two pups on the same day in 2005.

but with Utah prairie dogs disappearing to the woods to forage within an hour of emerging for the morning, and often not arriving back into the home territory until happy hour at 5–6 p.m., opportunities for infanticide were abundant. We spent thousands of hours at the study colony sitting around and waiting to see if someone would kill a baby. Thus, when an infanticide occurred, it was quite an event—one that members of the Dog Squad observed 48 times in their 11 years of research at BCNP.[25]

Not every Dog Squad member could observe an infanticide when it occurred, because his or her tower was not always close enough to the carnage. I went through two complete field seasons and never saw one. Each day (or year) without an infanticide built the tension. In 2004, I thought I was going to document my first infanticide. A week after R21 started his murderous rampage, another nonreproductive yearling male called Rear-Legs-37 (R37) occasionally strayed from his clan territory just north of my tower to an area bordering the South Pole. One day, he spent an hour going in and out of burrows, and I held my breath. But R37 never emerged with an unweaned pup, nor did he exhibit aboveground diagnostic signals of infanticide like having blood on his face or licking his claws. Indeed, we never saw these diagnostic signals unless a Utah prairie dog had just committed infanticide.[26]

Not only did the actual killing of pups pique our interest, but so did the cannibalism, which occurred after over 90 percent of the infanticides witnessed during the 11 years at BCNP.[27] The victim was not always consumed, but when it was, it was quite a feast for the marauder. Estimating conservatively, just half of a pup that is within a few weeks of emergence would provide at least 2–2.5 ounces (60–70 g) of meat. For a two-pound (almost 1,000 g) male Utah prairie dog, that is about one-sixteenth of his body weight—the equivalent of a 200-pound (90 kg) man eating a 12- to 13-pound (5.5–6 kg) burger in just half an hour!

Infanticide has often been dismissed as a freakish behavior occurring in response to disturbance, unnatural circumstances, or overcrowding.[28] This rationale is not appropriate for Utah prairie dogs. Complex diagnostic behaviors such as licking the claws and dust bathing are sometimes coupled with the act of infanticide, and this coupling suggests that infanticide is favored by natural selection.[29] In addition, infanticide affected 15 percent of Utah prairie dog litters, which indicates that the behavior is not isolated.[30] But the reason why natural selection would act to favor infanticide remains unclear.

Most cases of infanticide involved a yearling or adult reproductive male that did not mate with the mother that spring, or a nonreproductive yearling male. But the most curious cases occurred when Utah prairie dog males killed the lactating offspring of females with whom they had copulated just five to seven weeks earlier. In other words, these marauding males might have been killing their own offspring![31] Are the chances of fathering offspring in these cases so small that males are more likely to reap another benefit from the killings? Is it possible that a male can somehow discriminate between his and another male's offspring, and kill only the latter?[32] Or are we analyzing things too much, and males simply do not remember anything from the mating season? These were the types of vexing questions that we discussed on the way home in the Squad Car during the period of infanticides.

Equally curious was when mothers seemed to defend their natal burrows only weakly during the time when infanticides occurred, spending much of their time in the woods foraging among the pines. Are infanticides so rare that they are not worth a defense? Does the larger size of males render a defensive effort worthless? We will probably never know.

In the cases of R17 and R21, perhaps each was trying to clear the way for his possible offspring in the next year. This seems to be a good rationale for males that will be reproductive after emerging from hibernation.[33] But with so many males in the colony, R17 and R21 were far from guaranteed to ever be the resident male in the clan territories where they killed unweaned offspring. Besides, R17 and R21 killed some female pups that were potential mates for the following year, which could have hurt their chance to reproduce.

Although it was unusual, we did see individuals other than the marauder benefit from cannibalizing recently killed juveniles. Rarely does the marauder consume the entire victim, and the abandoned carcass is then available to other colony members. A raven commonly flies off with an abandoned juvenile carcass, however, so opportunities for cannibalism by noninfanticidal Utah prairie dogs are rare.

Reproductive success of marauders should increase if natural selection favors infanticide. John has seen no such trend, but the rare nature of infanticide limits analysis to only four dozen instances. The mysterious proclivity of some rogue Utah prairie dogs to kill unweaned juveniles, occasionally their own potential offspring, is one of the many challenges facing future researchers.

Young-of-the-Year

Oh, those bowsers! Late spring at the "Canyon of the Dogs" was a wild time. After a relatively monotonous four or five weeks of dogging it in the towers, we finally saw the pups start to appear aboveground. Litter sizes when babies first appear aboveground range from one to seven, but the most common litter sizes are four and five. Each pup weighs around half a pound (150–250 g), with male pups weighing in a bit heavier.[34]

They are the cutest animals ever, but sometimes over 200 pups first appeared aboveground over a period of only 10 days, and every single one needed to be trapped, marked, and processed (fig. 5.11). John would often begin a day of "baby season" by announcing, "Buckle up for a long, exciting day at the study colony."

We assumed that pups coming out of a nursery burrow defended by a female belonged to that female. And the vast majority of the time, this was the case. But sometimes what happens underground stays underground. On rare occasions, 10 or more juveniles emerged from the same burrow. Mixing of offspring evidently had occurred, and we could not assign each baby to its mother (fig. 5.12a–c). We did not know whether the "extra" pups arrived in the burrow of their emergence on their own volition, or with help from their mothers. Perhaps the mother defending the exploding burrow kidnapped the pups.[35] Why she would do that is anyone's guess, but in the rare cases when mixing takes place underground before the pups emerge, not much can be ruled out.

Whatever is occurring in these situations, it is clear that females generally accept foster offspring from within the clan either before or after they emerge. Soon after pups first mix with other litters, they begin to spend the night together in the same burrow with any of several mothers that usually are in the clan. Rarely, pups even spend the night with mothers whose pups have not yet appeared aboveground.[36]

Nursing

Utah prairie dog pups are not quite weaned when they appear aboveground. Weaning does not occur until about one to two weeks after pups see the aboveground world for the first time, and juveniles in some litters continue to nurse, at least occasionally, for as long as four weeks after first emergence from the natal burrow.[37] Our use of the term "lactation" to

FIGURE 5.11. *Fuzzy factor*. Utah prairie dog pups emerge in mid-June and are pretty much the cutest animals ever.

FIGURE 5.12 *(clockwise left to right). Mix and match.* Sibling Utah prairie dog pups generally emerge from the same natal burrow. After a day or two of exploring the world aboveground, litters from different mothers move beyond the immediate region around their natal burrows and begin to interact. Here, a Black-Butt-5-X (BB5X, left) has joined a litter of Front-Legs-o-Xs (FoXs) for an afternoon of looking for predators, and later, some FoXs make friends with nonsibling pups.

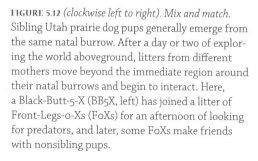

FIGURE 5.13. *Nursing along.* A female nurses her pup while on the ground in a fetal position *(left)*; Front-Legs-0 (Fo), with a faded marker, nurses her pup from a more conventional upright posture *(right)*.

refer to the period between birth and first emergence from the natal burrow is therefore convenient, but not fully accurate. Preemergent Utah prairie dog pups depend on mother's milk, but mothers will also bring some plants underground for them to munch. By the same token, emergent pups get nourishment primarily by foraging, but it is usually a week or two before they completely cease nursing.[38]

Unfortunately for the Dog Squad, most nursing occurs belowground. Just after parturition, we saw mothers enter their natal burrows during the day, apparently to nurse their helpless young. And for about a week after this, we routinely saw females emerge late for the day and submerge early for the night to tend to their motherly duties. But once pups have emerged, they sometimes nurse aboveground late in the day, just before adults and juveniles submerge for the night.

John has witnessed aboveground nursing over 800 times, observing it in Utah prairie dogs for the first time when Female-Back-Stripe (BS) nursed her pup in 1995. In order to nurse, a pup will approach a lactating female, nuzzle her chest, and dip his or her head to latch onto a teat. Mom usually stands upright

as if vigilant for a predator but sometimes stays on all fours (fig. 5.13a–b). Mothers may also nurse several of their pups simultaneously. Female Utah prairie dogs have 10 nipples in two vertical columns of 5 down the chest and abdomen, and they break off nursing by changing postures or scurrying a foot or two from the area, either because something occurs in the colony or because they are out of milk.[39]

Female-Wide-Apart-9 (WA9) was one of the great aboveground nursers of all time. Her exploits began in 1998. One of WA9's offspring would sniff and kiss her and then nuzzle her chest as if to ask for milk. Female-WA9 would then stand up in the classic upright position and present the large, turgid teats on her belly to her offspring. The WA9X would have its fill, usually for 5 to 10 minutes, and then run off. Mother WA9 would then return to her foraging activities in a clan territory behind John's tower.

This aboveground nursing by Female-WA9 occurred most nights for a week or so, sometimes with two WA9Xs joining in the feast. Then one night, something unusual happened. A 55X, the offspring of another mother from WA9's clan, approached WA9. Just like the

FIGURE 5.14. *Wet nurses*. Communal nursing involves females providing milk to nearby pups that are not necessarily their own. Here, a female is starting to nurse three pups with at least two different markers.

FIGURE 5.15. *Milkmaid*. Female-78 nurses a Front-Legs-o-X (FoX).

WA9X, she nuzzled WA9's chest fur. And lo and behold, WA9 once again lifted herself, presented her nipples, and let the juvenile nurse. Female-WA9 was nursing another mother's pup, and she seemed to be doing so willingly.

Over the next seven years, John saw many instances of this "communal nursing" during the three to four weeks after pups first appeared aboveground (figs. 5.14 and 5.15). About one-quarter of aboveground nursings involved a mother suckling another mother's offspring. The majority of these instances featured pups that nursed alone. Many pups nursed from whatever lactating female in their clan was nearby, instead of limiting themselves to only their mother.[40] Some

riving them out. Male Sweet-16 chases archrival yearling Male Rear-Legs-12 (R12) from his clan.

tand by your clan. Female clan mates check for predators on a clear morning in late June.

Up close and personal. After some finishing touches on his burrow, a Utah prairie dog stands vigilant and looks for predators with dirt on the brim of his nose.

surmountable. Male Sweet-16 pummels his less experienced adversary Male Rear-Legs-33 (R33) during an epic siege that settled glorious battle for clan dominance.

ly as a fox. A red fox snags a Utah prairie dog during a surprise attack.

It's a boy. John Hoogland informally checks the sex of a study subject by viewing its underside.

Kissing cousins. Two female clan mates say "hi" on a warm day in June.

Nest egg. A female Utah prairie dog brings nesting material to a burrow where her pups will be born.

Great scenery. A rainbow traces the sky over Utah's Paunsaugunt Plateau.

Bright-eyed. Utah prairie dog pups are pretty much the cutest animals ever.

Eat up! A female Utah prairie dog chows down on grasses during a warm summer afternoon in an effort to bulk up prior to hibernation.

Good to be home. Female Triple-Stripe (TS) is released to her clan territory after receiving her unique marker in the Squad Van.

Red Yogi. With intense eyes and folded paws, "Red Yogi" stands under southern Utah's tall grasses.

mothers were particularly inclined to nurse communally. One mother (50) nursed foster offspring (i.e., the offspring of other females) in five consecutive years; and two mothers (5-Stripe and 64) nursed foster offspring in three successive years. The feats of champion nurser Wide-Apart (WA) were historic—she nursed a whopping 17 foster offspring in 2003, along with nursing foster offspring in four consecutive years.

Because litters also commingle underground overnight, and because communal nursing aboveground is commonplace, it is likely that communal nursing also occurs underground. When pups move into a burrow with the pups of another mother, the mother follows and spends the night with them. Communal nursing underground or at night is likely in these cases.[41]

Communal nursing is fascinating on several levels. For one thing, nursing seems to be a behavior that humans relate to well.[42] From a scientific standpoint, questions exist as to why natural selection would favor the nursing of foster offspring. Milk is, after all, a limited resource, and one would think that mothers would dispense it only to their own offspring.[43]

Several factors have probably been important in the evolution of communal nursing. For one thing, pups are still in their natal burrows and have not mixed with other litters before first emergence, except in very unusual circumstances. Communal nursing therefore occurs only during the one to two weeks after a litter emerges, which minimizes the energetic cost of giving milk to foster pups. Furthermore, foster offspring are almost always from other mothers in the home territory. This means that foster mothers are often genetically related to foster offspring. While they do not share as many genes with foster offspring as they do with their own offspring, suckling nondescendant kin might be an important way to help individuals that share the mother's genes.[44]

Nursing foster offspring might also be adaptive for another reason. Just after they emerge, pups cannot run as fast as adults, do not respond to alarm calls as quickly, and can be carried away by predators more easily because they weigh less.[45] By suckling the pups of other females, a mother increases the chance that other pups will cluster around her own offspring, so that her own babies will be less likely to be captured if a predator attacks.[46]

Because each litter is isolated in a separate home nursery burrow for five to six weeks after the pups are born, it seems that mothers could easily learn to distinguish between their own offspring and those of other mothers if such discrimination were important. Whether females actually make this discrimination after first emergence from the natal burrow is something that we will probably never know.[47]

Playtime

Life as a pup is fast and fleeting. Luckily, a little time for playing can be squeezed in during the arduous fight for survival. Pups have playmates of both sexes and all ages. On occasion, a pup that has been weaned for three to four weeks squares up with a partner that has been weaned for only one to two weeks. The result is a decided awkwardness between the two, usually a sniff and then some mild agitation with sparring, followed by the smaller pup squealing and running away to escape an encounter that was doomed from the outset.[48]

Play interactions occur in a variety of forms (fig. 5.16a–b). Usually two individuals are involved, but groups of three or four sometimes play together. One pup might chase another, pounce when appropriate, and wrestle the "tagged" pup for a minute until they either stop or resume the chase. Or, two pups kiss and sniff, and then one jumps on the

FIGURE 5.16. *Child's play*. Pups from different litters engage in amicable interaction and feign fighting.

other and feigns hostility. The recipient battles back, ambushing in retaliation, and they joust, wrangle, and roll down the hill of a burrow mound in a furry tumbleweed of fury.

Other pairs size each other up by standing slightly upright as they face each other. They bite one another playfully and look for an opportunity to tackle the other or grab hold of a body part. A mischievous chomp of fur on the scruff of the neck or an illegal hand to the face sometimes occurs, but if one pup goes overboard, the other squeals a bit and ends the scrum by running away.[49] All of this activity is in addition to the amicable social

interaction that pups initiate with clan mates as they learn to recognize members of the natal territory (fig. 5.17).

To the casual observer, playing among pups seems to have little purpose other than relaxation, exercise, and cheap thrills. But play is an activity carefully crafted by millions of years of natural selection. Play is what some scientists call "incomplete behavior," which means it is a way of practicing survival skills or other tasks in which young will engage later in life.[50]

One example is defense of the home territory from invaders.[51] With their play-fights, males can practice the skills needed to jockey for position around an estrous female or to acquire and maintain residency with a clan. And females can hone their sparring abilities so that one day, they can oust invaders from their home territory.

Play copulation is another example of incomplete behavior.[52] A rendezvous that involves sexual practice usually starts with a playful bite or shove, followed by a tumble where one pup somehow lands on the other pup's back. Using a motion that needs no description, the top pup, almost always a male, will instigate sexual play (fig. 5.18).

Pups who are recipients of play copulatory thrusting by males are not always female. Male Utah prairie dog pups occasionally seem to either not know or not be concerned with the sex of their copulatory play partner. Around a half dozen male-male homosexual play interactions occur a year, but I have seen adults that appear to be engaging in such conduct only one time—in that case, both participants were female (fig. 5.19).[53]

Utah prairie dog pups do not always play with each other. They are quite inquisitive about practically any foreign object in the colony, and so are their adult counterparts. Especially if the item is shiny, Utah prairie dogs will attack such objects as invaders of the clan territory. Gear belonging to Dog Squad members that colony residents ambushed,

FIGURE 5.17. *Like father, like son*. Pup Front-Legs-o-X (FoX) enjoys a kiss with Male-Rear-Legs-41 (R41), one of his possible fathers.

FIGURE 5.18. *Playing the fool*. Two pups play-copulate by burrow UP.

FIGURE 5.19. *Not what it looks like?* Elaine photographed apparent pseudocopulation or some other bizarre behavior involving two adult females (note the design-oriented markers that denote females) during mating season in 2005. The event remains unexplained.

scrutinized, and seized included earmuffs, gloves, notebooks, novels, toothbrushes, walkie-talkies, and writing utensils.

Two ruffians even took umbrage at the paintbrushes that we used to apply their unique markers. Ring-Around-Rump-4 (RR4) was the ringleader and conspirator who recruited baby Racing-Stripe (RSX) as a confederate in the infamous Brush Theft of June 2004. The dynamic duo exacted their revenge on "Mr. Brushy" by inspecting and dragging their archnemesis into a burrow in their clan territory. We never saw Mr. Brushy again, but luckily, we had a replacement.

Snacks that field assistants brought to the colony were also considered fair game by playful pups and adults. The Dog Squad quickly learned not to leave any nut-based items on the ground because of several unsubstantiated reports of peanut butter thefts at the colony, all post–juvenile emergence, when the furry rapscallions had few concerns other than food. Apples were a favorite of kleptomaniac Utah prairie dogs, and we kept them away too. Despite these minor aggravations, it was unfortunate from an entertainment standpoint that Utah prairie dogs played less as they got older.

Preparing for Winter

Nourishment acquired after the reproductive cycle helps Utah prairie dogs change out their coats. Adults molt all of their fur twice a year, once each for their summer and winter pelages. Each molt takes about one to two weeks to complete. The color of winter and summer pelages is almost identical. Winter fur is thicker than summer fur and helps protect Utah prairie dogs from the frigid Rocky Mountain winters.[54]

Females that are raising litters are often the last of the adults to molt and enter hibernation, while younger animals that do not breed are among the first to molt and start hibernating.[55] Hibernation for Utah prairie dogs is not a mere temporary torpor. Rather, it is a full-fledged physiological change with drastic reductions in metabolic rate, heartbeat, and body temperature. During this time, Utah prairie dogs remain asleep for long periods and are not easily aroused.[56]

Our other academic commitments and the necessity of making a living precluded us from watching the Utah prairie dogs until hibernation. Whether they simply disappeared into a burrow one day only to remain unseen until mating season is unknown. We suspect that, as we saw in reverse when they emerged from hibernation, a two- to three-week period occurs when individuals spend more and more time in their burrow per day, going in and out of torpor until they achieve an extended period of sleep and decreased metabolism. We know that several members of a clan sometimes hibernate together in the same burrow, because three or four individuals sometimes aroused together from hibernation at the same burrow entrance.[57] And it also seems that despite hibernation, many Utah prairie dogs do not survive the long, frigid winter of BCNP each year.[58]

Because good nutrition is not readily available the entire year, and because they are preoccupied with mating activities during other times of the year, Utah prairie dogs must gain weight during the dog days of summer. Eating as much as they can before hibernation provides the food necessary to make the fat needed to survive until the thaw of the next year.[59] Pups that are heavy when they first appear aboveground at nine weeks old

FIGURE 5.20. *On thin ice*. Utah prairie dog pups that are on the light side, like these rascals, are less likely to survive the winter and become yearlings than their heavier counterparts.

are more likely than pups of lower body mass to survive the winter. But voracious feeding during the summer is crucial for all pups and adults if they are to survive until the following spring (fig. 5.20).[60]

For adults, the advent of sleepytime is different depending on sex and reproductive status. Males and nonreproductive animals offer almost no parental care, so they fatten up for most of the spring after mating season. They have the luxury of dipping into hibernation early because they possess enough energy, which means they no longer need to absorb the risk of predation that comes from foraging aboveground. Reproductive females, however, stretch out the summer as much as they can. They have been preoccupied with child rearing

FIGURE 5.21. *Being defensive*. Utah prairie dog pups must defend against the omnipresent threat of predation, just like adults.

and need time to catch up with the males and nonreproductive females.[61]

Under a constant threat of predation during the summer (fig. 5.21) and facing the possibility of starvation over the winter, only about half of the pups survive to the following year. But tremendous variation exists in the number of pups that become yearlings.[62] No matter who survives, or at least stays in the colony, each spring is a new beginning. All clan territories are up for grabs, and slightly different combinations of individuals make up clans each year. Every March, the extravaganza we call mating season begins again, just as it has for thousands of years.

After leaving the field site for the year, I never saw some of my friends again. But memories of their antics stayed with me. As the field season came to an end, I thought of the prairie dogs I got to know, and I wondered about their future.

SLOW

PRAIRIE DOG
XING

6

The Last Stand of Tic-Tac-Toe

Along the railroads the [prairie dogs] have been so accustomed to the trains
that they no longer take fright as the great noisy engine rushes madly by . . .
they are best observed, perhaps, from the windows of passing trains . . . it is
extraordinary how soon animals lose their fear of naturally terrifying objects when
such objects come and go frequently without doing them bodily violence.
—C. HART MERRIAM, *Yearbook of the United States Department of Agriculture*, 1902[1]

☽

*Among my most beloved experiences was releasing a pup that was marked and processed
for the first time. New friends sometimes died quickly, but I had the opportunity of
watching many pups grow, learn the ropes, fatten up, and become core members of the
colony. When I released a new study animal, I considered that one day it could develop
into a fertile female who would produce descendants that would define the colony for
years to come, or a male who could grow to become leader of an entire clan.*

*For this reason, leaving the study site in mid-July was always heartbreaking. The
feeling was particularly distressing following John's last year of studying Utah prairie
dogs in 2005. Every member of the Dog Squad realized that we would never know the
fates of some of our favorite animals.*

*How long would Black-Butt-9 continue to live, having already set the Utah prairie
dog longevity record in the wild? We always believed that her durability was due in part
to her producing only one emergent litter during her eight years, sparing her the energy
expenditure and bodily deterioration associated with raising pups to term. She was such
a flexible, laid-back type, and her independence in living peacefully on the western edge
of the colony was extraordinary. How disappointing it was that we would never know
the exact year of her death.*

*Would in-training protégé yearling males that we watched grow up before our eyes,
like Rear-Legs-18 (R18), Rear-Legs-26 (R26), and Rear-Legs-40 (R40), who gained
weight and showed signs of the aggression necessary to be the central figure in a clan,
ever become the big dogs at the colony?*

*Would the pups with disadvantaged childhoods, who came from litters ravaged by
infanticide or predation, or who were switched from burrow to burrow or forced into
foster care by the death of their mother, persevere and earn their yearling markers?*

*Would females that failed to produce a litter suffer the same fate in the future,
or eventually become successful mothers?*

*We would never know the fortunes of many of our rodent comrades. Not so when it
came to a female named Tic-Tac-Toe.*

She was a healthy female pup, the third captured from a litter of four born in 2003 to 4-Stripe-Back-Stripe. Tic-Tac-Toe's mother was called 4SBS for short, and John nicknamed her "Tiger" because of the pattern of stripes on her back. Tiger did not wean a litter in 2002, but her 2003 success profoundly affected the makeup of her clan. Emerging from their burrow on a mild, clear morning in early June, Tic-Tac-Toe (née 4SBSX), her sister, and two brothers had an uneventful underground childhood in a relatively incident-free area just south of a service road that split the colony in two. Partly because of Tiger's competence as a mother, neither infanticide nor predation occurred in or near Tic-Tac-Toe's natal burrow.

Arousing from hibernation earlier than most other females and at an above-average weight, Tiger learned from her mistakes during yearlinghood and did not repeat them as a sophomore. In 2003, she copulated in the early part of mating season and obtained a beautiful nursery burrow that was centrally located in the colony, affording her litter good protection from predators. Tiger's full figure made her a winner in fights and a good nurser. Consequently, each of her pups weighed almost half a pound (190–200 g), a solid size for Utah prairie dog youngsters.[2]

Marked with a miniature version of the charismatic striping pattern that defined their mother, Tic-Tac-Toe and her siblings were not avid aboveground nursers and enjoyed chewing on nearby grasses. Within just 24 hours of their emergence, they were interacting with another litter birthed by 6-Stripe-Racing-Stripe (6SRS), also containing four pups. 6SRS also had a great litter going, with some pups weighing in at over half a pound (more than 250 g), and she suffered only one blemish during her journey from conception to weaning—an infanticidal attack on her litter early in May before the pups emerged. A nonreproductive yearling male carried the fifth pup aboveground. The other four were

spared, for reasons that we were never able to decipher.

Tic-Tac-Toe also interacted frequently with the resident males of the clan, 33 and Rear-Legs-45. The unusual two-male setup was tenuous, a result of the failure of the elder 33 to oust R45 from the territory. Like their time underground, the summer days after Tic-Tac-Toe and her siblings emerged were care-free. They copied the adults in their clan by showing vigilance for predators and kissing, sniffing, and playing. Every evening was happy hour when Tic-Tac-Toe's family members such as Female-Head-3 and sexually immature yearling Male-Rear-Legs-17 (R17) returned from foraging in the woods and joined the others for nightly social activity.

Toward the end of 2003, a disruptive incident finally occurred. A raven attacked a nearby clan territory, frightening all of the Utah prairie dogs within 45 to 55 yards (40 to 50 m). Many emitted alarm calls, including Tiger (33 and R45, like typical males, looked at the raven, put their heads down, and then resumed eating without so much as standing up, much less calling).[3] It was a close call for Tic-Tac-Toe, who was foraging during the incident and seemed unnerved at her first experience with a predator. She was fairly close to the attacker, and her life could easily have ended. But when the raven came, she heeded the alarm from her tiger-striped mother, looked up briefly, and darted toward the nearest burrow.

Including Tic-Tac-Toe, all four pups in Tiger's litter were lively, heavy, and looked like the real deal. With hibernation and our annual departure from the site looming, John thought the chances of seeing them and the 6SRSXs as yearlings the next year were excellent. And when John returned in March 2004 (and I joined the Dog Squad), we found that most of those pups had survived the winter. But some substantial changes to the clan's makeup were obvious after just a week of observation.

FIGURE 6.1. *Born again.* Tic-Tac-Toe, pictured here in 2005 (the year when Elaine was photographing Utah prairie dogs at BCNP), emerged as a yearling in 2004 to a snow-covered clan with a drastically different composition than the prior year.

2004

The most salient change in Tic-Tac-Toe's clan for 2004 was the exodus of females. Female-Head-3, after being a loser the year prior, defected to a larger clan about 30 yards (more than 24 m) away that straddled the service road. Female-6SRSX, whom we marked FRB as a yearling, moved with her. Their mother, 6SRS, was no longer with us, perhaps a victim of predation or the cold winter. Only two female returnees from the clan were captured and marked—the now yearling Tic-Tac-Toe (fig. 6.1) and her mother, Tiger, who was back for a third year and who replaced 6SRS as the clan's oldest female.

As with any year, a round-robin of males occurred. The prairie dog formerly known as R17 graduated to his sophomore year, became sexually mature, and battled for glory in an area north of his natal territory after being assigned a new, permanent number. His role as a nonreproductive yearling male in Tic-Tac-Toe and Tiger's clan was filled by three pups from 2003—Rear-Legs-41 (R41), son of the late 6SRS, and the duo of Rear-Legs-37 (R37) and Rear-Legs-42 (R42), Tiger's sons (and Tic-Tac-Toe's littermate siblings). Their appearance made Tiger three for four on pup survival from 2003, a 75 percent success rate that was well above the success most females had that year.

The battle for who would be 2004 resident male for the Tiger–Tic-Tac-Toe clan was an interesting one. The iconic two-year-old I-15 dominated the entire area between my tower and the South Pole for about a week, but even he could not own that much terrain for the entire mating season. I-15 eventually relinquished small concessions—a two-female clan on the southeast edge of the colony to the chubby yet feisty Ought-4, and the medium-sized clan graced with Head-3 and FRB to Male-23, known among Dog Squad members for his short temper and predilection to run long distances and emit territorial calls.

I-15's final concession, a necessity as he focused on becoming the first mate to each of seven females in a massive clan at the south end of the colony where he eventually settled, was the Tiger–Tic-Tac-Toe clan. A yearling but reproductive male named Rear-Legs-25 (R25) cruised over and found his niche with Tiger and Tic-Tac-Toe, sniffing and kissing the mother-daughter twosome frequently to assess their sexual receptivity. Relative to the members of the larger clan that became I-15's domicile, Tiger and Tic-Tac-Toe emerged from hibernation later and their days of sexual receptivity were also a little later. Besides the clan's size, this timing probably also played a role in I-15's halfhearted retaliation against R25 once he came forward to claim Tiger and Tic-Tac-Toe. The Tiger–Tic-Tac-Toe gig was a good starter territory for a dog like R25 in his first year of clan leadership, and the experienced I-15 had bigger fish to catch.

On March 27, Tic-Tac-Toe copulated with R25, who turned out to be her only mate. Eventually, R25 succeeded in copulating with both Tiger and Tic-Tac-Toe—mother and daughter. But while Tiger had other suitors and elicited elaborate courtship behavior from them, Tic-Tac-Toe enjoyed a singular rendez-vous with the strapping young yearling that involved almost no fanfare. After only a slight increase in the number of social interactions, Tic-Tac-Toe and R25 went missing for a "BD" at noon and emerged from burrow 2Q, one right after the other, 42 minutes later. Unlike her veteran mother, Tic-Tac-Toe did little to get away and seek another partner, leaving an

easy mate-guarding task for R25. After a few adversarial dealings with Male-23 from the nearest territory over, R25 effortlessly ensured that Tic-Tac-Toe sired only his offspring.

With mating out of the way, Tic-Tac-Toe came into her own over the following weeks. Only two females were in the clan territory of about 25 square yards (more than 20 m^2), so several viable nursery burrows were available for both her and Tiger. Collecting nest material was also low maintenance, because the clan territory bordered a small grassy area containing vegetation that was a few inches high. No trips to the woods were necessary, and Tic-Tac-Toe was able to eschew these journeys, and the predation risk that came with them, in favor of a few easily collected loads from nearby. Despite the omnipresence of predators and a few attacks in the coming months, Tic-Tac-Toe remained alive.

The clan's central location with good access to resources turned out to be a lifesaver. In contrast, I-15, who almost became Tic-Tac-Toe's mate, was a prolific breeder with short-lived success. He became one of my favorites as he mated with the females behind my tower during mating season. But one morning in May, as I arrived at the colony and went to my tower, I saw the classic reamed-out burrows with fresh diggings of dirt in I-15's territory. Some often-used burrows were closed, and some smaller, more infrequently used burrows were blown wide open, a clear sign that an American badger had come during the night and feasted by plugging the Utah prairie dog escape routes.[4] The night before, I had seen I-15 atop the traps I had set, gloriously scanning his vast domain, basking in the afterglow of banishing other males from the area. That day I looked carefully the entire morning, ignoring my usual objectivity and hoping that he would appear, but he never did.

Another casualty of the badger attack was I-15's protégé, nonreproductive yearling male minion Rear-Legs-02 (R02), who was just learning the ropes of the clan. Sadly, he was

FIGURE 6.2. *Playing around.* For the outgoing Tic-Tac-Toe, dustpans, notebooks, and other field equipment were fair game.

finally rounding out because of his sneaky, intermittent trips into my bucket of whole oats while I was looking the other way. R02 was beginning to show real potential for clan leadership. Instead, the badger cut short his quest to someday rule a clan of his own.

The final victim of the carnage was another of I-15's crucial partners—his "wife," Black-Butt-2 (BB2), an early-morning riser, who made a name for herself by sometimes getting livetrapped before I had even placed the entire set of traps on the ground. She was gone, but I saw her young emerge a day later from a burrow close to BB2's original nursery burrow—the one that was opened wide overnight by the badger and was probably the site of BB2's demise. I cannot say that BB2 "sacrificed" herself, but it was nevertheless clear that while sleeping with her vulnerable young, she was the first line of defense for the burrow.

The badger attacks happened in the territory just south of R25's females, and Tic-Tac-Toe dodged a bullet once again. The same central proximity that saved her life also placed her close to my tower and made her a Dog Squad favorite. Every day, Tic-Tac-Toe created memories and photo opportunities to last a lifetime. Even routine behaviors, like suddenly standing up, urgently on guard and vigilant, were entertaining. Other times, as if she were aware of her fame, she put on a show. Somehow, Tic-Tac-Toe almost always picked the time I was watching her to nibble a piece of grass while erect, vocalize for no apparent reason, or bait Tiger over for a kiss. Her other hobbies included fussing with equipment that we failed to elevate from the ground (fig. 6.2), scouring for oats that we dropped, and remaining aboveground when we descended from the tower to set live traps. She also defended her territory vigorously (fig. 6.3).

FIGURE 6.3. *Out of character*. Tic-Tac-Toe had a calm disposition but still rebuffed invaders of her clan (pictured is a clan defense from 2005).

And as it became warmer, Tic-Tac-Toe enjoyed a good sunbathe atop the burrow mound just above where her offspring were developing. She stretched and then flattened herself like a pancake, extending her arms in front of her.

It was during her pregnancy that Tic-Tac-Toe developed an obsession with oats that set her apart from other Utah prairie dogs. While not quite at the level of BB2, Tic-Tac-Toe was a definite oataholic whom we captured frequently. At the height of her addiction, she took excursions into the territory that straddled the service road, inhabited by her seceding relatives Head-3 and FRB, to set off traps that were meant for the females in that territory.

Tic-Tac-Toe's method of obtaining oats was unorthodox. Rather than inserting herself into an open trap to lightly detach her snack without tripping the treadle, she developed a penchant for simply pushing the trap over, setting it off on its way down the burrow mound, and recovering the goods. She commonly did this to five or six traps and then walked right into the next trap and set it off. The tipping and subsequent capture sometimes became so disruptive that I had to give her a "time out." Keeping her in the trap, I sequestered her in the shade of my tower, occupied her with a handful of oats, and humbly reconstructed my trapping matrix.

Although the study colony was off-limits to tourists, Tic-Tac-Toe managed to become a favorite with the few travelers that mistakenly ventured into the area. One afternoon in late April 2004, I returned from the Squad Van to find some British vacationers who had ignored the signs posted by park personnel and were observing from my tower. Wanting to see a uniquely American animal, they somehow managed to find the colony. I obliged by showing them the impounded Tic-Tac-Toe, who was oblivious to her imprisonment and enjoying her refreshments. She was unlike anything they could find in England. Once again, Tic-Tac-Toe performed before a live audience, first chittering, then nuzzling the edge of the trap, and bobbing her head to look around alertly. Her eyes met with the young British boy, who smiled, pointed at Tic-Tac-Toe, and cheerily yet inexplicably proclaimed, "Ducky! It's a ducky!" Of course Tic-Tac-Toe knew nothing of her celebrity, and had she, I suspect she would have traded it for a handful of oats.

Tic-Tac-Toe stopped her exploits long enough to give birth during a mundane parturition. Thirty days after she copulated with R25, she woke up late, had something to eat, and was not seen again until that afternoon. Both observations were consistent with Tic-Tac-Toe birthing the pups that morning, and she returned to the burrow early to nurse them that night. When I tried to capture her to confirm a precipitous weight loss, the usually trap-happy Tic-Tac-Toe had no interest in being trapped, another sign that she was preoccupied with rearing her pups.[5]

For the entire colony, 2004 was a big year for pups. Over 200 of the little rascals overtook the colony that year, and we captured them all. Tiger's pups were not among them, as she abandoned her nursery burrow in late May, unable to produce litters in consecutive years. But about two weeks after Tiger's failure, Tic-Tac-Toe's four rambunctious young pleased me by emerging and quickly succumbing to live traps. More were always better when it came to babies.

While some of the pups weighed a bit less than average,[6] all members of the Tic-Tac-Toe litter were active and seemed healthy. For the next few weeks, Tic-Tac-Toe and her litter of two males and two females played on burrow mounds, foraged, kissed and sniffed other clan members, and watched for predators. During alarm calls, Tic-Tac-Toe made sure that the young knew the ropes. If one was distracted during the alert, she nuzzled the pup until he or she obliged by standing vigilant or joining in the chorus. Weaning came quickly, as did the growth of the pups. Within a few days of emergence, the young began to eat grass.

Head-3 and FRB both moved away from their relatives to a new territory before mating season, but the relocation worked for only one of them. The older Head-3 yielded a litter of two hefty pups, both with excellent chances of surviving for years to come, but the yearling FRB and one of her three pups both disappeared in late June.

The fate of FRB's other two pups after the possible predation of their mother was uncertain. They grew quickly but were not fully weaned, having emerged later than Tic-Tac-Toe's litter. Without their mother, they could not nurse to completion and could both starve if they were not mature enough to eat grass.

Not interfering in such a situation took all the scientific objectivity I could muster. Instead, I let nature take its course, and the results were riveting. After I did not see them for a day and feared the worst, I discovered that the two remaining FRB pups were still alive. One stayed in its natal territory and was nursing and going to bed with Female-71, who lived next to FRB and birthed a litter of two stout offspring (fig. 6.4). She now effectively had three pups to care for, and because the extra pup was born in the home territory, 71 either did not recognize or was not concerned with baby FRB's status as a foster offspring.[7]

The whereabouts of the other FRB pup were also interesting. Tic-Tac-Toe and her litter apparently adopted the pup, because they were interacting, waking up, and going to bed with it in their natal burrow. Whether the FRBX made a break for the Tiger–Tic-Tac-Toe territory underground or somehow slipped through the cracks as litters from both clans commingled was unclear. Regardless of how it happened, the mothers did not drive away the FRB pup as an invader.

Instead, baby FRB was welcomed as a de facto fifth member of Tic-Tac-Toe's litter and obtained all the perks that came with that status, including a "selfish herd" that offered protection from predators. Tiger, Tic-Tac-Toe, the four TTTXs, and the foster pup ate grass together contentedly and without interference from predatory attacks until our departure

FIGURE 6.4. *Earth mother.* Female-71, pictured here in 2005, was the most senior female of the clan adjacent to that of Tic-Tac-Toe and Tiger in 2004. She nursed an FRBX that was left without a mother.

that July. I spent the rest of the field season amazed that in the midst of tough times, Tic-Tac-Toe took care of her family, even the offspring of relatives that had absconded from the home clan territory.

2005

As with every year, significant changes occurred in Tic-Tac-Toe's home territory in 2005. The alterations in clan makeup seemed to be catalyzed by Tiger's death over the winter. Her death left Tic-Tac-Toe as the only female in that territory, because none of her four pups from 2004 survived into 2005. Tic-Tac-Toe could find a new clan and try again or live by herself in the same territory where she had lived in 2004 (fig. 6.5).

The males of the old Tiger–Tic-Tac-Toe clan from 2004, as usual, all jumped ship.

Rear-Legs-37 (R37), Tic-Tac-Toe's littermate sibling, was missing in action. He was probably a casualty of the winter, or maybe a vagabond looking to take root in another colony. R25, Tic-Tac-Toe's only sexual partner and now a sophomore, was awarded with a name change and moved to a larger territory with more females. Rear-Legs-42 (R42) was also captured and became one of our all-time favorites after his permanent number became 22. After an epic battle on a five-foot snowdrift with an upstart reproductive yearling male named Junior (R15), 22 conquered what had been I-15's large clan of females before his death (fig. 6.6a–b).

Tic-Tac-Toe seemed unfazed by the alterations and moved into the territory that straddled the service road.[8] It was obviously her best option, and far better than absorbing the predation risk associated with living by herself. Not only was it the largest territory

FIGURE 6.5. *Out in the cold*. With her clan mates from 2003 and 2004 dispersed or dead, Tic-Tac-Toe (shown a few days following hibernation after she received her yearly dye mark) found herself cold and lonely in March 2005.

FIGURE 6.6. *Double Deuces*. 22 (shown here in summer 2005 eating grass) won an epic battle with Junior (Male-Rear-Legs-15, or R15) that gave him the large clan behind my tower and made him the successor to I-15 *(left)*. Despite the loss to 22 and his yearling status, Junior, also shown in summer 2005, was a male to be reckoned with *(right)*.

FIGURE 6.7. *Pioneer.* On her own with no close relatives in the colony, Tic-Tac-Toe embarked to find a new clan to join shortly after emerging from hibernation in 2005 *(top)* and, after experimentation with nearby females *(bottom)*, eventually settled in a clan not far from her location of birth.

FIGURE 6.8. *Making new friends*. (From right to left) Male-7 (the eventual resident male of the clan), Female-71, and Male-Rear-Legs-36 (R36) became Tic-Tac-Toe's new family during mating season in 2005. The three amigos are shown here during summer of that year.

and clan anywhere near her, but she already had relatives who had established precedent by moving there (fig. 6.7a–b). Granted, FRB was long gone and Head-3 was never seen again after we did a census in July 2004. But the clan still contained Female-71, a good-sized two-year-old who had nursed FRB's pup. This connection meant that moving next door was the best Tic-Tac-Toe could do to be with "family."

The 71 clan was also a good fit for Tic-Tac-Toe because she did not always exhibit animosity when interacting with these females. Tic-Tac-Toe and 71 seemed to tolerate each other, and despite their different matrilines, they sometimes kissed amicably if they met at the boundary of their clan territories. Once she joined the clan, Tic-Tac-Toe was loyal to it and defended the territory vigorously. Along with her new family of 71, 51,

and Male-Rear-Legs-36 (R36), Tic-Tac-Toe waited to see which sexually mature male would arrive and take over the clan territory (fig. 6.8).

A few contenders emerged. Junior was a spanking reproductive yearling who had dispersed from his natal territory, which was adjacent to the boundary of the 71 clan. He lost a "clash of the ages" with 22 but otherwise looked good in confrontations with other males. He might have been a fit for Tic-Tac-Toe's new clan, but Junior instead focused on ousting the four-year-old Ought-4 from his residency in a small clan on the southeast edge of the colony. It did not take long for me to see that the grizzled Ought-4, though at a good weight and in decent condition, had lost a step. The difference in his combat ability from the year prior was subtle, but enough that the resourceful upstart Junior proved too much for him, driving him away from his old home where he woke up from hibernation. Two days after they started warfare, Ought-4 was looking for a new home.

With the overpowering two-year-old 22 well entrenched in the larger clan behind the tower, past-his-prime Ought-4 was ostracized and chose to hang around the edge of Tic-Tac-Toe's clan territory. He could not penetrate it well, because two-year-old Male-7 was kissing and sniffing 71 and Tic-Tac-Toe. Back and forth Ought-4 went between 7's and Junior's clans, unable to ensconce himself anywhere and forced farther and farther to the edge of the colony. His proximity to the periphery ended up being costly. With almost no advantages from the "selfish herd," he lost his life a few days later to a northern goshawk.

Meanwhile, Male-7 was a robust and sociable companion who resided in the territory of the 71 clan virtually uncontested, making him an acceptable and logical mate for Tic-Tac-Toe. He spent two weeks claiming her clan, constantly patrolling the territory boundaries, emitting territorial calls, and clobbering any male that approached him. I waited patiently for Tic-Tac-Toe's estrus day. I trapped her and observed her vulva to be swollen and closed, so I knew that her estrus was imminent. I waited a day, then another.

Then came the morning of March 31. The day started with Tic-Tac-Toe and 7 awaking from the same burrow system, which, combined with the number of days she was aboveground, led me to believe that Tic-Tac-Toe's day of estrus was looming or had arrived. All day, 7 courted Tic-Tac-Toe with scores of kisses and sniffs and kept her in close proximity. I never observed them submerging into a burrow together, but I suspected that the wedding was imminent or had already occurred.

Running around the territory all morning as he had for two weeks, 7 emitted more territorial calls and made a pass at a few opportunities to be the second or third mate for females in adjacent clans as he monitored

Tic-Tac-Toe. At 2:20 p.m., he seemed to have little awareness of anything as he ran back across the road toward his burrow after checking out an estrous female outside his clan territory.

Although the road was off-limits to the public and posted as such, tourists did occasionally make their way down to the colony through either misguided curiosity or irresponsibility. Such was the case on this day, as a trespassing but slowly traveling vehicle recognized 7's reverie and stopped considerately to let him cross.

Cross he did, running in front of the stopped car to gain access to his home territory. But as he traversed the service road, Tic-Tac-Toe inexplicably ran toward the back wheels of the automobile. Perhaps it was because she was estrous and was moving toward 7 for another kiss. Possibly it was because Tic-Tac-Toe had moved from a clan territory farther away from the service road and was inexperienced with the nuances of traffic. Or maybe something else was going on in Tic-Tac-Toe's head.

In any event, I can remember running toward the road and yelling for the oblivious driver to remain stopped. But the distance between the tower and the tragedy was too great. By the time I reached the area, the car was gone, and so was Tic-Tac-Toe.

Five minutes later, John came to record the incident. With a trap labeled, he attached a slip of paper to the handle—Tic-Tac-Toe: Roadkill, 2:20 p.m. And then he transferred Tic-Tac-Toe's carcass into the trap.

After John's somber message to the other Dog Squad members over the radio, we were left with no choice but to take Tic-Tac-Toe to the Squad Van for some final paperwork and to say our good-byes. It was a grisly, troubling task, but at least we would learn of Tic-Tac-Toe's final condition. Two assistants stayed at the colony in case any copulations occurred while John was in the Squad Van.

FIGURE 6.9. *Widower*. Male-7 wandering away from the road and toward the area under my tower after Tic-Tac-Toe's passing. He probably would have sired some of Tic-Tac-Toe's offspring were it not for her unfortunate accident.

Tic-Tac-Toe was taken in her prime. Successful in defending herself through several major predation events over two years, she eventually proved to be no match for careless humans. Adding to the indignity, she appeared to be sexually receptive or close to it on the day of her death. Her goal was to produce viable offspring that would inhabit the home territory for years into the future, but instead she passed away lonely with no descendants. She had come close in 2004, and had she lived, she might have achieved her objective in 2005. Now, we would never know.

Neither would her potential mates. I returned to my tower following the autopsy, leaving Tic-Tac-Toe in the van to await a return to her home territory the following day, and 7 seemed concerned. His change in behavior was clear, as he ran around his territory for

hours looking into burrows and calling, trying in vain to locate the female with whom he had interacted just a few minutes before and who almost certainly would have conceived his offspring (fig. 6.9).

The following day we arrived at the colony, went to the van, secured Tic-Tac-Toe's corpse, and walked to her burrow before the other Utah prairie dogs woke up. We were filled with sadness not only over Tic-Tac-Toe's death, but also because her demise reminded us of the days we had spent together. As we stood in her home territory, we remembered how Tic-Tac-Toe enriched our times at the colony, and the lessons she taught us. We recalled how she put everything she had into her litter during her first year, trying to learn the ins and outs of motherhood. She was so resourceful when she built her nest, fervently collecting grasses in the woods and stopping to arrange them in her mouth before diving into the burrow. We recollected how Tic-Tac-Toe took good care of her family, holding no grudges even though the life journey of her relatives took them away from their birth clan.

Most of all, we remembered how Tic-Tac-Toe was adaptable enough to disperse when her situation called for change. She handled the relocation of family members and the death of her mother and pups so well, calmly shifting to an adjacent territory and socializing with new clan members, disregarding past territorial disputes.

For one last stand, we placed Tic-Tac-Toe's crumpled body on the ground near the burrow where she had spent her last night. How would we remember Tic-Tac-Toe? Certainly not lying motionless next to her burrow. We would always have the morning of March 27, 2004, the day she conceived her only litter. For those few moments in time, Tic-Tac-Toe was the most important female in the colony. Now, perhaps she would be food for a badger, fox, or hawk. In the morning, the sun greeted us with one less prairie dog gracing the meadow.

7

Save the Prairie Dogs

The beauty and genius of a work of art may be reconceived, though its first
material expression be destroyed; a vanished harmony may yet again inspire the
composer; but when the last individual of a race of living beings breathes no more,
another heaven and another earth must pass before such a one can be again.
—C. WILLIAM BEEBE, *The Bird*, 1906[1]

One does not sell the earth upon which people walk.
—CRAZY HORSE[2]

☽

In Through the Looking Glass, *Lewis Carroll offers a metaphor for perpetual lack
of progress. The protagonist, Alice, receives an invitation to play croquet with the Red
Queen,[3] representing the queen piece on a chessboard. Their conversation is unusual:*

> *"Well, in our country," said Alice, still panting a little, "you'd generally get to
> somewhere else—if you run very fast for a long time, as we've been doing."*
> *"A slow sort of country!" said the Queen. "Now, here, you see, it takes all
> the running you can do, to keep in the same place. If you want to get somewhere
> else, you must run at least twice as fast as that!"[4]*

*Sometimes, it is easy to feel conflicted about Utah prairie dog conservation. For progress
to occur, all pieces must be exactly in place on the environmental and bureaucratic
chessboards, and when they are, an unforeseen variable can suddenly change the strategy of the efforts. For example, someone might submit a new application for development, or an unusually cold winter or a sudden lack of funding might occur, or the law
might change.*

*Tic-Tac-Toe's death serves as a reminder that humans are a major threat to Utah
prairie dogs. Her death also underscores the complexity of conservation efforts, and the
omnipresence of human influence on nature, even in protected areas. Saving Utah prairie dogs is complicated, because one cannot simply declare land or animals untouchable
without appropriate context. To communicate this reality, some say that wildlife managers do not manage wildlife—they manage people.[5] That is an important distinction
because it means that we must move forward with practical, not just idealistic, methods*

of conserving Utah prairie dogs. Perceptions are part of reality—and some negative perceptions about Utah prairie dogs are unlikely to change.

During a croquet match, a player must slap a ball through a series of horseshoe-shaped wickets in the ground. Or, the player can hit and displace another contestant's ball into an unfavorable position. Such is the reality of the fight to save Utah prairie dogs. We must maneuver through "hoops," while groups of people with different convictions, or sometimes vested interests, struggle for position. How we respond to this competition will define the role of Utah prairie dogs in the modern West for years to come.

The very mention of Utah prairie dogs still conjures up fervent opinions from just about everyone I meet in Utah. While I was on the Dog Squad, no experience away from the field was complete without the requisite interactions with locals, who somehow spotted me as a partial-year resident immediately. The all-you-can-eat pancake breakfast in the next town over was a classic example, among others–barbershops, car repair facilities, grocery stores, even libraries.

I attended the all-you-can-eat pancake breakfast several times on my rare mornings off. Usually a waiter came over, did not recognize me, and inevitably asked what I was doing in the area. "Studying the Utah prairie dogs over in the park," I would say. And that was usually the end of any hope of peaceful pancake consumption.

"Do you shoot them?"

The question came frequently and with a chuckle even though the federal listing of Utah prairie dogs as a threatened species proscribes such activities.

"Nope. I sit in towers and watch them."

"Why would you do that? Is there something wrong with you?"

I began to explain their captivating social behavior, but rarely was anybody interested. Before I knew it, eavesdropping strangers, including ranchers, tourists, and townspeople with little stake in the argument, were talking between tables to debate the conservation status of Utah prairie dogs. They took stances of save the darn prairie dogs or shoot the

darn prairie dogs, but hardly ever anything in between.

For every interested layperson who wanted to learn about Utah prairie dogs, I also found at least one member of the anti–prairie dog persuasion. And for every seemingly balanced person I talked to, I encountered a zealot from either pole. Usually, the conversation I incited went on like a town hall debate for half an hour until, mercifully, the waiter came over with the check. His send-off was particularly inflammatory one morning in June 2004.

"You can watch those gophers as much as you want," he said while calculating the damage, "but they'll always be [expletive] rats to me."

Five minutes later as I rose to leave, a tourist from Colorado who had overheard the ruckus finished his bison sausage and approached me. He was on his way to see the Utah prairie dogs of Bryce Canyon, and we exchanged pleasantries and bonded over football. His view on the controversy was a bit different.

"I appreciate what you do, trying to learn about nature," he said. "Some of these people around here walk around like they are nature."

Dog-Gone

Utah prairie dogs were once common throughout valleys in the southern and central portions of Utah. With an estimated historic population of 95,000 individuals,[6] some colony sites likely had thousands of Utah prairie dogs. Then came eradication programs initiated by coalitions of ranchers and the federal government, including the 1930 poisoning of over 123,000 acres in five Utah counties.[7] Accuracy of Utah prairie dog counts is debated among interested citizens,[8] but in any case, today's cumulative population size for Utah prairie dogs appears to be between 3,000 and 13,000 adults.[9] The USFWS continues to list Utah prairie dogs as a species threatened with extinction due mostly to threats associated with loss of habitat from human development and plague. The current classification of Utah prairie dogs as threatened protects them from overt extermination.[10]

Good news for Utah prairie dogs came when the USFWS reported in 2011 that Utah prairie dog populations have been steady or increasing over the last decade.[11] Each year, the Utah Division of Wildlife Resources (UDWR) records visual counts of Utah prairie dogs across their entire current range in the spring.[12] Five of the seven highest counts after federal listing have occurred since 2005.[13] And recent reports of almost 6,000 adults from spring counts are a substantial improvement from an all-time low of 2,160 adults counted in the 1970s.[14]

While these increases are perhaps encouraging, they do not ensure the long-term recovery or survival of Utah prairie dogs. Nor do they indicate that the species is realizing its intended ecological function over the entirety of its natural range. Utah prairie dogs remain threatened by habitat destruction and modification, development and urbanization, geological exploration, vehicles, plague, and illegal shooting and poisoning. Approximately 75 percent of Utah prairie dogs occur on non-federal lands that are likely to be developed in the future, presenting a major challenge to conservation.[15] Continued improvement and implementation of conservation plans is therefore crucial for Utah prairie dogs and their grassland ecosystem.

None of the Dog Squad's research directly concerned endangered species policy, and an entire book could be devoted to Utah prairie dog conservation and management alone. But Utah prairie dogs are so linked with their threatened status that no discussion of Utah prairie dogs can ignore the fight to save them. In my story's final pages, I explain why Utah prairie dogs are no longer dominant animals in the meadows of southern Utah. I then discuss some of the misconceptions about Utah prairie dogs that, in part, led to their extermination and precipitous decline. I continue by detailing how Utah prairie dogs are likely beneficial to the environment. Finally, I explain what wildlife biologists and other interested parties are doing to save Utah prairie dogs for future generations.

Why Have So Many Utah Prairie Dogs Disappeared?

One of the biggest reasons that Utah prairie dogs occupy a small fraction of their former range is humans who dislike them. Besides their resemblance to another widely detested animal, the rat, and the misconception that they reproduce quickly, a common reason for despising and destroying prairie dogs of all species has been the claim that horses and cattle break their legs in burrows (fig. 7.1). Prairie dogs have also been charged with other crimes, such as digging and burrowing in sacred graveyards or worship grounds, damaging airport runaways and recreational fields, invading golf courses and gardens, chewing wires, and interfering with electrical transmission lines.[16] Some farmers and ranchers say that prairie dogs attract predators such as coyotes and foxes that might prey on livestock or domestic animals.[17] Another common complaint is that burrow mounds create an uneven ground surface and wreak havoc on farm equipment (fig. 7.2).[18]

FIGURE 7.1. *Excavation*. Many ranchers despise Utah prairie dogs because they fear that livestock and horses will break their legs in burrows.

But perhaps the most common complaint about prairie dogs is that they compete with cattle and other livestock for forage (fig. 7.3). In 1902, C. Hart Merriam supported this assertion when he wrote that "32 [black-tailed] prairie dogs consume as much grass as 1 sheep, and 256 [black-tailed] prairie dogs as much as 1 cow."[19] Because widespread killing of prairie dogs started well before this statement, it is debatable whether ranchers actually needed Merriam to come to this conclusion about prairie dogs before they carried out their extermination plans. Also debatable is the calculation itself, because many conclude that it overestimates the competition between prairie dogs and cattle.[20]

In any case, probably the most important and provocative question regarding Utah prairie dogs is whether they compete with

livestock for food. Unfortunately, no one has a decisive answer to this question because of a lack of scientific research—particularly controlled experiments that manipulate vegetation and the density of livestock. Some research on this topic is available for Utah prairie dogs, but better data on competition between prairie dogs and livestock come from black-tailed prairie dogs.

With that disclaimer, data from a few studies are relevant. Specifically, Utah prairie dogs increase the time they spend foraging and devote less time to looking for predators when exposed to simulated foraging by cattle, particularly in areas with forage utilization rates of over 80 percent. Reduced vegetation from cattle foraging is also related to decreased individual growth rates in Utah prairie dogs.[21] As for black-tailed prairie dogs, they consume some grasses and forbs that cattle also eat, and they can reduce the overall mass of vegetation available for cattle in an area.[22] Utah prairie dogs probably also munch certain plants that cattle would otherwise ingest.

These studies may imply that abhorrence of Utah prairie dogs is not totally irrational or without historical basis. Financial effects of this competition are unclear, but the potential for monetary loss has obviously been salient enough to make the presence of Utah prairie dogs inconsistent with the vision for land ownership of many American citizens over the last 150 years. This issue has made Utah prairie dogs easy targets for extermination.[23]

Utah prairie dogs have also disappeared because of sylvatic plague, a virulent disease caused by bacteria that probably first arrived in the United States around the turn of the twentieth century via commercial ships from China. When Utah prairie dogs contract the disease from infected fleas, drastic reduction of colony size, and often total elimination of all residents, usually occurs.[24] The spread of plague among Utah prairie dogs has also increased fear among the public that plague from Utah prairie dogs will be transmitted to

FIGURE 7.2. *Leveling the playing field*. Some irrigated agricultural fields in southern Utah contain Utah prairie dogs, like this one just outside Cedar City. Many farmers complain that Utah prairie dogs destroy cropland and interfere with the use of equipment. Photo by Brian Slobe.

FIGURE 7.3. *American compromise*. At the heart of the controversy involving Utah prairie dogs is the question of whether they compete with cattle.

FIGURE 7.4. *Dusting.* Workers apply dust to a black-tailed prairie dog at Thunder Basin National Grassland, Wyoming, during a translocation. Dusting kills fleas that spread plague and other diseases. Photo by Jill Majerus, courtesy of the World Wildlife Fund.

people, especially children, another factor that has led to the hatred and extermination of Utah prairie dogs.[25]

Plague has caused some major challenges for John's research. He became concerned about plague at the study colony in BCNP after nine individuals in the same immediate area died aboveground or disappeared after appearing disoriented in May 2001. When three of those carcasses came back from a lab after testing positive for plague, BCNP officials allowed John and the Dog Squad to infuse a flea-killing insecticide called Pyraperm into every burrow entrance of the colony. This seemed to stop the outbreak, because no other individuals showed symptoms that year, and the number of fleas counted on captives in the Squad Van decreased dramatically.[26]

One might think that because Utah prairie dogs live in congested colonies with kissing, sniffing, and cannibalism, plague would be transmitted directly from individual to individual. But after elimination of the fleas, no additional cases of plague appeared that year or the next. Thus, while plague-infected Utah prairie dogs probably directly transmit the disease to other Utah prairie dogs in some cases, the presence of fleas was necessary for most incidents of transmission.[27] Indeed, the same method of killing fleas with Pyraperm also halted an outbreak of plague at the study colony in 1998, after two pups that were acting strangely died aboveground and the Centers for Disease Control and Prevention (CDC) confirmed that they tested positive for plague.[28]

The virulent nature of plague has made flea dusting crucial for the long-term persistence of Utah prairie dog colonies. Pyraperm remains active for about six weeks after application, but newer flea dusts, such as DeltaDust, can remain active for up to six months.[29] Such methods can probably be used on all species of prairie dog (fig. 7.4). Indeed, Bryce Canyon officials, who originally dusted burrows for fleas every three years, now do so every year because of the history of plague susceptibility at colonies in the park. The increased frequency seems to be helping, because plague has not ravaged any of the Utah prairie dog colonies at BCNP over the last few years.[30] And similar programs, such as intensive dusting in Dixie National Forest, have also yielded more stable Utah prairie dog colonies.[31] But even with careful monitoring and dusting, incidents of plague remain a threat to Utah prairie dogs.

Are Utah Prairie Dogs Guilty as Charged?

Although Utah prairie dogs are often blamed for consuming forage marked for cattle and livestock, studies indicate that grazing may be compatible with Utah prairie dog presence under certain conditions. Such is the case when the amount of forage consumed by livestock is not so high as to become competitive with Utah prairie dogs. Indeed, livestock and Utah prairie dogs may compete only in instances of low productivity in the habitat, such as during a hot summer or on arid rangelands with little moisture.[32]

We can project results from black-tailed prairie dogs onto the less-studied Utah prairie dogs regarding their benefits to the environment if we do the same for the question of whether they compete with livestock for food. Among those benefits is maintenance of the grassland ecosystem and improved habitat for livestock via destroying the seeds of some woody plants.[33] In addition, black-tailed

prairie dogs increase the digestibility, protein content, and productivity of grasses, particularly at young colony sites.[34] Digging by black-tailed prairie dogs aerates the soil so that it conserves rain as groundwater, and burrowing redistributes nutrients by mixing subsoil and topsoil. Black-tailed prairie dogs can also control noxious weeds and native invaders that come into a habitat that has been damaged or overgrazed.[35] Because of these benefits, bison and pronghorn often prefer to forage at colony sites.[36]

Along with their benefits to plant communities, all prairie dog species attract hunting predators such as red foxes, northern goshawks, and golden eagles to colony sites. Utah prairie dog burrows provide shelter and nesting habitat for myriad other animals such as American badgers, long-tailed weasels, and hundreds of insect or arachnid species. And the number of insects probably contributes to making Utah prairie dog colonies an excellent place to bird-watch. Species such as western bluebirds (*Sialia mexicana*), western meadowlarks (*Sturnella neglecta*), and dark-eyed juncos (*Junco hyemalis*) frequently occur at Utah prairie dog colony sites.[37]

Besides the pivotal ecological relationships that would disintegrate in the absence of Utah prairie dogs (figs. 7.5a–b and 7.6a–f), it is important to realize that Utah prairie dogs have persisted for hundreds of thousands of years without widespread detriment to the environment. Thus, regardless of whether Utah prairie dogs are officially a "keystone species," they have an important role in the grassland ecosystem that is likely beneficial.

Regarding alleged cases of livestock or horses breaking their legs in Utah prairie dog burrows, I am aware of no official statistics on the frequency of such incidents. They probably do occur every so often, but John investigated this possibility anecdotally for black-tailed prairie dog burrows by talking to scores of ranchers. When a burrow-induced injury to livestock or horses was alleged, he usually

FIGURE 7.5. *Utah prairie dog allies*. Birds are frequent sights at Utah prairie dog colonies. Two examples are red-tailed hawks *(left)* and owls *(right)*.

found upon cross-examination that the wounded animal sometimes foraged in a field with black-tailed prairie dogs and somehow sustained a leg injury. Another common conversation transpired as follows: "Well, none of my cows have broken a leg in a burrow, but it happens all of the time. Talk to the rancher down the road. A few of his cattle have been injured from prairie dog burrows." John followed up, only to uncover a similar response and begin a vicious cycle.[38] During the pancake breakfast and other events in southern Utah, I initiated several conversations with ranchers concerning Utah prairie dog burrows, almost all of which yielded the same results (fig. 7.7).

A major reason for these findings is that burrows usually have a large mound of soil at each entrance, which a hoofed mammal can easily see and simply walk around. The harmonious existence of bison and Utah prairie dogs in the same areas[39] also suggests that leg fractures from hoofed mammals stepping into a burrow are rare. Dog Squad assistants, however, have occasionally stepped into Utah prairie dog burrows, thankfully injuring only their pride and not their legs.

In addition, the public should not be overly concerned about contracting plague from Utah prairie dogs (or the other species of prairie dog). I recommend obvious precautions

FIGURE 7.6. *(clockwise from upper left) The more, the merrier*. Utah prairie dog colonies are centers of ecological activity. Allies of Utah prairie dogs include chipmunks, coyotes, deer, pronghorn, moths, and voles.

FIGURE 7.7. *Watch your step.* Even though incidents of livestock or humans incurring injury from burrows appear to be rare, the reputations of all five species of prairie dog have suffered from the possibility of such occurrences. The concern extends even to places frequented by tourists who enjoy seeing prairie dogs, like this one with black-tailed prairie dogs in South Dakota. Photo by Theodore G. Manno.

such as refraining from contact with wild prairie dogs. But the reputation of Utah prairie dogs with respect to plague seems overblown. Cases of humans contracting plague from any species of prairie dog are extremely rare, and many people do not realize that other animals that are far less reviled, such as foxes and bobcats (*Lynx rufus*), can also carry fleas.[40]

Utah prairie dogs, although occasionally in conflict with human interests, are almost certainly beneficial to the grassland ecosystem and are not guilty of every high crime and misdemeanor of which they are accused. The inescapable conclusion is that the poisoning and vast reduction of Utah prairie dog populations that took place during the last century was inappropriate, misguided, and poorly

conceived. It follows that we should work hard to conserve all species of prairie dog now, before it is too late.

Save the Prairie Dogs

Parowan, Utah, is nestled along Interstate 15, a wagon-trail-turned-highway with speed limits of up to 80 miles (130 km) per hour. Often, on the way home after "doggin' it," assistants who did not bring vehicles to the field tended to wind up at the bus station here at the end of the field season. But Parowan, Cedar City, and the towns nearby were of interest to us for other reasons, too. Specifically, Utah prairie dogs are not an unusual sight in the region, even though they have been annihilated from most of their historical range.[41]

Many community members, however, are not interested in spotting Utah prairie dogs because they consider them to be in conflict with human activities. Their burrows pop up from the grounds of ranches; they scurry across airline runways; they run over graves in cemeteries; they sprint along Parowan's Main Street; they create holes in the infield of softball facilities; they steal golf balls from public courses; and they dig tunnels near areas of development in Cedar City (fig. 7.8a–b).[42] As a result, the national-level concern for Utah prairie dogs as a threatened species is often not apparent among human inhabitants of the I-15 corridor.[43]

Studies indicate that most Utahans, including those in agricultural areas, believe that the fundamental objectives of the ESA are appropriate. Only a small minority believe that all Utah prairie dogs should be killed. However, the percentage of the population that believes in Utah prairie dog protection *über alles* is also small, and some businesses such as golf courses, cemeteries, and airports are particularly averse to the presence of Utah prairie dogs nearby.[44]

At first glance, it might appear that the continued conflict between humans and Utah prairie dogs results purely from fear of the monetary loss and land devaluation that may occur from Utah prairie dog interference with agriculture or development. Ostensibly, the issue involves mostly competition with livestock, but surveys indicate that many landowners are concerned not just about finances but also about how the ESA is used and interpreted. Often citing the Fifth Amendment of the US Constitution, which states that private property cannot "be taken for public use, without just compensation,"[45] they worry that the ESA's overall mission has been corrupted and used to threaten their property rights. In other words, it appears that many Utahans are concerned about their independence as

FIGURE 7.8. *House of cards.* One source of conflict between Utah prairie dogs and humans is the presence of Utah prairie dogs on lands that are marked for development, like these areas on the outskirts of Cedar City. Photo by Brian Slobe.

landowners and the bureaucracy of the ESA rather than Utah prairie dogs per se.[46]

The reader can decide whether this attitude represents a progressive and rugged individualism or an irrational close-mindedness. Either way, it is apparent to me that conservation of Utah prairie dogs necessitates direct landowner involvement and communication between people of different persuasions, along with targeting incentives for landowners toward conservation objectives rather than mere compensation.[47] I can accept this approach, because while I am an ardent Utah prairie dog lover, I am also a practical person. I realize that while my exposure to Utah prairie dogs is all from sitting in towers to watch them, the experience of them may be quite different for someone who is trying to make his or her living via farming, ranching, or developing—especially in places like Iron County, Utah, where the population is largely rural.[48] That is why I emphasize that conservation solutions must be as fair to landowners as possible and involve improvement of Utah's grassland ecosystem as a whole.

Current Utah prairie dog conservation efforts aim to reconcile environmental protection with human activities (tables 7.1 and 7.2). After federal listing as endangered in 1973 and an all-time low population of just over 2,000 adults,[49] the UDWR coordinated with the USFWS and led a massive translocation of Utah prairie dogs from private to public lands, establishing many new colonies.[50] Meanwhile, the protections offered by the ESA allowed Utah prairie dogs to steadily increase in numbers. By 1984, Utah prairie dogs were still rare, but the population gains were substantial enough to warrant downlisting from endangered to threatened.[51]

Managing a species that was suffering thinned ranks but was nevertheless clashing with human interests required some creative problem solving. During the 10 years following the 1984 downlisting, two recovery strategies that addressed these conflicts came to prominence. The first was implemented in 1984 when the USFWS applied an exception to the typical protections offered by the ESA under Section 4(d) of the act. Under this policy, adult and juvenile Utah prairie dogs can be "taken" (defined by the ESA as harming or harassing a species, including killing individuals) in some locations and with certain restrictions if deemed a nuisance, and "incidental take" may be approved by the USFWS if it is the result of an otherwise lawful activity but not its purpose.[52] The second came in 1991 when

the USFWS delineated three distinct recovery units (RUs) and established specific criteria for their monitoring and management as part of an official Utah Prairie Dog Recovery Plan. Goals for population numbers and protected acres of habitat were calculated using mathematical formulas for the number of reproductive individuals needed to maintain a genetically diverse and viable population, and the area needed to support that population (table 7.1).[53]

By 1994, a revised strategy was needed to combat the low survivorship of translocated Utah prairie dogs and to address the omnipresent threat of plague. The Utah Prairie Dog Recovery Implementation Team (UPDRIT) investigated these issues and shifted the focus of the Recovery Plan toward response to plague; public involvement; and habitat improvement, creation, and monitoring, an approach that continues to be implemented today (table 7.1).[54] Whereas prior recovery efforts were focused almost entirely on federal lands, a Revised Recovery Plan was completed and published in 2012 with the intent of working with private landowners to conserve habitat as a means of Utah prairie dog recovery.[55] Thus, the Revised Recovery Plan emphasized several relatively new conservation mechanisms such as Habitat Conservation Plans (HCPs), Safe Harbor Agreements (SHAs), and protection of Utah prairie dog habitat through conservation easements in an effort to reconcile Utah prairie dog conservation with the interests of farmers, ranchers, and developers (table 7.2; fig. 7.9a–b).[56]

Some of these tactics may involve authorizing lethal take. As a scientist, I understand the rationale behind this allowance, but as a Utah prairie dog lover, it is hard for me to talk about killing Utah prairie dogs that would likely exhibit the individual qualities of study animals like Black-Butt-2, I-15, or Tic-Tac-Toe. Indeed, these arrangements remain controversial in some circles, especially because restrictions on take have decreased since the

TABLE 7.1. Timeline of Important Events in Utah Prairie Dog Management and Conservation

Year	Action or event	Consequences
1973	Endangered Species Act (ESA) signed into law	Utah prairie dogs are among the original species to receive federal protection, and they are listed as an endangered species. Poisoning, shooting, drowning, and other overt killing of Utah prairie dogs becomes illegal.
1976	All-time low Utah prairie dog population count	Only 2,160 adult Utah prairie dogs are left from a population that once numbered an estimated 95,000 (<3% of the former range).
1970s and 1980s	Large-scale translocations of Utah prairie dogs to public lands	Over 12,800 Utah prairie dogs are translocated to public lands. Survivorship of translocated animals is below 10% in most colonies, suggesting the need for more habitat development and monitoring.
1984	Utah prairie dog ESA listing changed from endangered to threatened and ESA 4(d) Special Rule Application	Utah prairie dogs are downlisted due to population increases and become a threatened species. Conflicts develop between Utah prairie dogs and agricultural and other human activities. As a result of the reclassification, conflicts involving Utah prairie dogs are addressed through allowance of a Special Rule to allow take of up to 5,000 adults and pups per year during the time after pups have emerged (June 1 to December 31), in parts of the Cedar and Parowan Valleys. USFWS reserves the right to prohibit take that is inconsistent with the conservation of the species, and Utah Code forbids using chemical toxicants for this purpose.
1991	Amendment to ESA 4(d) Special Rule	The range on which Utah prairie dogs may be taken is extended to any private land, although practice is to permit take only where Utah prairie dogs are causing damage to irrigated agricultural land. Limits on take are increased to 6,000 adults and pups per year. Take must still occur after population has increased from the emergence of pups (June 1 to December 31), and USFWS continues to reserve the right to prohibit take that is inconsistent with the conservation of the species. Utah Code forbids using chemical toxicants for this purpose.
1991	Official Utah Prairie Dog Recovery Plan implemented	A Utah Prairie Dog Recovery Plan is implemented by USFWS. The plan's primary recovery criterion is to establish Utah prairie dog populations on public lands across three Recovery Units: West Desert, Paunsaugunt, and the Awapa Plateau.
1994	Utah Prairie Dog Recovery Implementation Team (UPDRIT) founded	An interdisciplinary team of governmental agencies, universities, and other representatives is formed to analyze the implementation of the Recovery Plan. The team finds that strategies in use may be flawed and that survivorship of translocated Utah prairie dogs is low. An Interim Conservation Strategy is drafted to bridge the gap over the next 5–10 years as new information is gathered.

TABLE 7.1. Timeline of Important Events in Utah Prairie Dog Management and Conservation (*continued*)

Year	Action or event	Consequences
1997	Interim Conservation Strategy implemented	As information is collected to determine the direction of future efforts, UPDRIT publishes an Interim Plan that promotes more habitat improvement, research, and public involvement.
2003	Forest Guardians (FG) submit Petition for Endangered Listing	On the grounds of continued habitat destruction and take of Utah prairie dogs, environmental group Forest Guardians and author Terry Tempest Williams petition USFWS to uplist the Utah prairie dog to endangered rather than threatened.
2006	Legal settlement on FG petition	After a 2004 notice of intent to sue from the petitioners and a 2006 complaint for injunctive and declaratory relief in District Court, a settlement is reached that requires USFWS to make 90-day ruling on petition in 2007.
2006	UPDRIT becomes Utah Prairie Dog Recovery Team	The UPDRIT is formalized into the Utah Prairie Dog Recovery Team.
2007	USFWS initiation of 5-year review	USFWS finds that the petition does not provide enough evidence that uplisting is warranted in its 90-day ruling. Nevertheless, a 5-year review of the status of Utah prairie dogs is initiated.
2009	Habitat Credits Exchange Program (HCEP) begins	As part of a pilot program administrated by the Panoramaland and Color Country Resource Conservation and Development Councils, mitigation "credits" are generated by willing landowners that sell a conservation easement on their property. Citizens participating in activities that require mitigation buy credits from this account and offset habitat degradation by funding habitat restoration, additional conservation easements, and other projects beneficial to Utah prairie dogs on private lands. The self-supporting effort results from a 2008 Natural Resources Conservation Service (NRCS) grant to fund the program's initiation.
2010	Utah Prairie Dog Revised Recovery Plan drafted	Revision of the 1991 Recovery Plan begins. Recovery criteria for three Recovery Units, based on new population research and an increase in public involvement and habitat monitoring, is the primary focus of the revision.
2010	Utah Prairie Dog Recovery Implementation Program (UPDRIP) founded	The UPDRIP, a public and private partnership, is formed to coordinate UPD recovery while accommodating land uses throughout the range of the species. Consisting of local, state, and federal governments, environmental groups, and farm bureaus, UPDRIP begins securing grant funding for recovery efforts and formulating long-term management visions. Participants include the USFWS, UDWR, US Forest Service (USFS), Bureau of Land Management (BLM), School and Institutional Trust Lands Administration (SITLA), Utah Farm Bureau (UFB), Paiute Tribe, Panoramaland Resource Conservation and Development Council (PRCDC), and Color Country Resource Conservation and Development Council (CCRCDC), among others.

TABLE 7.1. Timeline of Important Events in Utah Prairie Dog Management and Conservation (continued)

Year	Action or event	Consequences
2010	US District Court vacates 2007 90-day finding	The court sends the 2007 90-day finding back to USFWS for further consideration. USFWS is directed to address whether the loss of historical range constitutes a significant portion of the range of the species.
2011	USFWS revised 90-day ruling on FG petition	Supplementing its report with additional information acquired since the 2007 90-day finding, USFWS rules again that the petition does not provide enough evidence that uplisting is warranted. No further review of the status of the Utah prairie dog is initiated.
2012	2nd Amendment to ESA 4(d) Special Rule	Increased presence of Utah prairie dogs in cemeteries, sacred grounds, and transportation facilities leads to changes in 4(d) rule allowing for take after barriers are installed. Permitted take limit is changed from 6,000 adults and juveniles annually to 10% of the annual post–juvenile emergence population over the entirety of the Utah prairie dog range (not to exceed 7% on agricultural lands). Starting date for season of take is changed to June 15. Take for activities associated with standard agricultural practices is exempted. If translocations are conducted without success, there are no timing, amount, or permit restrictions on take of Utah prairie dogs from areas where they threaten human safety or disrupt human cultural or burial sites.
2012	Final Utah Prairie Dog Revised Recovery Plan approved and implemented	The final revision of the Utah Prairie Dog Recovery Plan, revised from the original plan in 1991, is approved and implemented. The plan includes revised recovery criteria for three Recovery Units (RUs) based on new population research, and updates actions such as increased public involvement and habitat monitoring. Most notably, USFWS sets the objective of at least 2,000 adults (at least 1,000 adults in spring counts) and 5,000 protected acres in each RU for five consecutive years. Utah prairie dogs must be on protected land to count toward this goal.
2040	Target date for recovery	Estimated year of Utah prairie dog recovery under the current Recovery Plan.

Sources: USFWS, *Utah Prairie Dog: Final Revised Recovery Plan*, i–122; Ritchie et al., *Prairie Dog Interim Conservation*, 3; USFWS, "Revised 90-day Finding," 36053–36068; Forest Guardians, "Petition"; Collier and Spillett, "Status," 27–39; Collier and Spillett, "Decline of a Legend," 83–87; Collier and Spillett, "Factors Influencing the Distribution," 151–158; Elmore and Messmer, *Public Perceptions*, 4; Keith Day, pers. comm.; UPDRIP, *2011 Work Plan*; UPDRIP, *Status Report*, 1–15; Bonzo and Day, *Administrative Monitoring Report*; ICC (Iron County Commission) and UDWR (Utah Division of Wildlife Resources), "Habitat Conservation Plan"; Thomas, "Habitat Conservation Planning," 105–130; USFWS, "Final Rule to Amend Special Rule," 27438–27443; Erica Wightman, pers. comm.

TABLE 7.2. Arrangements and Techniques for Utah Prairie Dog Management and Conservation

Arrangement	Definition	Recent Developments
Translocation	Utah prairie dogs are trapped and released at a location away from conflict with humans.	Because of the historically high mortality rate of relocated Utah prairie dogs (starvation, plague), post-translocation habitat and population monitoring techniques are now more prevalent. Utah prairie dogs are dusted for fleas before release and quarantined to check for other diseases; cages are used to prevent Utah prairie dogs from escaping their new environment; and visual censuses occur after translocation to monitor population number and check for signs of undue predation or disease. Techniques such as vacuuming or flooding prairie dogs from their burrows have been used in translocations of black-tailed prairie dogs, but not Utah prairie dogs. Research concerning whether survivorship of transplants increases if clans are moved together indicates no advantage for Utah prairie dogs (although research for black-tailed prairie dogs is conflicting); the issue can be circumvented by moving individuals from the same and adjacent burrow entrances jointly and relocating them to the same area of the new site.
Habitat Conservation Plan (HCP)	Under Section 10 of the ESA, HCPs involve a landowner or governmental entity that agrees to participate in activities such as translocation, habitat creation or monitoring, fencing, prescribed burning, seeding, or purchase of conservation easements that will conserve Utah prairie dogs, concurrently with actions that may result in incidental take (e.g., construction, agriculture).	USFWS has active HCPs with the Cedar City Golf Course/Paiute Indian Tribe and Iron County. A new "rangewide" HCP has been proposed to cover several counties and allow for development of lands with fewer restrictions on take than the current Iron County HCP. The rangewide HCP will cost an estimated $26 million to implement, mostly from mitigation fees and government agency contributions, and participating counties are seeking other funding.
Safe Harbor Agreement (SHA)	SHAs implement measures for Utah prairie dog conservation on private property while making compromises between conservation and other land uses. Landowners are awarded immunity from federal regulations regarding Utah prairie dogs on their property in exchange for implementing techniques such as translocation (to or from the landowner's property), habitat creation or monitoring, fencing, prescribed burning, seeding, or purchase of conservation easements that improve the grassland ecosystem as a whole (for livestock and Utah prairie dogs). Incidental take may also be a component.	"Programmatic" SHAs now have associated permits that authorize governments and other entities to enroll a large number of individual property owners in the SHA program. USFWS and the Utah Division of Wildlife Resources (UDWR) also participate in SHAs with individual ranchers.

TABLE 7.2. Arrangements and Techniques for Utah Prairie Dog Management and Conservation (continued)

Arrangement	Definition	Recent Developments
Conservation Easement (CE)	CEs are a preservation agreement between a landowner and a government agency for various purposes, such as conservation or restricting development. CEs can also be used as a mitigation strategy in HCPs and SHAs to offset habitat loss.	Beginning in 2009, the Habitat Credits Exchange Program (HCEP) generates "credits" by purchasing conservation easements for Utah prairie dogs. Commercial builders, developers, landowners, or any other buyers in "need of" incidental take can purchase enough credits to mitigate the take and proceed with their project unrestricted. Voluntary buyers (i.e., those not desiring take but nevertheless concerned about conservation) may soon be able to buy credits and retire them for conservation-related, nonmitigation purposes. HCEP may also start an Adopt-a-Prairie-Dog program and award credit purchases of $100 or more with a plush Utah prairie dog and a certificate.
Conservation Bank (CB)	Conservation banks are permanently protected lands that provide mitigation such as burning, plague dusting, and/or seeding to offset the impacts of habitat loss. USFWS approves a specific number of habitat or species credits that bank owners may sell in exchange for protecting and managing the land. CBs can also be components of HCPs or SHAs.	The Iron County HCP was amended to include mitigation credits from SITLA CBs for county projects. SITLA is an independent agency that manages trust land for Utah's public institutions. A permanent conservation easement is on the SITLA property and held by UDWR. Much like the HCEP, SITLA earns credits that it uses or sells to other parties to offset impacts to Utah prairie dogs from various projects. Iron County also owns the Little Horse Valley CB west of Cedar City. Little Horse has no Utah prairie dogs but is adjacent to public lands with colonies of Utah prairie dogs that will likely expand, making it an important area in Utah prairie dog recovery.

TABLE 7.2. Arrangements and Techniques for Utah Prairie Dog Management and Conservation (continued)

Arrangement	Definition	Recent Developments
ESA Section 7 Consultation (S7)	Federal agencies carrying out any action that may affect an ESA listed species such as Utah prairie dogs consult with USFWS under the "Interagency Cooperation" clause of the ESA. If it is determined that the agency's action may affect the species in question negatively after an informal consultation, USFWS continues with biological assessments, formal consultations, and official biological opinions resulting in recommendations for protecting the listed species. USFWS may approve incidental take if actions may adversely affect a species but do not threaten its persistence.	USFWS and the Federal Aviation Administration (FAA) completed an S7 in 2008 to assess impacts to Utah prairie dogs by southern Utah airports such as Bryce Canyon, Cedar City Regional, Loa-Wayne Wonderland, Panguitch Municipal, and Parowan. An airport mitigation account holds contributions from the FAA (around $950,000) committed to Utah prairie dog conservation through this consultation, offsetting incidental take and trapping and translocation by UDWR. USFWS has received board approval from SITLA to purchase 800 acres of habitat on Johnson Bench, Garfield County, from this funding, with The Nature Conservancy holding the title to manage the property for Utah prairie dogs.

S7 consultations have also assessed mitigation fees for impacts to Utah prairie dogs during the building of transmission lines, and the Utah Department of Transportation, as it pursues a programmatic S7 for mitigation of Utah prairie dogs for the next 20 years, will be purchasing almost $250,000 worth of credits from the HCEP in 2013 as part of an S7. |

Sources: Bill Branham, pers. comm.; Cedar City Corporation and Paiute Tribe of Utah, Habitat Conservation Plan, 5–6; Curtis, "Factors Influencing Relocation Success," 1–82; ICC and UDWR, "Habitat Conservation Plan," 104; Keith Day, pers. comm.; Hoogland, "Conservation of Prairie Dogs," in Hoogland, Conservation of the Black-Tailed Prairie Dog, 185–187; USFWS, Recommended Translocation Procedures, 1–13; Long, et al., "Establishment," 188–209 (with sidebar by Debra Shier containing results contradicting Long, et al. 2006); USFWS, "Revised 90-day Finding," 36065–36066; Mackley, "Effects of Habitat Modifications"; Player and Urness, "Habitat Manipulation," 517–523; Hoogland, "Alarm Calling," 438–449; Hoogland, "Black-Tailed, Gunnison's," 917–927; Manno, "Utah Prairie Dogs Vigilant," 553–558; Bonzo and Day, Administrative Monitoring Report;

Thomas, "Habitat Conservation Planning," 105–130; Henetz, "Lawsuit"; USFWS, Safe Harbor Agreements; USFWS and UDWR, Safe Harbor Agreement: Allen Henrie; Williams, Finding Beauty, 220–221; PRCDC and USFWS, Programmatic Safe Harbor; Erica Wightman, pers. comm.

Note: Of the two conservation banks that permanently protect prairie dog habitat on nonfederal lands, one is in the Awapa Plateau Recovery Unit (RU) (State of Utah School and Institutional Trust Lands Administration [SITLA], about 800 acres), and the other is in the West Desert RU (Little Horse Valley, about 220 acres).

FIGURE 7.9. *Par for the course*. Managers and patrons of the Cedar City Golf Course (CCGC) have experienced conflict with Utah prairie dogs for years *(top)*. The UDWR has moved Utah prairie dogs off the CCGC since 1996, but the rodents persist *(bottom)*. In 2007, the CCGC became a partner with the Paiute Indian Tribe in an HCP containing arrangements that mitigate removal of Utah prairie dogs from the golf course. Photos by Brian Slobe.

4(d) rule's 1984 inception.[57] Despite criticism by advocacy groups of the 4(d) rule application to Utah prairie dogs, and despite the doubt some Utahans have about the accuracy of Utah prairie dog counts,[58] the USFWS reported in 2010 that the 4(d) rule is not in conflict with Utah prairie dog conservation because populations have increased since its implementation almost three decades ago. Meanwhile, many consider a comprehensive plan involving the complete absence of lethal control to be impractical, and it has not been implemented.[59]

In 2010, a new coalition of government officials, citizens groups, and universities called the Utah Prairie Dog Recovery Implementation Program (UPDRIP) was founded to support initiatives like monitoring for plague, habitat maintenance, fencing, translocations, HCPs, and SHAs.[60] Then in August 2012, the USFWS approved a revision to the 4(d) rule application that allows unlimited take where Utah prairie dogs are deemed to pose a safety threat to humans, and defines more clearly the restrictions on take in other instances (table 7.1).[61] Perhaps these new arrangements will yield effective compromises between interested parties, as conflicts between humans and Utah prairie dogs continue (table 7.3).

Other Conservation Issues

Some readers may wonder why prairie dogs of any species are not simply given birth control. One method of contraception—removing all of the males in a colony—would involve a level of effort on par with that of the Dog Squad. Even if all males were captured, immigrants would likely come and impregnate most of the females anyhow. In addition, efforts to feed black-tailed prairie dogs oats laced with a now illegal synthetic estrogen called diethylstilbestrol (DES) have fallen into disrepute because of secondary effects. Other animals that ingest the DES, whether directly by eating the

oats or indirectly by eating the prairie dogs, in turn cannot reproduce.[62]

One prospect that I suggest for saving a few Utah prairie dogs, particularly those destined for lethal take, involves placing them in zoos. While Utah prairie dogs are wild animals and conservation in their natural habitat is paramount, this option seems preferable to killing them. Indeed, Utah prairie dogs (and their black-tailed cousins, which are found in zoos across the United States) are endearing and seem to adjust well to properly managed exhibits. In addition, the social activity of captive prairie dogs can inspire new biologists and show the positive and fun side of the species, leading to indirect outreach and conservation effects.[63] Hogle Zoo in Salt Lake City has recently discontinued housing Utah prairie dogs after doing so for many years, and currently, Utah prairie dogs are not found in zoos.[64]

Another unpracticed option for conservation that I hesitate to mention is the allowance of regulated and limited recreational shooting of Utah prairie dogs on private lands. The rationale is that landowners with Utah prairie dogs on their property would possibly maintain a colony because of the financial incentives of allowing shooting. Otherwise, the rancher might just (illegally) kill all of the Utah prairie dogs on his land. Shooting of unprotected prairie dog species is practiced in other states, but recreational shooting of Utah prairie dogs is illegal because of their threatened status (fig. 7.10).[65]

Especially painful to me is the thought that animals that I see as individuals with personalities would be killed for "sport" if ranchers encourage recreational shooting of their Utah prairie dogs. But while I make clear my disappointment in humanity over someone who would blow away my favorite animals for no good reason, I am resigned to the unrelenting desire for participation in this despicable behavior.[66] Indeed, hunters are more likely than nonhunters to favor conservation.[67]

TABLE 7.3. Some Notable Conflicts between Utah Prairie Dogs and Humans

Location	Conflict	Resolution, strategies implemented, or updates
Bryce Canyon City/Ruby's Inn	The city is trying to improve its water treatment and distribution capacity in response to increased usage, partly from surging tourism. Utah prairie dogs reside above the underground portions of the infrastructure that need to be upgraded, and in the best areas to expand a sewer treatment system that falls short of state standards.	Bryce Canyon City is currently developing an HCP, but costs are limiting the amount of mitigated property and are removing funds needed for the infrastructure projects. A preliminary draft has been accepted by USFWS, strategic properties near Bryce City have been acquired with a Federation Aviation Administration (FAA) mitigation fund and grant, and the city is reviewing other mitigation options.
Cedar City	Utah prairie dogs are living on the Cedar City Golf Course (CCGC). Managers of CCGC are frustrated because Utah prairie dogs are digging up the grounds and there is potential for injury to golfers.	UDWR has relocated Utah prairie dogs off the CCGC since 1996. With the adult population over 300, a 2007 HCP for the property was implemented (jointly with Paiute Tribal Lands, see below), and a mitigation site (Wild Pea Hollow, WPH) was purchased by the county. In 2011, the Utah Prairie Dog Recovery Team approved more mitigation sites and increased translocations as over 600 adult and juvenile Utah prairie dogs were trapped and removed from the CCGC. Translocation is ongoing until all Utah prairie dogs are removed from the property, but officials do not view translocation as a comprehensive strategy, as Utah prairie dogs persist on the property. Exclusion barriers surrounding the CCGC have been discussed but not yet pursued as CCGC managers and the city develop possibilities for funding the project.
Enoch	Citizens are concerned that Utah prairie dog colonies could spread plague to humans and stymie economic growth. Insisting that Utah prairie dog colonies should exist only outside of the town limits, and claiming that it already contributes to conservation and mitigation of take through tax dollars, Enoch has adopted a land use ordinance that prohibits property owners from dedicating space to Utah prairie dog habitat through a conservation easement or otherwise.	The Utah Prairie Dog Recovery Team has clarified that it does not support the presence of isolated Utah prairie dog colonies within city limits, preferring to improve connectivity of Utah prairie dog habitat. As the overall goal is delisting of Utah prairie dogs, and certain habitat protections on private property (such as CEs or SHAs) could contribute, the Iron County commissioner has discussed this ordinance with the Enoch City Council. The county is concerned that not allowing conservation arrangements to occur in Enoch would affect the success of the new Rangewide HCP, and that Enoch should contribute to mitigation in the same fashion as other towns if residents receive take.

TABLE 7.3. Some Notable Conflicts between Utah Prairie Dogs and Humans (continued)

Location	Conflict	Resolution, strategies implemented, or updates
Equestrian Point	Utah prairie dogs are present on parcels intended for development, as well as in an area with a ballpark and the Bridal Path, which connects residents of a neighborhood to a park. Owners of two of the parcels have applied for an HCP with take, but the number of Utah prairie dogs on the property means that other strategies are also needed. An owner of one parcel has complained of being unable to sell his land because it has decreased in value after Utah prairie dogs moved onto the property after his purchase.	UDWR trapped 110 Utah prairie dogs from the park and Bridal Path in 2009–2010 and continues trapping in these areas. Owners have been offered credits through the HCEP.
Hatch, Todd's Junction, and Tropic	While building a transmission line from Hatch to Todd's Junction, Garkane Energy stopped construction and commenced an ESA S7 with USFWS when it found Utah prairie dogs on the corridor of the line. It also consulted with USFWS regarding a transmission line from Tropic to Hatch.	Garkane Power purchased $55,000 worth of credits for mitigation from the HCEP. Some are applied to the Tropic-Hatch project, and the remainder will be "banked" (saved for later) and applied to other projects if results of future consultation deem it necessary.
Paiute Tribal Lands	Utah prairie dogs exist on the tribe's pow-wow grounds, ball field, and other recreational areas.	The Tribe is a joint applicant in the CCGC HCP of 2007. As per the HCP, mitigation site WPH must be maintained as suitable Utah prairie dog habitat or hold at least 70 individuals for two consecutive years before the Tribe is allowed to take Utah prairie dogs. Complications have occurred as the Utah prairie dog population at WPH crashed, and sagebrush took over the site in 2006–2007, rendering it unacceptable as Utah prairie dog habitat.
		Rather than buy credits from the HCEP, the Tribe acquired funding for vegetation treatments that were implemented in 2011 and will likely improve vegetation for a potential population of Utah prairie dogs in 2–3 years. UPDRIP is researching funding opportunities for a barrier to keep Utah prairie dogs away from the pow-wow grounds in the meantime.

TABLE 7.3. Some Notable Conflicts between Utah Prairie Dogs and Humans (*continued*)

Location	Conflict	Resolution, strategies implemented, or updates
Paragonah	Utah prairie dogs are burrowing around gravesites and walking on paths in the cemetery.	Over 128 individuals have been removed since 1997 and UDWR traps and relocates Utah prairie dogs off the cemetery and other sites in Paragonah each summer. A small population persisted because Utah prairie dogs dug under a fence intended to exclude them from the property. In response, Iron County, USFWS, UDWR, and the town recently completed a 6-foot-deep belowground barrier fence (previously 2 feet deep) with funds from Endangered Species and FAA mitigation funds. With the completion of the fence, take has been authorized.
Parowan	Utah prairie dogs are present on the runway of the municipal airport. Concern exists over the soft spots in the ground caused by burrowing that are a hazard when heavy planes land on the runway. Airport managers want all Utah prairie dogs trapped and relocated so that soft spots can be repaired.	Under the Iron County HCP, over 70 Utah prairie dogs were trapped from the Parowan Airport by UDWR during 1997–1999. Another 129 Utah prairie dogs were removed in 2011 under a new take permit issued by USFWS.
		Airports are also permitted a certain amount of incidental take following an ESA S7 with USFWS to assess Utah prairie dog impacts. USFWS provided $274,000 of ESA Section 6 funding (with matching funds from the state and Parowan City) to fence the Parowan Airport. The fence is completed and take has been authorized.

Sources: Bill Branham, pers. comm.; Cedar City Corporation and Paiute Tribe of Utah, *Habitat Conservation Plan,* 5–6; ICC and UDWR, "Habitat Conservation Plan," 104; Keith Day, pers. comm.; Henetz, "Lawsuit"; USFWS, *Safe Harbor Agreements;* USFWS and UDWR, *Safe Harbor Agreement: Allen Henrie;* Williams, *Finding Beauty,* 220–221; PRCDC and USFWS, *Programmatic Safe Harbor;* USFWS, *Utah Prairie Dog: Final Revised Recovery Plan,* i–122; UPDRIP, *2011 Work Plan;* UPDRIP, *Status Report,* 1–15; Bonzo and Day, *Administrative Monitoring Report;* Steed, "Just Shoot Them," 1–33; Erica Wightman, pers. comm.

Note: This table lists particularly controversial or newsworthy cases and is not comprehensive.

FIGURE 7.10. *No shooting.* "Varmint shooting," however cowardly and repulsive to the author, is nevertheless popular in states containing prairie dog species such as black-tailed prairie dogs that are not listed as endangered or threatened. This sign is here because of an order issued to prohibit the shooting of prairie dogs in certain areas of Thunder Basin National Grassland in Wyoming. Photo by Ruthanne Johnson, courtesy of the Humane Society of the United States.

FIGURE 7.11. *Red Yogi.* As a Utah prairie dog stands vigilant atop his burrow, he sees a landscape much different from the one his ancestors saw before Western settlement.

In 2005, John concluded his research on Utah prairie dogs. With every pup trapped and released and our equipment packed away, it was time to say good-bye to the study colony for good. On the evening before our departure, the study animals assembled for their daily happy hour and began to drop into their burrows one by one.

Soon, a husky old female was the only one left. The last dog on the meadow bobbed her head up, stood vigilant, and emitted a final call toward the woods, scanning her surroundings one last time prior to submergence for the night. I wondered whether this would be the public's image of the Utah prairie dog 50 or 100 years from now—the final Utah prairie dog in the world, calling into the distance, defenseless against predation or crying out for a mate that would never appear (fig. 7.11).

Finally, the female submerged for the night, and I pondered the future of the species as I climbed into the Squad Car to drive away from the colony for the last time. Five years later, I saw some encouraging signs for the long-term survival of Utah prairie dogs.

In 2010, I attended an event at BCNP that is now an annual special occasion: Utah Prairie Dog Day, a celebration to honor the contributions of Utah prairie dogs to the grassland ecosystem. The event offers an opportunity for folks to learn about Utah prairie dogs and see them in the wild.

It was Utah-based author Terry Tempest Williams who pioneered a day for prairie dogs to be integrated with the more traditional celebration of Groundhog Day on February 2. The campaign continued when Utah student Luke Zitting collected about 1,000 signatures in support of his 2010 resolution to the state legislature to officially recognize Utah Prairie Dog Day.[68] The holiday is perhaps now the single most important day of the year for prairie dog conservation, with annual events in cities like Denver and Aurora (for black-tailed prairie dogs).[69]

Appropriately, February 2 is close to the anniversary of the petition to upgrade the Utah prairie dog from threatened to endangered,[70] and every year, a Prairie Dog Report Card is released by the environmental group WildEarth Guardians. The report gives grades to states on the basis of how much their habitat conservation, shooting regulations, poisoning policies, and fights against plague are helping prairie dogs. Unfortunately, Utah received a C-minus in 2013,[71] but my hope is that Prairie Dog Day, in concert with the new recovery actions, can help improve things for Utah prairie dogs.

Prairie Dog Day and Groundhog Day are observed by a few former Dog Squad members each year. February 2 is also the birthday of one of John's sons.[72] The coincidence made John want to give his newborn the fitting middle name "Cynomys." His wife vetoed the idea.

While Prairie Dog Day is typically celebrated on February 2, Utah Prairie Dog Day at BCNP occurs in May or June to coincide with weather that is conducive to celebration and viewing Utah prairie dogs. Students and their families enter the park free and have an opportunity to interact with a special surprise guest that I will not reveal here. Utah prairie dog viewing sessions occur throughout, with afternoon and evening interpretive programs. At night, the extravaganza continues with a program called "Prairie Dogs and Other Cool Critters." But the hallmark event is an art contest for the kids.[73]

Offering positive and educational encounters with Utah prairie dogs and opportunities to view them in their natural habitat is one of the best ways to build support for Utah prairie

dogs and their conservation (fig. 7.12a–b). Nonlocal children attending Utah Prairie Dog Day are usually naive about the controversy surrounding Utah prairie dogs; most local children are aware of their family's hatred toward Utah prairie dogs but seem to want to learn more about the critters nevertheless. Either way, ensuring that Utah's future inhabitants grow to view Utah prairie dogs positively is crucial in the fight to save them. And with the evident interest children show in Utah prairie dogs during Utah Prairie Dog Day, it is no wonder that many attendees are interested in saving the Utah prairie dog for future generations.

Perhaps the most important rationale for conserving Utah prairie dogs is their importance to an entire ecosystem. After all, the rarity of Utah prairie dogs cannot be excused as a natural occurrence. They have suffered a calculated genocide with bullets, gas, and poison that has killed millions.[74] How right or wrong it was, I will not discuss. What is done is done. But allowing the decline of Utah prairie dogs to continue unchecked toward extinction would create a dangerous precedent of allowing ourselves to choose to purposely and methodically eradicate a species and destroy an ecosystem for whatever reasons we see fit, however spurious. Let us remember that Utah prairie dogs do not belong to property owners, or environmental activists, or even governmental agencies. They belong to the people of the United States of America, and coming together on solutions to prevent their demise should be the duty of all citizens.[75]

Utah prairie dogs should also be conserved because they have inherent value and fascinating social behavior that both biologists and laypeople appreciate. Their unique behaviors have contributed to the understanding of several key evolutionary issues that I have described in previous chapters, such as coloniality, alarm calling, communal nursing, kin recognition, social interaction, and infanticide. Utah prairie dogs can therefore help us

FIGURE 7.12. *Fund-raising.* A Utah prairie dog educational display at the BCNP Visitor Center *(left)*. One tactic for conserving Utah prairie dogs is encouraging ecotourism—people come to see Utah prairie dogs in their natural habitat and are charged a fee to do so, thus removing concern that Utah prairie dogs interfere with financial development. National parks like BCNP are an example of this strategy, but private landowners may be able to benefit from ecotourism as well. In *(right)*, UPDRIP coordinator Bill Branham enjoys a summer afternoon with "Pete" the prairie dog at BCNP. Pete provides a positive image of Utah prairie dogs to those who want to learn about Utah's grassland ecosystem. Right photo courtesy of Bill Branham.

understand other social species, including our own.

It encourages me that Utah prairie dog conservation appears to be an attainable goal toward which some people are already working. Acting on behalf of animals that cannot speak for themselves, the Prairie Dog Coalition (PDC) campaigns against poisoning programs, supports humane control solutions, responds to action alerts of exterminations, and provides educational resources.[76] A vaccine against the plague that can be delivered

to prairie dogs via feed pellets is showing promise while a method for its distribution is being optimized.[77] And officials are constantly honing and implementing management and conservation plans, often using the detailed biological information on the species that now exists. From dispelling myths that lead to intolerance of Utah prairie dogs, such as quick reproduction, automatic colony expansion, frequent broken legs of cattle and horses in burrows, and unabated competition for forage with livestock; to knowing when Utah prairie dogs breed so as to not disturb them with lethal control at a critical juncture; to determining that Utah prairie dog families share burrows so that we can be more accurate with population counts—with so many conservation implications, scientific knowledge has been key in the fight to save Utah prairie dogs.[78]

The recent decision to continue the listing of Utah prairie dogs as threatened (table 7.1) does not put a damper on my enthusiasm. It would be easy for my knee-jerk reaction to the ruling to be one of discouragement, but as much as I am conditioned to protect Utah prairie dogs, I concede that the USFWS probably made a sensible, judicious, and evenhanded decision within the context of southern Utah's current landscape. Given the grand scale of the political and economic implications, the dialogue I encountered at the pancake breakfast, and constraints brought on by the legal pigeonholes of the ESA, the determination must have been challenging. With great reluctance, I acknowledge that what is best for Utah prairie dogs is not necessarily reasonable or practical.[79]

As a Utah prairie dog stands vigilant and looks toward the horizon, it sees a changing landscape. Whether it will see a progressive frontier in which its brethren can play a role is uncertain. A future obstacle to sustained recovery of Utah prairie dogs will be continued controversy over their management. Despite the latest ESA ruling, some landowners believe they still are not being treated fairly. Issues include a perceived double standard under the ESA when incidental take from development or ranching is compared with other disturbances to Utah prairie dogs, such as roadkills by tourists (figs. 7.13a–c and 7.14).[80] Some local governments remain suspicious of recent studies that reaffirm Utah prairie dogs as a distinct species, asking for more DNA testing that might delineate Utah prairie dogs and their closest evolutionary cousins, white-tailed prairie dogs, as a single

FIGURE 7.13. *Look both ways.* The proximity of Utah prairie dog colonies to roads, both within BCNP and in towns across southern Utah, creates problems for dispersing Utah prairie dogs *(top and middle)*. Some Utah prairie dogs even frequent burrows that are directly beneath roads *(bottom)*.

FIGURE 7.14. *Watch your speed*. Personnel at BCNP place speed limit signs and educate the public about driving carefully in the park.

species that does not warrant federal listing.[81] Because Utah prairie dogs live only in Utah, a few folks argue against federal jurisdiction over the species.[82] Many ranchers fear restrictions under the ESA and balk at taking steps to receive financial aid.[83] And some Utahans are not happy about contributing financially to mitigate take. They argue that conservation groups should put forth their own money as reparations to landowners for damage caused by Utah prairie dogs, in lieu of involvement with private insurance or the government.[84]

Others seem to claim that some of the current conservation efforts are merely cosmetic and that federal agencies should do more to protect Utah prairie dogs. They believe that arrangements involving incidental take and translocations are really just window dressing disguised as the status quo of annihilating

Utah prairie dogs, and that the end of lethal control is essential to long-term recovery. They debate the population counts by the USFWS,[85] and they argue that even more efforts should be geared toward protecting Utah prairie dogs where they already exist, in lieu of translocations.[86]

In the end, no easy, definitive answers exist. That is why I have risked offending proponents from all angles of the debate in writing this chapter in a manner that embraces the conflict and attempts to find middle ground. I admit that I am conflicted over many of these issues myself, and I share the concern of many ranchers and developers over human–Utah prairie dog clashes. But this concern is within the context of a desire for sustainable, environmentally responsible agriculture and industry, and I therefore also favor as much protection as possible for species like the Utah prairie dog that are threatened with extinction (fig. 7.15).

Gray areas of the Utah prairie dog debate are particularly relevant for the 75 percent of Utah prairie dogs that live on nonfederal lands.[87] The USFWS seems to realize through its Revised Recovery Plan and recent actions to purchase and protect habitats that exiling almost all of these Utah prairie dogs to a few sheltered areas would not be true conservation—especially when, despite improved methodology, many Utah prairie dogs perish after translocation.[88] In addition, the lack of connectivity inherent in establishing Utah prairie dog populations at a limited number of locations can lead to local extinctions of Utah prairie dog colonies,[89] making some increased population counts either temporary or mere technicalities.

Conservation should therefore continue to involve reasonable efforts to protect Utah prairie dogs where they already exist, as well as creation of habitat for potential translocations. It follows that involving landowners in creative multiple-use land arrangements that improve the ecosystem for livestock and Utah

FIGURE 7.15. *Canyon of hope*. Western settlement has been tough for Utah prairie dogs. Good conservation will require compromise and cooperation among ranchers, agriculturists, naturalists, and government officials.

prairie dogs alike, with SHAs or otherwise, seems like an appropriate focus of forthcoming conservation efforts. Such methods should be complemented with the most comprehensive protection of Utah prairie dogs possible on public lands, with measures taken against roadkills, plague, and so forth.

While I agree with many of the approaches in the Revised Recovery Plan that invoke landowner involvement, I also share the concern of some advocacy groups regarding the amount of take from the rangewide population.[90] Leaving aside my repulsion at killing Utah prairie dogs, I am resigned to tolerating a certain amount of take as a concession to allow Utah prairie dogs some protection on the private lands that make up most of their current habitat. However, the existing level of potential lethal control (10 percent of the rangewide population) seems hard to

rationalize. I understand that such activities occur after the population has ballooned with young-of-the-year, that this amount has not yet been realized, and that recent Utah prairie dog populations are reported to be increasing.[91] Nevertheless, with Utah prairie dogs occupying a small fraction of their former range and other nonlethal methods being available to mitigate conflict such as translocation and fencing, I hope that lethal take will not increase. If it must occur at all, killing Utah prairie dogs should happen rarely and only after every other option has been exhausted.[92]

Regardless of one's opinions on details surrounding the conservation of Utah prairie dogs, we must find a way to move forward collectively. Especially because most people believe in the fundamental mission of the ESA,[93] we cannot waste the immense potential to save Utah prairie dogs, and to coincidentally improve southern Utah's grassland ecosystem. Indeed, Utah prairie dogs have shown us that they are amazingly resilient through their ability to survive persecution over the last 150 years. These underdogs will obviously persevere if we give them the slightest opportunity, as towns of them still line the valleys of southern Utah even though they have been killed by the thousands. It is unlikely that Utah prairie dogs will ever reassume their former range, but if we continue working together, the battle to save Utah prairie dogs is one we can win. Let's give 'em a chance.

As Utah prairie dogs make a last stand against extinction, I hope this book will inspire people to see their colonies not as meaningless dots on the landscape, but as the final strongholds of important rodents with a role in America's history. Perhaps those who

happen upon the prairie dog colonies among Utah's red rocks will now react to the residents with curiosity instead of disdain. Maybe they will even stop to observe the hustle and bustle of the big city.

With enough patience, they will see individuals with social lives, a dynamic communication system, and other meaningful behaviors that have been carefully crafted over millions of years via natural selection. And for those who witness the society of critters in which a kiss is a handshake, conservation will take on newfound importance, destroying the environment will become unacceptable, and Utah prairie dogs will bear no resemblance to the "rats" that have been killed indiscriminately for so long. If only for a moment, they will look across the valleys of Utah, close their eyes, and imagine how it once was—a nation of prairie dogs, as far as the eye could see.

Of Predators and Prairie Dogs

My internal compass has always pointed west. Growing up in urban Philadelphia, I always envisioned traveling to the American Southwest. Joining John Hoogland's Dog Squad provided not only the opportunity of a lifetime for a Utah-style safari, but also the chance to observe a species threatened with extinction.

I thought the experience would be as glamorous as the animal-related shows on television, but the Dog Squad was really hard work. My body needed to adjust to the altitude of over 8,000 feet (almost 2500 m), and freezing temperatures combined with deep snow and cramped living quarters were a major challenge. What also surprised me was the lack of diversion from Utah prairie dogs, as Panguitch, the nearest town of any size, was a bit different from Philadelphia. The hamlet offered little more than some fast food and Mormon church services.

Fieldwork required dedication, practice, constant observation, solitude, and lots and lots of patience. Keen eyesight was also a necessary skill for Utah prairie dog research. Sniffing, kissing, fighting, nest building, mating, infanticide—these were interactions needing documentation, and they occurred quickly. But no behavior was harder to observe than the predation of Utah prairie dogs. Daydreaming during lulls in activity was unacceptable because a red fox or northern goshawk could appear at any second and pounce on a nonvigilant Utah prairie dog.

Although I was sad to see the demise of my study animals, I was amazed at how my observations helped us understand nature. For years, the public has assumed that natural selection weeds out the old and the weak. But with Utah prairie dogs, most victims of predations were in good condition—either reproductive males too preoccupied with sex to escape attacks, or pregnant females who could not run fast. And this is just one misconception about Utah prairie dogs, which are often reviled as plague-spreading vermin that breed like rabbits–a notion also undermined by research.

What else will we discover about Utah prairie dogs? Only time will tell. That is why open-mindedness, particularly regarding the incompatibility of Utah prairie dogs with cattle, is an important part of conservation. So is bringing people with different convictions to the bargaining table, a task that is challenging but feasible. Many people are surprised to find out that directly after my experience on the Dog Squad, I traveled to New Mexico to work at a guest ranch without a thought that my interests in ranching and conservation might be mutually exclusive. Now, as a ranch-guide author, I still regard my time on the Dog Squad as some of the best days of my life, and a period when my interests in the American West developed. I therefore maintain that people of varying interests can compromise and improve Utah's grassland ecosystem as a whole to make life better for livestock, wildlife, and humans.

LILI DEBARBIERI,
Dog Squad Class of 2005
Author, *A Guide to Southern Arizona's Historic
Farms and Ranches: Rustic Southwest Retreats*

August 2, 2012

Hi Theo,

My seventh year with white-tailed prairie dogs here at the Arapaho National Wildlife Refuge (ANWR) in northern Colorado has been informative, but discouraging. Upon my arrival in March, our study colony had fewer individuals than ever before (53). All the females but one mated, but few of them weaned a litter, probably for at least one of three reasons: (a) this year has been ANWR's driest since the Oligocene—so the white-tailed prairie dogs have almost nothing to eat; (b) many of the 2012 females mated with close relatives; (c) the presence of Barbara the badger directly in front of my tower might have encouraged many females to abort their young before parturition. Around my tower I had 14 females, but only two gave birth. Overall we had only 12 litters and 53 babies—the lowest numbers ever here at ANWR.

The woes have continued. Barbara concentrated mostly on Wyoming ground squirrels until late May, when she turned her attention to white-tailed prairie dogs. The results have been devastating. She has taken at least 4 of our adults, but several other adults are also missing. Of the 53 weaned babies, we now have only 22. We have seen Barbara capture about 15 of our babies, but we think that she is probably responsible for ALL of the disappearances. And the babies have been aboveground for only four weeks! I fear that almost none of the babies will survive until March 2013.

Originally I planned to work with the white-tailed prairie dogs here for about 7-8 years. But because the white-tailed prairie dog population here at ANWR is currently so low, and because I will have so few to study in 2013, I am making plans to initiate new long-term research with Gunnison's prairie dogs at Valles Caldera National Preserve (VCNP) in northern New Mexico. I will transfer all my equipment to VCNP in September or October

2012, and will start full-time research in March 2013. I can hardly wait to get started!

Soon, I will be busy recruiting for my next Prairie Dog Squad. Responses to recent advertisements I have placed on various job websites have been impressive—perhaps because opportunities for employment and graduate education are currently so bleak. Before making a final decision about the 2013 Prairie Dog Squad, I have encouraged each potential recruit to contact you and other former research assistants. I hope that you can respond, but I do not expect you to craft a personal reply for each request. Instead, perhaps you can write and save a paragraph or two on your computer, and then just send your short description to each recruit that contacts you. And please be candid about the highs and lows of your experience.

Below is the sort of generic response that I would send. I thank you for your assistance, which is certain to help me to assemble a dandy 2013 Prairie Dog Squad.

Cordially,

John Hoogland

Hi [insert name here],

I am responding to your e-mail about the possibility of helping John Hoogland to study Gunnison's prairie dogs in New Mexico. I assume that you are emailing me because you have just had a frontal lobotomy. Why else would you want to join the 2013 Prairie Dog Squad for 4 months, largely at your own expense?

John Hoogland is an egomaniacal slavedriver. He thinks, talks, and dreams about nothing—emphasis on NOTHING—but prairie dogs.

You wonder about days off. Stop wondering, because you will get none. You might get off early one day if winds will exceed 120 miles (75 km) per hour, because John is afraid of high winds. He should be afraid of electrical storms as well because lightning once struck his tower while he was in it. But he's not. If you are really lucky, you might get a delayed departure time one day, because John's 1986 jalopy is a piece of junk that frequently does not start in cold weather.

So you think that you have been cold before? Wow, you have no idea what cold is like until you try to document prairie dog matings during mid-March in the mountains at an elevation of 8,100 feet (2469 m)! John will tell you that he wears 8 layers on the bottom, 11—yep, a whopping 11—layers on top, 2 wool hats and 2 hoods, handwarmers, and toewarmers. And he will advise you to purchase a pricey contraption that practically suffocates you as it tries to recycle warmth from your exhalations. Jogging or some other form of activity might allow you to survive northern New Mexico's freezing conditions, but sitting still in your observation tower and watching prairie dogs fornicate just doesn't do the trick.

John will tell you that prairie dogs sometimes commit infanticide. Don't believe him! I watched every day from dawn to dusk during the 5–6 weeks when pups were still underground, and never observed a single murder in two years. John says that he has documented infanticides, but I conclude that he must be fabricating data and have considered reporting his scientific misconduct.

Yes, those prairie dog babies are cute. But they all emerge from their burrows at the same time. Trying to catch them brings new meaning to the terms chaos, pandemonium, and exhaustion. By the time that John asks you to enter his 25-year-old van to mark the last baby, you will never want to see another prairie dog in your life. Oh, that marking van! The temperature approaches 120°F (49°C) during the period in June when you will be marking babies. The stench from all those prairie dog droppings will make you want to faint, so that John will need to cajole a different victim to enter the van for eartagging and marking.

Oh, did I tell you about the town where you will be living? John refers to it as a "metropolitan" area, but the population is a measly few hundred people. The locals refer to John's female research assistants as "The Gopher Girls." But don't muse about going to the bars in Albuquerque and don't worry about being harassed by the local girl-watchers, because John will monopolize your time every day from dawn until dusk. When you get home at night, you are too exhausted to do anything except eat a TV-dinner and then crawl into bed.

John is fond of saying that "prairie dog research is not a job. It's an adventure." He's certainly correct about the job part, because the term "job" implies salary, right? And he is correct about the second part, too: prairie dog research is an adventure, all right—one that you will want to forever forget.

I hope that I have answered all your questions and concerns about the 2013 Prairie Dog Squad. Enjoy!

Sam Squaddie, Dog Squad Class of 2005

Stand by Your Clan

Preface

1. Pennsylvania chocolate tycoon Milton Hershey bought a dozen black-tailed prairie dogs in 1905 from two German settlers named Franz and Louise Zinner. The prairie dogs became the first animals in the zoo Hershey was building for his utopian, company-based town, which also included an amusement park, a new chocolate factory, hotels, a museum, a stadium, and other services. The zoo maintains a black-tailed prairie dog colony below the town's hallmark yellow silos to this day. Hershey Archives, "History of the Hershey Zoo," accessed May 17, 2012, http://www.zooamerica .com/about_us.php.

Chapter 1

1. University of Nebraska Press/University of Nebraska, Lincoln Libraries-Electronic Text Center, *The Journals of the Lewis and Clark Expedition*, entry from June 5, 1805, retrieved February 5, 2005, http://lewisandclarkjournals .unl.edu/.
2. Spencer F. Baird, *Mammals of the Boundary* (Washington, DC: United States and Mexican Boundary Survey, 1859), 40.
3. University of Nebraska, *Journals of Lewis and Clark*, entry from September 17, 1804.
4. Natasha B. Kotliar, Brian J. Miller, Richard P. Reading, and Timothy W. Clark, "The Prairie Dog as a Keystone Species," in *Conservation of the Black-Tailed Prairie Dog: Saving North America's Western Grasslands*, ed. John L. Hoogland (Washington, DC: Island Press, 2006), 53–64.
5. See, for example, William F. Andelt, "Methods and Economics of Managing Prairie Dogs," in Hoogland, *Conservation of the Black-Tailed Prairie Dog*, 129–38; William C. Jameson, "On the Eradication of Prairie Dogs: A Point of View," *Bios* 44 (1973): 129–35; C. Hart Merriam, "The Prairie Dog of the Great Plains," *Yearbook of the United States Department of Agriculture* (1902): 262–70; D. Randall, "Poison the Damn Prairie Dogs!" *Defenders* 51 (1976): 381–83; D. Randall, "Shoot the Damn Prairie Dogs!" *Defenders* 51 (1976): 378–81.
6. This number may be an estimate that applies to all species of prairie dog. See Raymond D. Burroughs, *The Natural History of the Lewis and Clark Expedition* (East Lansing: Michigan State University Press, 1961), 95–125; and Ernest T. Seton, *Lives of Game Animals*, vol. 4 (New York: Doubleday, 1929). Utah prairie dogs once inhabited approximately 700 sections in 10 areas of southern Utah, and the decline in the number of these sections occupied by Utah prairie dogs is estimated at 87 percent. See John J. Pizzimenti and G. Donald Collier, "*Cynomys parvidens*," *Mammalian Species* 52 (1975): 1.
7. Indeed, the Utah prairie dog is the only non-fish vertebrate endemic to Utah (viz., found in Utah only); see Pizzimenti and Collier, "*Cynomys parvidens*," 1–3.
8. Ibid.
9. No one can truly know how many prairie dogs once inhabited the meadows of Utah. Regarding the 95,000 figure, the US Fish and Wildlife Service (USFWS) wrote in 2011 that it did not consider this to be a reliable estimate because "it was derived from informal interviews with landowners and not actual survey data." USFWS, "Revised 90-day Finding on a Petition to Reclassify the Utah Prairie Dog from Threatened to Endangered," *Federal Register* 76 (2011): 36055.
10. G. Donald Collier, "The Utah Prairie Dog: Abundance, Distribution, and Habitat Requirements" (PhD diss., Utah State University, 1975): 15–17; G. Donald Collier and J. Juan Spillett, "Factors Influencing the Distribution of the Utah Prairie Dog, *Cynomys parvidens* (Sciuridae)," *Southwestern Naturalist* 20 (1975): 151; USFWS, "Proposal to Amend Special Rule Allowing Regulated Taking of the *Cynomys parvidens*," *Federal Register* 55 (1990): 6022.

11. USFWS, "Amendments to List of Endangered Fish and Wildlife," *Federal Register* 38 (1973): 14678.

12. USFWS, "Final Rule to Reclassify Utah Prairie Dog as Threatened with Special Rule to Allow Regulated Taking," *Federal Register* 49 (1984): 22330–34.

13. Ibid.

14. The origin of "prairie dogging" is unclear. The term seems to have become substantially more common after it was depicted in the syndicated comic strip *Dilbert*, if it was not first "invented" or articulated there. Scott Adams, *Dilbert 2.0: 20 Years of Dilbert* (Kansas City, MO: Andrews McMeel, 2008), 151.

15. Kim Long, *Prairie Dogs: A Wildlife Handbook* (Boulder, CO: Johnson Books, 2002), 22.

16. Josh Smith, "Utah Legislature: Murray Students Push for Praises of Prairie Dogs," *Deseret News*, February 2, 2010.

17. H. Thomas Goodwin, "Pliocene-Pleistocene Biogeographic History of Prairie Dogs, Genus *Cynomys* (Sciuridae)," *Journal of Mammalogy* 77 (1996): 407–11; Richard G. Harrison, Steven M. Bogdanowicz, Robert S. Hoffmann, Eric Yensen, and Paul W. Sherman, "Phylogeny and Evolutionary History of the Ground Squirrels (Rodentia: Marmotinae)," *Journal of Mammalian Evolution* 10 (2003): 249–76; John J. Pizzimenti, "Evolution of the Prairie Dog Genus *Cynomys*," *Occasional Papers of the Museum of Natural History, University of Kansas* 39 (1975): 1–73.

18. John L. Hoogland, "Sexual Dimorphism in Five Species of Prairie Dogs," *Journal of Mammalogy* 84 (2003): 1254–66.

19. Pizzimenti and Collier, "*Cynomys parvidens*," 1–3.

20. Pizzimenti, "Evolution of the Prairie Dog," 1–73; Harrison et al., "Phylogeny," 249–76.

21. Pizzimenti, "Evolution of the Prairie Dog," 1–73.

22. University of Nebraska, *Journals of Lewis and Clark*, entry from September 7, 1804.

23. Ibid.

24. Ibid., March 24, 1805.

25. Elliot Coues and Joel A. Allen, *Monographs of North American Rodentia*, vol. 2 (Washington, DC: United States Survey of the Territories, 1877), 1–1091; Josiah Gregg, *Commerce of the Prairies*, vol. 2 (New York: Henry G. Langley, 1844), 228–30; Washington Irving, *A Tour on the Prairies* (London: John Murray, 1835), 295, 297; Ernest T. Seton, "The Prairie

Dogs (*Cynomys ludovicianus*) at Washington Zoo," *Journal of Mammalogy* 7 (1926): 229–330.

26. John J. Audubon and John Bachman, *The Quadrupeds of North America*, 3 vols., reprinted in one volume as *Audubon's Quadrupeds of North America* (Secaucus, NJ: Wellfleet, 1989), 144. Citations refer to the reprint.

27. Pizzimenti and Collier, "*Cynomys parvidens*," 3.

28. Dee Brown, *Bury My Heart at Wounded Knee: An Indian History of the American West* (New York: Sterling Publishing, 2009), 46; Waldo R. Wedel, *Prehistoric Man on the Great Plains* (Norman: University of Oklahoma Press, 1961), 134.

29. See, for example, Barre Toelken, "Coyote, Skunk, and Prairie Dogs," in *Coming to Light: Contemporary Translations of the Native Literatures of North America*, ed. Brian Swann (New York: Random House Digital, 1996); Barre Toelken, *The Anguish of Snails: Native American Folklore in the West* (Logan: Utah State University Press, 2003), 149, 176. I thank Mr. Toelken for this excerpt and for discussing these stories with me in an e-mail message on March 12, 2012.

30. Carma Lee Smithson and Rober C. Euler, *Havasupai Legends: Religion and Mythology of the Havasupai Indians of the Grand Canyon* (Salt Lake City: University of Utah Press, 1994), 16.

31. Frances Densmore, "Northern Ute Music," *Smithsonian Institution, Bureau of American Ethnology* 75 (1922): 201.

32. Theo H. Scheffer, "Historical Encounter and Accounts of the Plains Prairie Dog," *Kansas Historical Quarterly* 40 (1945): 527–37; Wedel, "*Prehistoric Man*," 134.

33. George Ord, "North American Zoology," in *A New Geographic, Historical, and Commercial Grammar*, vol. 2, 2nd ed., ed. W. Guthrie (Philadelphia: Lippincott, 1815), 292.

34. Constantine S. Rafinesque, "Museum of Natural Sciences. 9. Synopsis of Four New Genera and Ten New Species of Crustacea, Found in the United States," *American Monthly Magazine* 2 (1817): 45.

35. Spencer F. Baird, *Mammals. Reports of Exploration and Surveys to Ascertain the Most Practicable and Economical Route for a Railroad from the Mississippi River to the Pacific Ocean*, vol. 8 (Washington, DC: United States War Department, 1858), xxxix, 331.

36. Joel A. Allen, "Mammals from Beaver County, Utah. Collected by the Museum Expedition of 1904," *Bulletin of the Museum of*

Science, Brooklyn Institute of Arts and Science 1 (1905): 119.

37. Merriam, "Prairie Dog," 257–70.

38. Pizzimenti and Collier, "*Cynomys parvidens*," 1.

39. NPS (National Park Service), "Utah Prairie Dog," accessed June 3, 2012, http://www.nps .gov/brca/naturescience/upd.htm.

40. John L. Hoogland, *The Black-Tailed Prairie Dog: Social Life of a Burrowing Mammal* (Chicago: University of Chicago Press, 1995), 12.

41. Gregg, *Commerce of the Prairies*, 228–30. Gregg made this comment in reference to black-tailed prairie dogs, but the descriptions also apply to Utah prairie dogs.

42. See also Harold J. Egoscue and Elizabeth S. Frank, "Burrowing and Denning Habits of a Captive Colony of the Utah Prairie Dog," *Great Basin Naturalist* 44 (1984): 495–98. See Hoogland, *Black-Tailed Social Life*, 26–36, and sources therein for comparisons to black-tailed prairie dog burrows, which, unlike the burrows of Utah prairie dogs, can have "rim craters" at their entrances.

43. Egoscue and Frank, "Burrowing and Denning Habits," 495–98.

44. Ibid.

45. Erin M. Lehmer and Dean E. Biggins, "Variation in Torpor Patterns of Free-Ranging Black-Tailed and Utah Prairie Dogs across Gradients of Elevation," *Journal of Mammalogy* 86 (2005): 15–21.

46. Gerardo Ceballos and Don E. Wilson. "*Cynomys mexicanus*," *Mammalian Species* 248 (1985): 1–3; Hoogland, *Black-Tailed Social Life*, 18–19.

47. Theodore G. Manno, "Why Are Utah Prairie Dogs Vigilant?" *Journal of Mammalogy* 88 (2007): 555–63.

48. D. Coleman Crocker-Bedford and J. Juan Spillett, *Habitat Relationships of the Utah Prairie Dog*, US Department of Agriculture, Forest Service, Intermountain Region Publication No. 0-677-202/4 (1981), 8.

49. Hoogland, "Sexual Dimorphism," 1254–66.

50. This quote was in regard to black-tailed prairie dogs but applies to all species of prairie dog. Ernest T. Seton, *Wild Animals at Home* (New York: Grosset and Dunlap, 1913), 21–22.

51. Merriam, "Prairie Dog," 262–70.

52. Steve C. Forrest and James C. Luchsinger, "Past and Current Chemical Control of Prairie Dogs," in Hoogland, *Conservation of the Black-Tailed Prairie Dog*, 116–17.

53. See Andelt, "Methods and Economics," 130; Forrest and Luchsinger, "Chemical Control,"

116–17, and sources therein for a review and history of extermination methods and the future direction of prairie dog control.

54. USFWS, "Amendments to List," 14678; USFWS, "Final Rule to Reclassify," 22330–34.

55. USFWS "Revised 90-day Finding," 36056–62.

56. Allan M. Barnes, "A Review of Plague and Its Relevance to Prairie Dog Populations and the Black-Footed Ferret," in *Proceedings of the Symposium on the Management of Prairie Dog Complexes for the Reintroduction of the Black-Footed Ferret*, ed. John L. Oldemeyer, Dean E. Biggins, and Brian J. Miller, (Biological Report, US Department of the Interior, US Fish and Wildlife Service, 1993), 33; Jack F. Cully and Elizabeth S. Williams, "Interspecific Comparisons of Sylvatic Plague in Prairie Dogs," *Journal of Mammalogy* 82 (2001): 894–905; John L. Hoogland, Stacey Davis, Sarah Benson-Amram, Danielle LaBruna, Brigitte Goossens, and Margaret A. Hoogland, "Pyraperm Halts Plague among Utah Prairie Dogs," *Southwestern Naturalist* 49 (2004): 376–83.

57. Natasha B. Kotliar, Bruce W. Baker, April D. Whicker, and Glenn Plumb, "A Critical Review of Assumptions about the Prairie Dog as a Keystone Species," *Environmental Management* 24 (1999): 177–92; Kotliar et al., "Prairie Dog as Keystone," 53–64.

58. Brian C. Steed, "Why Don't We Just Shoot Them?: An Institutional Analysis of Prairie Dog Protection in Iron County, Utah," Y673 Fall Mini-Conference (2005), 6; USFWS, *Utah Prairie Dog* (Cynomys parvidens) *Final Revised Recovery Plan* (Denver: US Fish and Wildlife Service, 2012), 3.5–18.

59. The following sources list keystone benefits provided by black-tailed prairie dogs: William Agnew, Daniel W. Uresk, and Richard M. Hansen, "Flora and Fauna Associated with Prairie Dog Colonies and Adjacent Ungrazed Mixed-Grass Prairie in Western South Dakota," *Journal of Range Management* 39 (1986): 135–39; Thomas M. Campbell III and Tim W. Clark, "Colony Characteristics and Vertebrate Associates of White-Tailed and Black-Tailed Prairie Dogs in Wyoming," *American Midland Naturalist* 105 (1981): 269–76; Tim W. Clark, Thomas M. Campbell, David G. Socha, and Denise E. Casey, "Prairie Dog Colony Attributes and Associated Vertebrate Species," *Great Basin Naturalist* 42 (1982): 572–82; Kotliar et al., "Critical Review," 177–92; Justin E. Kretzer and Jack F. Cully,

"Effects of Black-Tailed Prairie Dog on Reptiles
and Amphibians in Kansas Shortgrass Prairie,"
Southwestern Naturalist 46 (2001): 171–77;
Mark V. Lomolino and Gregory A. Smith,
"Terrestrial Vertebrate Communities at Black-
Tailed Prairie Dog (*Cynomys ludovicianus*)
Towns," *Biological Conservation* 115 (2004):
89–100; Brian J. Miller, Gerardo Ceballos,
and Richard P. Reading, "The Prairie Dog and
Biotic Diversity," *Conservation Biology* 8 (1994):
677–81. I infer many of the same benefits with
Utah prairie dogs.

60. UPDRIP (Utah Prairie Dog Recovery Imple-
mentation Program), *2011 Work Plan* (Cedar
City: Southern Utah University, 2012);
UPDRIP, *Utah Prairie Dog Issues Status Report*
(Cedar City: Southern Utah University,
2012), 1–15.

61. John Hoogland, "Black-Tailed, Gunnison's,
and Utah Prairie Dogs All Reproduce Slowly,"
Journal of Mammalogy 82 (2001): 917–27.

62. Mark E. Ritchie, Marilet Zablan, Michael
Bodenchuk, Ron Bolander, Rebecca Bone-
brake, Kate Grandison, and Ken McDonald,
Utah Prairie Dog Interim Conservation Strategy
(Salt Lake City: US Fish and Wildlife Service,
1997), 9.

63. Manno, "Utah Prairie Dogs Vigilant," 555–63;
Mary A. Wright-Smith, "The Ecology and
Social Organization of *Cynomys parvidens*
(Utah Prairie Dog) in South-Central Utah"
(master's thesis, Indiana University, 1978).

64. Hoogland, "Black-Tailed, Gunnison's," 917–27;
John L. Hoogland, "Alarm Calling, Multiple
Mating, and Infanticide among Black-Tailed,
Gunnison's, and Utah Prairie Dogs," in *Rodent
Societies*, ed. Jerry O. Wolff and Paul W. Sher-
man (Chicago: University of Chicago Press,
2007), 438–49; Manno, "Utah Prairie Dogs
Vigilant," 555–63.

65. Manno, "Utah Prairie Dogs Vigilant," 555–63.

66. Hoogland, "Black-Tailed, Gunnison's," 917–27.

67. Hoogland, "Alarm Calling," 438–49.

68. During the recruitment process, John sends
two "scare letters" to potential Dog Squad
members to weed out those who are unfit for
the experience. This is the first installment.
The second is reprinted in Terry Tempest
Williams, *Finding Beauty in a Broken World*
(New York: Pantheon, 2008), 92–94. The
author is the same "Theo" who is mentioned
sporadically over pages 94–204.

Chapter 2

1. Ann G. Harris, Esther Tuttle, and D. Sherwood Tuttle, *Geology of National Parks*, 5th ed.
(Dubuque, IA: Kendall Hunt Publishing, 1997),
46; Michael Joseph Oswald, *Your Guide to the
National Parks: A Complete Guide to All 58 Parks*
(Whitelaw, WI: Stone Road Press, 2012), 402.
The geologic term "hoodoo" was used by early
geologists who thought the rock formations
could cast a spell with their "magical" spires
and arches.

2. As told by Indian Dick to a ranger at BCNP,
in Lorraine Salem Tufts, *Secrets in the Grand
Canyon, Zion, and Bryce Canyon National Parks*,
3rd ed. (North Palm Beach, FL: National Photographic Collections, 1998), 73. Indian Dick's
story is unclear as to exactly why oral tradition
reflects that the Legend People were turned
to stone. In addition, tribal elders explained
to Bryce Canyon interpretive ranger Kevin
Poe that the authentic version of the story
is sacred to the Paiutes and therefore should
be told only by their people. A version of the
story that speaks to the Legend People being
punished for living too heavily on the land was

created by Ranger Poe in 1999 and approved
by Southern Paiute elders. Thus, Ranger Poe
was given permission to tell this story of
the Legend People provided that he alter the
authentic oral tradition. Jan Stock, e-mail to
author, January 9, 2013.

3. Harris, Tuttle, and Tuttle, *Geology of National
Parks*, 44–46, 53; Oswald, *Guide to the
National Parks*, 402; Tufts, *Secrets in the Grand
Canyon*, 71–73.

4. Oswald, *Guide to the National Parks*, 402.

5. I am talking about BCNP and the area around
it generally here. I am not suggesting that the
actual location of our study colony was completely pristine. See Williams, *Finding Beauty*,
97, 160–61, 187, 197.

6. NPS (National Park Service), *Bryce Canyon
Visitors Guide* (Washington, DC: National Park
Service, 2012).

7. Harris, Tuttle, and Tuttle, *Geology of
National Parks*, 44; Tufts, *Secrets in the Grand
Canyon*, 71–73.

8. NPS, *The Hoodoo: Park Planner, Hiking and
Shuttle Guide* (Washington, DC: National

Park Service, 2005); NPS, *Bryce Canyon Visitors Guide*.

9. Hoogland, *Black-Tailed Social Life*, 57–59.

10. Data-taking procedures described in this chapter are similar to those Hoogland used in his study of black-tailed prairie dogs in South Dakota, with adjustments for the nuances of Utah prairie dogs. References for technical descriptions of all methods described in this chapter are as follows: John L. Hoogland, "Prairie Dogs Disperse When All Close Kin Have Disappeared," *Science* 339 (2013): 1205–7; Hoogland, *Black-Tailed Social Life*, 37–68, 96, 125–30, 149, 223, 404–7; Manno, "Utah Prairie Dogs Vigilant," 556–58. The safety of the study animals was paramount during these procedures; methods followed guidelines of the American Society of Mammalogists for animal care and use.

11. I later studied Columbian ground squirrels in Canada and used a mounted badger to elicit alarm calls for comparison with mating calls. I named the badger Chubs Jr., and after my study, I gave Chubs Jr. to a graduate student at the University of California, Los Angeles, where he (Chubs Jr.) is currently employed eliciting alarm calls from yellow-bellied marmots. The original Chubs is still with John and is currently being used in experiments with Gunnison's prairie dogs in New Mexico. I cannot remember exactly, but I believe that an assistant named Sara Druy first coined the original name "Chubs" in 2004.

12. I refer to the burrow from which pups emerge as the "nursery burrow" for the mother, and the "natal burrow" for the pups.

13. Hoogland expressed this sentiment in Williams, *Finding Beauty*, 177.

14. John L. Hoogland and Paul W. Sherman, "Advantages and Disadvantages of Bank Swallow (*Riparia riparia*) Coloniality," *Ecological Monographs* 46 (1976): 33–58.

15. John L. Hoogland, "The Evolution of Coloniality in White-Tailed and Black-Tailed Prairie Dogs (Sciuridae: *Cynomys leucurus* and *Cynomys ludovicianus*)," *Ecology* 62 (1981): 252–72.

16. "The manufacturer claims that the smoke (mostly zinc chloride) is non-toxic." Steven Vogel, Charles P. Ellington Jr., and Delbert L. Kilgore Jr. "Wind-Induced Ventilation of the Burrow of the Prairie-Dog, *Cynomys ludovicianus*," *Journal of Comparative Physiology* 85 (1973): 1–14.

17. Hoogland researched black-tailed prairie dogs at Wind Cave National Park from 1975 to 1989. Hoogland, *Black-Tailed Social Life*, 37–38.

18. See, for example, Hoogland, "Evolution of Coloniality," 252–72; Hoogland, "Sexual Dimorphism," 1254–66; John L. Hoogland, "Philopatry, Dispersal, and Social Organization of Gunnison's Prairie Dogs," *Journal of Mammalogy* 80 (1999): 243–51; Hoogland, "Alarm Calling," 438–49; Hoogland, "Black-Tailed, Gunnison's," 917–27.

19. For reasons that are unclear, Utahans have some of the highest per capita consumption of Jell-O in the world. Katty Kay, *Utah Loves Jell-O—Official*, BBC News, February 6, 2001, http://news.bbc.co.uk/2/hi/americas/1156021 .stm.

20. Many practicing members of the Church of Jesus Christ of Latter-day Saints eschew "hot drinks" as per Doctrine and Covenants 89:9.

Chapter 3

1. Francis Galton, *Gregariousness in Cattle and Men* (London: Macmillan, 1871), 352–57.

2. The phenomenon in Milgram's study actually applied to a portion of the US population. Stanley Milgram, "The Small-World Problem," *Psychology Today* 1 (1967): 61–67.

3. I later researched the social connections of Columbian ground squirrels. Certain squirrels interacted with many other individuals, others with very few. Theodore G. Manno, "Social Networking in the Columbian Ground Squirrel," *Animal Behaviour* 75 (2008): 1221–28.

4. Utah prairie dog clans are similar to, but should not be confused with, black-tailed

prairie dog coteries. Coteries are unique in their frequency of infanticide and religious allegiance of female individuals to a home territory with boundaries that almost never change. In contrast, female Utah prairie dogs sometimes move from one home territory to another, and the boundaries of clans are more flexible. Arrangements of most other ground-dwelling squirrels, where females have their own territory and several female territories are overlapped by a dominant male, should also not be confused with coteries. Scientific descriptions of Utah prairie dog clans, and comparisons to coteries, can be found in:

John L. Hoogland, "Philopatry, Dispersal,"
243–51; Hoogland, "Alarm Calling," 438–49;
John L. Hoogland, Kristen E. Cannon, Lili-
ana M. DeBarbieri, and Theodore G. Manno,
"Selective Predation on Utah Prairie Dogs,"
American Naturalist 168 (2006): 546–52;
Hoogland, "Black-Tailed, Gunnison's," 917–27;
Manno, "Utah Prairie Dogs Vigilant," 555–63.

5. Annual local dispersal by males is also a
mechanism of inbreeding avoidance in black-
tailed prairie dogs. Although probably not as
salient, because it is not rare for Utah prairie
dog females to switch clans, the similar Utah
prairie dog mating system involving stationary
females with males that disperse at sexual
maturity tends to prevent males from mating
with related females. John L. Hoogland, "Prairie Dogs Avoid Extreme Inbreeding," *Science*
215 (1982): 1639–41.

6. Fission, fusion, and lack of allegiance to clan
territories by female Utah prairie dogs are
being reported for the first time here. See also
Hoogland, "Prairie Dogs Disperse," 1205–7.
Similar phenomena in black-tailed prairie dog
coteries, which occur much more rarely, are
reported in Theodore G. Manno, F. Stephen
Dobson, John L. Hoogland, and David W.
Foltz, "Social Group Fission and Gene Dynamics among Black-Tailed Prairie Dogs (*Cynomys ludovicianus*)," *Journal of Mammalogy* 88
(2007): 448–56. Fissioning also occurs in other
mammalian societies. Napoleon A. Chagnon,
"Genealogy, Solidarity, and Relatedness: Limits
to Local Group Size and Patterns of Fissioning in an Expanding Population," *Yearbook of
Physical Anthropology* 19 (1975): 95–110.

7. George W. Kendall, *Texan Santa Fé Expedition* (London: Sherwood, Gilbert, and Piper,
1846), i, 192.

8. Irving, *Tour on the Prairies*, 117–18.

9. This social interaction is essentially the same
"kiss" that occurs among black-tailed prairie dogs (Hoogland, *Black-Tailed Social Life*,
61) and other species of ground-dwelling squirrels (e.g., Theodore G. Manno and Stephen
Dobson, "Why Are Male Columbian Ground
Squirrels Territorial?" *Ethology* 11 (2008):
1049–60).

10. This social interaction is essentially the same
"sniff" that occurs among black-tailed prairie
dogs (Hoogland, *Black-Tailed Social Life*,
60–61, 234–35) and other species of ground-
dwelling squirrels (e.g., Manno and Dobson,

"Columbian Ground Squirrels Territorial,"
1049–60).

11. Manno, "Utah Prairie Dogs Vigilant," 557.

12. These hostile interactions, not described in
detail in the scientific literature for Utah
prairie dogs, are essentially the same as the
chases and fights of other prairie dog species
(Hoogland, *Black-Tailed Social Life*, 136–38,
225–27, 248–49) and other species of ground-
dwelling squirrels (e.g., Manno and Dobson,
"Columbian Ground Squirrels Territorial,"
1049–60).

13. Manno, "Utah Prairie Dogs Vigilant," 557.

14. These interactions are similar to those of
black-tailed prairie dogs. Hoogland, "Sexual
Dimorphism," 1254–66; Hoogland, *Black-Tailed
Social Life*, 206–7.

15. Manno, "Utah Prairie Dogs Vigilant," 555–63.

16. These intermediate vigilance postures were
used in a study of vigilance by Hoogland on
white-tailed prairie dogs, but not in Manno's study of vigilance for Utah prairie dogs.
John L. Hoogland, "The Effect of Colony Size
on Individual Alertness of Prairie Dogs," *Animal Behaviour* 27 (1979): 394–407.

17. Manno, "Utah Prairie Dogs Vigilant," 555–63.

18. Ibid.

19. William D. Hamilton, "Geometry for the
Selfish Herd," *Journal of Theoretical Biology* 31
(1971): 295–311. Also see H. Ronald Pulliam,
"On the Advantages of Flocking," *Journal of
Theoretical Biology* 38 (1973): 419–22.

20. Steven L. Lima, "Back to the Basics of Anti-
Predatory Vigilance: The Group-Size Effect,"
Animal Behaviour 49 (1995): 11–20; Romy
Steenbeek, Ruben C. Piek, Marleen van Buul,
and Jan A. R. A. M. van Hoof, "Vigilance in
Wild Thomas's Langurs (*Presbytis thomasi*):
The Importance of Infanticide Risk," *Behavioral
Ecology and Sociobiology* 45 (1999): 137–50.

21. See theory in Ben Hirsch, "Social Monitoring
and Vigilance Behavior in Brown Capuchin
Monkeys (*Cebus apella*)," *Behavioral Ecology and
Sociobiology* 52 (2002): 458–64.

22. See theory in Joanna Burger and Michael
Gochfield, "Vigilance in Ostriches (*Struthio
camelus*): Mate Competition or Antipredator
Behavior?" *Ostrich* 59 (1994): 14–20; Steenbeek
et al., "Vigiliance in Thomas's Langurs," 137–50.

23. Manno, "Utah Prairie Dogs Vigilant," 555–63.

24. Many of these vocalizations have not been
reported in the scientific literature and are
described here for the first time. For technical

descriptions and scientific data concerning Utah prairie dog alarm calls, see Hoogland, "Alarm Calling," 438–49 and comparisons to black-tailed prairie dogs therein. Gunnison's prairie dog vocalizations, especially alarm calls, have been studied in more depth. They have calls that might differentiate among predators. See Constantine N. Slobodchikoff, *Prairie Dogs: Communication and Community in an Animal Society* (Cambridge, MA: Harvard University Press, 2009), 65–92.

25. Hoogland, "Alarm Calling," 438–49. For comparisons with black-tailed and Gunnison's prairie dogs, see Hoogland, *Black-Tailed Social Life*, 163–86 and John L. Hoogland, "Why Do Gunnison's Prairie Dogs Give Antipredator Calls?" *Animal Behaviour* 51 (1996): 871–80.

26. Hoogland, "Alarm Calling," 438–49.

27. Hamilton, "Geometry for the Selfish Herd," 295–311.

28. Hoogland, "Alarm Calling," 438–49; Manno, "Utah Prairie Dogs Vigilant," 555–63. For theoretical analysis, see Burger and Gochfeld, "Vigilance in Ostriches," 14–20; and Hamilton, "Geometry for the Selfish Herd," 295–311.

29. Field data on nepotistic ground squirrel calls were presented by Christopher Dunford, "Kin Selection for Ground Squirrel Alarm Calls," *American Naturalist* 111 (1977): 782–85; and Paul W. Sherman, "Nepotism and the Evolution of Alarm Calls," *Science* 197 (1977): 1246–53. These two scientists worked independently.

30. William D. Hamilton, "The Genetical Evolution of Social Behavior. I and II," *Journal of Theoretical Biology* 7 (1964): 1–52.

31. Hamilton, "Genetical Evolution of Social Behavior," 1–52; Hoogland, "Why Do Gunnison's," 871–80; John L. Hoogland, "Nepotism and Alarm Calling in the Black-Tailed Prairie Dog (*Cynomys ludovicianus*)," *Animal Behaviour* 31 (1983): 472–79.

32. Alan Carter, "Evolution and the Problem of Altruism," *Philosophical Studies: An International Journal for Philosophy in the Analytic Tradition* 123 (2005): 213–20; Charles R. Darwin, *On the Origin of Species by Means of Natural Selection, or, the Preservation of Favoured Races in the Struggle for Life* (New York: D. Appleton, 1869), 102–3.

33. The same phenomenon exists in black-tailed prairie dogs. David Francis Costello, *The World of the Prairie Dog* (Philadelphia: Lippincott, 1970), 37.

34. Hoogland, "Alarm Calling," 438–49.

35. Hoogland, "Prairie Dogs Disperse," 1205–7; Hoogland, "Alarm Calling," 438–49; Hoogland et al., "Selective Predation," 547; Hoogland, "Black-Tailed, Gunnison's," 917–27; Manno, "Utah Prairie Dogs Vigilant," 555–63.

36. Monte G. Garrett and William L. Franklin, "Prairie Dog Dispersal in Wind Cave Park: Possibilities for Control," in *Fifth Great Plains Wildlife Damage Control Workshop: Proceedings*, ed. R. M. Timm and R. J. Johnson (Lincoln: Institute of Agriculture and Natural Resources, University of Nebraska, 1981), 185–98. The phenomenon of long-distance dispersal has not been well studied for Utah prairie dogs. Garrett and Franklin's study on black-tailed prairie dogs showed that individuals disperse singly, can travel as far as 4.5 miles (around 7 km), are highly vulnerable to predation, and usually attempt to move into an established colony rather than initiate a new colony. Even though males do most of the dispersing within the colony, females and males are about equally likely to move between colonies. Most long-distance dispersers of both sexes are yearlings, but they can be any age or reproductive status except young-of-the-year. Finally, the most common period for long-distance dispersal is the month or so after the pups emerge from their natal burrow. Perhaps future researchers will find that some of these patterns apply to Utah prairie dogs as well. Also see Craig J. Knowles, "Observations on Prairie Dog Dispersal in Montana," *Prairie Naturalist* 17 (1985): 33–40.

37. Hoogland et al., "Selective Predation," 546–52.

38. Ibid.

39. Ibid., 547–48.

40. Ibid., 547.

41. Ibid., 548.

42. William D. Hamilton and Robert M. May, "Dispersal in Stable Habitats," *Nature* 269 (1977): 578–81.

43. Hoogland, "Prairie Dogs Disperse," 1205–7.

44. I wrote a similar inset for *Nature Alberta* magazine regarding my research on Columbian ground squirrels. Theodore G. Manno, "Squirrel-esque!—The Natural Wonders of Columbian Ground Squirrel Breeding Season in Kananaskis Country," *Nature Alberta*, Summer 2007. I thank Dennis Baresco, editor of *Nature Alberta*, for permission to piggyback on that material for this book.

Chapter 4

1. Darwin, *Origin of Species*, 62.

2. Michelle L. Haynie, Ronald A. van den Bussche, John L. Hoogland, Dennis A. Gilbert, and Robert D. Bradley, "Parentage, Multiple Paternity, and Breeding Success in Gunnison's and Utah Prairie Dogs," *Journal of Mammalogy* 84 (2003): 1244–53.

3. John L. Hoogland, "Estrus and Copulation among Gunnison's Prairie Dogs," *Journal of Mammalogy* 79 (1998): 887–97; Hoogland, "Alarm Calling," 438–49.

4. These hostile interactions are similar to those described for black-tailed prairie dogs; see Hoogland, "Black-Tailed Social Life," 76–79.

5. Investigators have independently discovered aboveground courtships in other prairie dogs or ground-dwelling squirrels. John L. Hoogland, "Estrus and Copulation," 887–97; Hoogland, Black-Tailed Social Life, 234–37; Eileen A. Lacey, John R. Wieczorek, and Priscilla K. Tucker, "Male Mating Behaviour and Patterns of Sperm Precedence in Arctic Ground Squirrels," *Animal Behaviour* 53 (1997): 767–79; Jan O. Murie, "Mating Behavior of Columbian Ground Squirrels. I. Multiple Mating by Females and Multiple Paternity," *Canadian Journal of Zoology* 73 (1995): 1819–26.

6. Previously unpublished for Utah prairie dogs, this phenomenon has been documented for black-tailed prairie dogs. Hoogland, *Black-Tailed Social Life*, 233–34, 236, 240, 257–58, 313–20.

7. Hoogland, "Alarm Calling," 438–49.

8. Previously unpublished for Utah prairie dogs, this phenomenon has been documented for black-tailed prairie dogs. Hoogland, *Black-Tailed Social Life*, 233–34, 236, 240, 257–58, 313–20.

9. Ibid. We had a head start on diagnostic signals to look for after Hoogland's previous studies, and with that framework, we looked for these other nuances of courtship that are specific to Utah prairie dogs.

10. A technical description of these diagnostic behaviors for Utah prairie dogs can be found in Hoogland, "Alarm Calling," 438–49; Manno, "Utah Prairie Dogs Vigilant," 557.

11. Hoogland, "Alarm Calling," 438–49; Manno, "Utah Prairie Dogs Vigilant," 557; also see Hoogland, *Black-Tailed Social Life*, 233–34, 236, 240, 257–58, 313–20.

12. Black-tailed prairie dogs also exhibit several BDs during a courtship. Hoogland, *Black-Tailed Social Life*, 227.

13. For a description of mating calls emitted by black-tailed prairie dogs, see R. Mark Grady and John L. Hoogland, "Why Do Male Prairie Dogs (*Cynomys ludovicianus*) Give a Mating Call?" *Animal Behaviour* 34 (1986): 108–12. Males of myriad other species call postcoitus to protect their "investment." Theodore G. Manno, Anna P. Nesterova, Liliana M. DeBarbieri, Stuart E. Kennedy, Kelsey S. Wright, and F. Stephen Dobson, "Why Do Male Columbian Ground Squirrels Give a Mating Call?" *Animal Behaviour* 74 (2007): 1319–27; Karen McComb, "Roaring by Red Deer Stags Advances the Date of Oestrus in Hinds," *Nature* 330 (1987): 648–49; Alan G. McElligott and Thomas J. Hayden, "Post-Copulatory Vocalizations of Fallow Bucks: Who Is Listening?" *Behavioral Ecology* 12 (2001): 41–46; Ryne A. Palombit, Dorothy L. Cheney, and Robert M. Seyfarth, "Male Grunts as Mediators of Social Interaction with Females in Wild Chacma Baboons (*Papio cynocephalus ursinus*)," *Behaviour* 136 (1999): 231–42; Noriko Tamura, "Postcopulatory Mate Guarding by Vocalization in the Formosan Squirrel," *Behavioral Ecology and Sociobiology* 36 (1995): 377–86.

14. Not previously reported for Utah prairie dogs, this contextual differentiation has been confirmed for other animals with postcopulatory male calls and alarm calls that sound similar. Manno et al., "Columbian Ground Squirrels Mating Call," 1319–27; Tamura, "Postcopulatory Mate Guarding," 377–86.

15. This incredible variability, not previously reported for Utah prairie dogs, has foiled efforts to find definite functions of mating calls in other squirrels as well. Grady and Hoogland, "Male Prairie Dogs," 108–12; Manno et al., "Columbian Ground Squirrels Mating Call," 1319–27; Tamura, "Postcopulatory Mate Guarding," 377–86.

16. Black-tailed prairie dogs have also been seen calling before or after copulation. Grady and Hoogland, "Male Prairie Dogs," 108–12. Not so for male Columbian ground squirrels, who call only before they inseminate a female. Manno et al., "Columbian Ground Squirrels Mating Call," 1319–27. Calling at both times complicates any determination of a function for the call.

17. McComb, "Roaring by Red Deer Stags," 648–49.

18. Manno, "Utah Prairie Dogs Vigilant," 557; also see Hoogland, *Black-Tailed Social Life*, 237.

19. Hoogland, *Black-Tailed Social Life*, 248–49.

20. John L. Hoogland, "Why Do Females Mate with More Than One Male?—Insights from Long-Term Research," *Journal of Mammalogy* 94 (2013): 731–44.

21. Ibid.

22. Haynie et al., "Parentage, Multiple Paternity," 1244–53. This percentage is much higher than for black-tailed prairie dogs. Hoogland, "Alarm Calling," 438–49.

23. Hoogland, "Alarm Calling," 438–49; Manno, "Utah Prairie Dogs Vigilant," 557. Also see Hoogland, *Black-Tailed Social Life*, 227–30 for technical descriptions of male mate guarding in black-tailed prairie dogs, which is similar to the mate guarding of Utah prairie dogs.

24. Haynie et al., "Parentage, Multiple Paternity," 1244–53; Hoogland, "Alarm Calling," 438–49; Manno, "Utah Prairie Dogs Vigilant," 557. For similar patterns in black-tailed prairie dogs, also see David W. Foltz and John L. Hoogland, "Analysis of the Mating System of the Black-Tailed Prairie Dog (*Cynomys ludovicianus*) by Likelihood of Paternity," *Journal of Mammalogy* 62 (1981): 706–12; for a discussion of first male sperm precedence in other ground squirrels, see Lacey, Wieczorek, and Tucker, "Male Mating Behaviour," 767–79; Anna P. Nesterova, Shirley Raveh, Theodore G. Manno, David W. Coltman, and F. Stephen Dobson, "Pre-Mating Behavioral Tactics of Columbian Ground Squirrels," *Journal of Mammalogy* 92 (2011): 861–70; Patricia L. Schwagmeyer and David W. Foltz, "Factors Affecting the Outcome of Sperm Competition in Thirteen-Lined Ground Squirrels," *Animal Behaviour* 39 (1990): 156–62.

25. Sarah B. Hrdy, *The Langurs of Abu: Female and Male Strategies of Reproduction* (Cambridge, MA: Harvard University Press, 1977), 101–41.

26. These phenomena, anecdotal for Utah prairie dogs, have been reported most prominently for Columbian ground squirrels. Manno and Dobson, "Columbian Ground Squirrels Territorial," 1049–60; Nesterova et al., "Pre-Mating Behavioral Tactics," 861–70.

27. A technical description of these data can be found in Hoogland et al., "Selective Predation," 546–52.

28. This is occasionally the case for other animals as well. See, for example, Hans Kruuk, "Predators and Anti-Predator Behavior of the Black-Headed Gull," *Behaviour* 11 (1972): 7–43; George B. Schaller, *The Serengeti Lion* (Chicago: University of Chicago Press, 1972), 209.

29. Aboveground copulation is also rare for black-tailed prairie dogs, white-tailed prairie dogs, and Columbian ground squirrels. Hoogland, *Black-Tailed Social Life*, 258–259; Theodore G. Manno, Liliana M. DeBarbieri, and Jocelyn Davidson, "Why Do Columbian Ground Squirrels Copulate Underground?" *Journal of Mammalogy* 89 (2008): 882–88.

30. Katherine E. Bruce and Daniel Q. Estep, "Interruption of and Harassment during Copulation by Stumptail Macaques, *Macaca arctoides*," *Animal Behaviour* 44 (1992): 1029–44; Michael W. Gratson, Gretchen K. Gratson, and Arthur T. Bergerud, "Male Dominance and Copulation Disruption Do Not Explain Variance in Male Mating Success on Sharp-Tailed Grouse (*Tympanuchus phasianellus*) Leks," *Behaviour* 118 (1991): 187–213.

31. John had this problem while studying black-tailed prairie dogs as well. Hoogland, *Black-Tailed Social Life*, 257–58.

32. Ibid., 233–34, 236, 240, 257–58, 315.

33. Manno, "Utah Prairie Dogs Vigilant," 557–58.

34. See also Williams, *Finding Beauty*, 143.

35. Harris, Tuttle, and Tuttle, *Geology of National Parks*, 44; Tufts, *Secrets in the Grand Canyon*, 71–73.

Chapter 5

1. William Blake, *Songs of Innocence and Experience* (London: William Blake, 1794), 43.

2. Hoogland, "Black-Tailed, Gunnison's," 917–27.

3. Hoogland originally used this term to describe black-tailed prairie dogs, but the term applies here as well. John L. Hoogland, "Black-Tailed Prairie Dog Coteries are Cooperatively Breeding Units," *American Naturalist* 121 (1983): 275–80.

4. Hamilton, "Genetical Evolution of Social Behavior," 1–52.

5. Jerram L. Brown, "Avian Communal Breeding Systems," *Annual Review of Ecology and Systematics* 9 (1978): 123–55; Stephen T. Emlen, "Cooperative Breeding in Birds and Mammals," in *Behavioural Ecology: An Evolutionary Approach*, 3rd ed., ed. John R. Krebs and Nicholas B. Davies (Oxford, UK: Blackwell Scientific Publications, 1991), 301–37.

6. I must place an asterisk on this statistic because the Dog Squad stopped studying at

BCNP in 2005 while BB9 was still alive, so she
might have lived beyond eight years.

7. Hoogland, "Black-Tailed, Gunnison's," 917–27.

8. Early reproduction is also advantageous in
other species. See, for example, Brian Mitchell
and G. A. Lincoln, "Conception Dates in Relation to Age and Condition in Two Populations
of Red Deer in Scotland," *Journal of Zoology
(London)* 171 (1973): 141–52. Ian Newton and
Mick Marquiss, "Seasonal Trend in the Breeding Performance of Sparrowhawks," *Journal of
Animal Ecology* 53 (1984): 809–29.

9. Manno, "Utah Prairie Dogs Vigilant," 557.

10. Unlike black-tailed prairie dogs (Hoogland,
Black-Tailed Social Life, 250–51), Utah prairie dogs often leave the home territory to
gather NM.

11. Stealing NM is not common for other species
of prairie dog but provides a major source of
NM for certain Utah prairie dog females each
year. This is hardly the first case of burglariz-
ing in the animal kingdom. Jose R. Garrido,
Cristina G. Sarasa, and Manual Fernandez-
Cruz, "Intraspecific Kleptoparasitism in the
Cattle Egret," *Journal of Field Ornithology*
73 (2002): 185–90; Jane Goodall, *The Chimpanzees of Gombe* (Cambridge, MA: Belknap
Press), 303–5.

12. Diagnostic behaviors for parturition in other
prairie dog species are almost identical to
those witnessed for Utah prairie dogs. John L.
Hoogland, "Duration of Gestation and Lactation for Gunnison's Prairie Dogs," *Journal
of Mammalogy* 78 (1997): 173–80; Hoogland,
Black-Tailed Social Life, 384–90; Hoogland,
"Black-Tailed, Gunnison's," 917–27.

13. Hoogland, "Black-Tailed, Gunnison's," 917–27;
Manno, "Utah Prairie Dogs Vigilant," 557.

14. Ibid.

15. Ibid.

16. Ibid.

17. Hoogland, "Black-Tailed, Gunnison's," 917–27.

18. Craig J. Knowles, "Reproductive Ecology of
Black-Tailed Prairie Dogs in Montana," *Great
Basin Naturalist* 47 (1987): 202–6.

19. Hoogland, "Black-Tailed, Gunnison's," 917–27.
The same pattern of lower probability of
conception and successful pregnancy exists
in black-tailed prairie dogs. Hoogland, *Black-
Tailed Social Life*, 287–92, 298–305. In much of
the animal kingdom, adults with reproductive experience are often more attractive to
potential mates and are usually better parents
when they have had parental experience.

See, for example, Anders P. Møller, "Mixed
Reproductive Strategy and Mate Guarding in a
Semi-Colonial Passerine, the Swallow *Hirundo
rustica*," *Behavioral Ecology and Sociobiology*
17 (1985): 401–8; Gordon H. Orians, "On the
Evolution of Mating Systems in Birds and
Mammals," *American Naturalist* 103 (1969):
589–603.

20. See indirect evidence for resorption in black-
tailed prairie dogs summarized in Hoogland,
Black-Tailed Social Life, 151, 362, 390.

21. Hoogland et al., "Selective Predation," 546–52.

22. Diagnostic behaviors for the onset of lactation
in other prairie dog species are about identi-
cal to those witnessed for Utah prairie dogs.
Hoogland, "Duration of Gestation," 173–80;
Hoogland, *Black-Tailed Social Life*, 384–90;
Hoogland, "Black-Tailed, Gunnison's," 917–27.

23. Hoogland, "Duration of Gestation," 173–80;
Hoogland, *Black-Tailed Social Life*, 384–90;
Hoogland, "Black-Tailed, Gunnison's," 917–27.

24. Sarah B. Hrdy, "Infanticide among Animals:
A Review, Classification, and Examination of
the Implications for the Reproductive Strategies of Females," *Ethology and Sociobiology* 1
(1979): 13–40.

25. During the 11 years, the Dog Squad saw 25 different males kill 48 pups at BCNP. Hoogland,
"Alarm Calling," 438–49.

26. In contrast, black-tailed prairie dogs committed infanticide more frequently. Whereas
marauding Utah prairie dogs almost always
brought their victims aboveground, black-
tailed prairie dogs nearly always committed
infanticide underground and exhibited aboveground diagnostic behaviors such as rubbing
the face and licking the claws. Rubbing the
face and licking the claws occurred after many
Utah prairie dog infanticides as well. Females
killing the lactating offspring of close kin, the
most common type of infanticide in black-
tailed prairie dogs and a behavior seen in only
a handful of other animals, does not occur in
Utah prairie dogs, as only males commit infanticide. To compare with Utah prairie dogs, see
John L. Hoogland, "Infanticide in Prairie Dogs:
Lactating Females Kill Offspring of Close Kin,"
Science 230 (1985): 1037–40.

27. Hoogland, "Alarm Calling," 438–49.

28. Hrdy, "Infanticide among Animals," 13–40.

29. George C. Williams, *Adaptation and Natural
Selection* (Princeton, NJ: Princeton University
Press, 1966), 8–20.

30. Hoogland, "Alarm Calling," 438–49.

31. This occurred in 9 (19 percent) of the 48 infanticides witnessed during John's 11 years of Utah prairie dog research at BCNP. In 8 of these cases, the female had mated with at least one other male, so perhaps these cases did not result in a male killing his own offspring. Hoogland, "Alarm Calling," 438–49.

32. Hrdy, "Infanticide among Animals," 13–40; Raymond Pierotti, "Infanticide versus Adoption: An Intergenerational Conflict," *American Naturalist* 138 (1991): 1140–58; Paul W. Sherman, "Reproductive Competition and Infanticide in Belding's Ground Squirrels and Other Animals," in *Natural Selection and Social Behavior*, ed. Richard D. Alexander and David W. Tinkle (New York: Chiron Press, 1981), 311–31.

33. Hrdy, "Infanticide among Animals," 13–40.

34. Hoogland, "Sexual Dimorphism," 1254–66.

35. Claudio Campagna, Burney J. Le Boeuf, and Humberto L. Cappozzo, "Pup Abduction and Infanticide in Southern Sea Lions," *Behavior* 107 (1988): 44–60; Neil J. Gemmell, "Kin Selection May Influence Fostering Behaviour in Antarctic Fur Seals (*Arctocephalus gazella*)," *Proceedings of the Royal Society B: Biological Sciences* 270 (2003): 2033–37; Masashi Kiyota and Hiroshi Okamura, "Harrassment, Abduction, and Mortality of Pups by Nonterritorial Male Northern Fur Seals," *Journal of Mammalogy* 86 (2005): 1227–36.

36. This conclusion is based on our observations of social interactions between Utah prairie dogs. Hoogland has done juvenile transfer experiments on black-tailed prairie dogs, which also have females defending a common territory. Black-tailed prairie dogs seem to discriminate only between juveniles that are or are not within the coterie and do not seem to discriminate between pups of close kin and those of distant kin. They appear to recognize pups from the coterie through direct social learning within the first month after the young emerge from their natal burrow. Hoogland, *Black-Tailed Social Life*, 210–14.

37. For details of various aspects of Utah prairie dog nursing, see John L. Hoogland, "Nursing of Own and Alien Offspring by Utah Prairie Dogs (*Cynomys parvidens*)." *Behavioral Ecology and Sociobiology* 63 (2009): 1621–34.

38. Ibid.

39. Ibid.

40. Ibid.

41. Ibid. For black-tailed prairie dogs, radioactive nucleotides confirmed that foster mothers transferred milk to foster offspring during underground communal nursing. Hoogland, *Black-Tailed Social Life*, 187–99.

42. Tom Walker, *The Way of the Grizzly* (New York: Voyageur, 1993), 139.

43. Hoogland, *Black-Tailed Social Life*, 94.

44. Hoogland, "Nursing Own and Alien," 1621–34.

45. Hoogland et al., "Selective Predation," 546–52.

46. Hoogland, "Nursing Own and Alien," 1621–34.

47. Ibid.

48. Similar patterns have been described for grizzly bears, and unrelated grizzly cubs will play as well. Walker, *Way of the Grizzly*, 115.

49. Manno, "Utah Prairie Dogs Vigilant," 555–63.

50. Alec Brownlee, "Animal Play," *Applied Animal Behaviour Science* 106 (2000): 307–312; Robert Fagan, "Selective and Evolutionary Aspects of Animal Play," *American Naturalist* 108 (1974): 850–858.

51. Brownlee, "Animal Play," 307–12.

52. Ibid.

53. Utah prairie dog pups are not the only animals that show homosexual play. For a review of the topic, see Volker Sommer and Paul L. Vasey, *Homosexual Behavior in Mammals: An Evolutionary Perspective* (New York: Cambridge University Press, 2006), 1–389.

54. Pizzimenti and Collier, "*Cynomys parvidens*," 2.

55. The Dog Squad did not watch Utah prairie dogs submerge into hibernation, but the energy expenditure involved with molting and lactation makes this pattern likely. A similar pattern occurs for other species of ground-dwelling squirrels. Peter Neuhaus, "Timing of Hibernation and Molt in Female Columbian Ground Squirrels," *Journal of Mammalogy* 81 (2000): 571–77.

56. Lehmer and Biggins, "Variation in Torpor Patterns," 15–21; Walker, *Way of the Grizzly*, 125–26.

57. Hibernation in groups also occurs among ground-dwelling squirrels. Walter Arnold, "The Evolution of Marmot Sociality: II. Costs and Benefits of Group Hibernation," *Behavioral Ecology and Sociobiology* 27 (1990): 239–46. Hibernation alone occurs as well. Peter J. Young, "Hibernating Patterns of Free-Ranging Columbian Ground Squirrels," *Oecologia* 83 (1990): 504–11.

58. Technically, we do not know because we never recorded exactly how many Utah prairie dogs started to hibernate each fall. It is therefore possible, though very unlikely, that the vast majority of Utah prairie dogs that start to hibernate survive.

59. Ellen Cheng, "Effects of Simulated Summer Grazing on Utah Prairie Dog (*Cynomys parvidens*) Growth Rates and Behaviors" (master's thesis, Utah State University, 2000).
60. Ibid.

61. Neuhaus, "Timing of Hibernation," 571–77.
62. Hoogland, "Black-Tailed, Gunnison's," 917–27; Mark E. Ritchie, "Biodiversity and Reduced Extinction Risks in Spatially Isolated Rodent Populations," *Ecology Letters* 2 (1999): 11–13.

Chapter 6

1. Merriam, "Prairie Dog," 259.
2. Hoogland, "Sexual Dimorphism," 1254–66.
3. Ravens sometimes kill baby Utah prairie dogs. In 2004, I witnessed a raven prey on BB2X. Williams, *Finding Beauty*, 117. I have also seen ravens kill Columbian ground squirrels. Manno, "Ground Squirrels Copulate Underground," 882–88.
4. This event from 2004, and others from that year, are not included with the incidents published in Hoogland et al., "Selective Predation," 546–52, which documents predations from 2005 only.
5. Hoogland, "Black-Tailed, Gunnison's," 917–22.
6. Hoogland, "Sexual Dimorphism," 1254–66.
7. Hoogland, "Nursing Own and Alien," 1621–34. For animals where pups or juveniles from different mothers do not share a common territory, recognition of individual litters is more likely. Michael D. Beecher, "Successes and Failures of Parent-Offspring Recognition in Animals," in *Kin Recognition*, ed. Peter G. Hepper (Cambridge: Cambridge University Press, 1991), 94–124; Lauryn Benedict, "Offspring Discrimination without Recognition: California Towhee Responses to Chick Distress Calls," *Condor* 109 (2007): 79–87; James F. Hare, "Juvenile Richardson's Ground Squirrels (*Spermophilus richardsonii*) Manifest Both Littermate and Neighbour/Stranger Discrimination," *Ethology* 104 (1998): 991–1002.
8. As per the female dispersal patterns described in Hoogland, "Prairie Dogs Disperse," 1205–7.

Chapter 7

1. C. William Beebe, *The Bird: Its Form and Function* (New York: H. Holt, 1906), 18.
2. Cited in Paul A. Johnsgard, *Prairie Dog Empire: A Saga of the Shortgrass Prairie* (Lincoln: University of Nebraska Press, 2005), 137.
3. Among the notable previous uses of this metaphor are Issac Asimov's illustration of the concept of predestination paradox and the Red Queen hypothesis in biology, which postulates that continuing adaptation is needed in order for a species to survive, even though the overall appearance of individuals within that species might not seem to change. Issac Asimov, *The Early Asimov: Or, Eleven Years of Trying* (New York: Doubleday, 1972), 477–98; Matt Ridley, *The Red Queen: Sex and the Evolution of Human Nature* (New York: Penguin Putnam, 1993), 1–416.
4. Lewis Carroll, *Through the Looking Glass and What Alice Found There* (London: MacMillan, 1871).
5. This sentiment has been expressed in various forms by several people. One example is Doug Wachob, associate executive director of the conservation research center at Teton Science Schools, who paraphrased this idea during a lecture at the Teton Science School in Jackson, Wyoming. Another example comes from Steed, "Just Shoot Them," 2.
6. Kenneth P. McDonald, *Analysis of the Utah Prairie Dog Recovery Program, 1972–1992*, Utah Division of Wildlife Resources Publication No. 93-16 (1993), 2. This figure is typically cited as the historical population and is perhaps the most accurate published estimate, but see note 9 in chapter 1 regarding the inherent limitations of this calculation.
7. USFWS, *Utah Prairie Dog* (Cynomys parvidens) *Recovery Plan* (Denver: US Fish and Wildlife Service, 1991), i–41.
8. R. Dwayne Elmore and Terry A. Messmer, *Public Perceptions Regarding the Utah Prairie Dog and Its Management: Implications for Species Recovery*, Berryman Institute, Publication No. 23 (Logan: Utah State University, 2006), 4.
9. USFWS, "Revised 90-day Finding," 36055–56. I have taken the most recent spring count (total from all three recovery units) of around 6,000 and multiplied by two as per D. Coleman Crocker-Bedford, "Utah Prairie Dog Habitat Evaluation," *Proceedings of the Utah Wildlife Society Technical Meeting* (1975): 1–7,

and have covered a range that is just below the recent counts and just above those counts multiplied by two. Because yearling Utah prairie dogs commonly mate and reproduce, I consider them to be adults for purposes of population estimates. I have cast a wide net with this range of numbers because officials can only estimate how many Utah prairie dogs exist today. Counting them one by one would require a Dog Squad–like effort for every colony in Utah and is therefore not practical. See note 12 below on the differences between spring counts and population estimates from different times of the year, and how "counts" are generated. See also Nathan Rice, "Saving Threatened Utah Prairie Dogs—On Private Property," *High Country News*, August 20, 2012.

10. USFWS, "Revised 90-day Finding," 36055.

11. Ibid., 36063.

12. Visual counts are taken during the spring and are therefore estimates of the number of adults that have survived the winter. Not all individuals are visible or aboveground at the same time, so spring counts are assumed to represent only about 50 percent of the population at the colony site. Crocker-Bedford, "Prairie Dog Habitat Evaluation," 1–7; USFWS, "Revised 90-day Finding," 36055–56; see also Dean E. Biggins, John G. Sidle, David B. Seery, and Andrea E. Ernst, "Estimating the Abundance of Prairie Dogs," in Hoogland, *Conservation of the Black-Tailed Prairie Dog*, 94–107. Under this assumption, a spring count of 6,000 over the entire range indicates a total of 12,000 adults. Population estimates can also include the young-of-the-year and will therefore be higher. These estimates are calculated by multiplying the spring count by two and integrating the proportion of successfully breeding adult females and the average litter size into another multiplier (USFWS, "Revised 90-day Finding," 36055). The USFWS notes that spring count surveys and population estimates are not true censuses and are instead "designed to monitor population trends over time." Hence, I indicate a wide range in my estimate for present-day Utah prairie dog populations.

13. USFWS, *Utah Prairie Dog: 5-Year Review, Summary and Evaluation* (West Valley City, UT: Utah Field Office, Ecological Services, 2012), 36–41.

14. See USFWS, "Proposal to Amend," 6022, for the 2,160 figure. As of 2010, the Awapa Plateau Recovery Unit had a spring count of 614 adult prairie dogs, the Paunsaugunt Recovery Unit had 835 adult prairie dogs, and the West Desert Recovery Unit had 4,199 adult prairie dogs. A high of over 7,500 was recorded in 1989, twice as many as the estimated count of 3,300 in 1973. These statistics are described in the reports as "rangewide counts." USFWS, *Utah Prairie Dog: 5-Year Review*, 36–41.

15. USFWS, *Utah Prairie Dog: Final Revised Recovery Plan*, 1.3–9.

16. UPDRIP, *Status Report*, 1–15.

17. Steed, "Just Shoot Them," 16.

18. Lynne Fox-Parrish, "Attitudes and Opinions of Landowners and General Citizens Relative to the Black-Tailed Prairie Dog" (master's thesis, Emporia State University, 2002); Berton L. Lamb, Richard P. Reading, and William F. Andelt, "Attitudes and Perceptions about Prairie Dogs," in Hoogland, *Conservation of the Black-Tailed Prairie Dog*, 108–14.

19. Merriam, "Prairie Dog," 258.

20. Carl B. Koford, "Prairie Dogs, Whitefaces, and Blue Grama," *Wildlife Monographs* 3 (1958): 35. Koford estimated using other data that 335 prairie dogs eat as much as one cow.

21. Ellen Cheng, "Effects of Summer Grazing"; Ellen Cheng and Mark E. Ritchie, "Impacts of Simulated Livestock Grazing on Utah Prairie Dogs (*Cynomys parvidens*) in a Low Productivity Ecosystem," *Oecologia* 147 (2006): 546–55; R. Dwayne Elmore and Terry A. Messmer, "Livestock Grazing and the Utah Prairie Dog: Implications for Managing the Awapa," Berryman Institute, Publication No. 24 (Logan: Utah State University, 2006), 1.

22. See, for example, Agnew, Uresk, and Hansen, "Flora and Fauna," 135–39; Richard M. Hansen and Ilyse K. Gold, "Blacktail Prairie Dogs, Desert Cottontails and Cattle Trophic Relations on Shortgrass Range," *Journal of Range Management* 30 (1977): 210–14; Miguel Mellado, Abundio Olvera, Adrian Quyero, and German Mendoza, "Dietary Overlap between Prairie Dog (*Cynomys mexicanus*) and Beef Cattle in a Desert Rangeland of Northern Mexico," *Journal of Arid Environments* 62 (2005): 449–58; Jerry D. Volesky, James K. Lewis, and Charles H. Butterfield, "High-Performance Duration and Repeated-Seasonal Grazing Systems: Effect on Diets and Performance of Calves and Lambs," *Journal of Range Management* 43 (1990): 310–15. For a detailed review of black-tailed prairie dog competition

with cattle, horses, and other livestock, see James Detling, "Do Prairie Dogs Compete with Livestock?" in Hoogland, *Conservation of the Black-Tailed Prairie Dog*, 65–88, and sources therein.

23. Steed, "Just Shoot Them," 2. The same applies to black-tailed prairie dogs and other species of prairie dog. James F. Carr, "A Rancher's View towards Prairie Dogs" in *Proceedings of the Black-Footed Ferret and Prairie Dog Workshop*, ed. Raymond L. Linder and Conrad N. Hillman (Rapid City: South Dakota State University, 2008), 168–71; Lamb, Reading, and Andelt, "Attitudes and Perceptions," 110.

24. For example, Hoogland originally attempted his study of Utah prairie dogs at the East Creek colony in BCNP, but the colony crashed and almost became extinct after the advent of plague. Williams, *Finding Beauty*, 176. See also Stanley H. Anderson and Elizabeth S. Williams, "Plague in a Complex of White-Tailed Prairie Dogs and Associated Small Mammals in Wyoming," *Journal of Wildlife Disease* 33 (1997): 720–32; Dean E. Biggins and Michael Y. Kosoy, "Influences of Introduced Plague on North American Mammals: Implications from Ecology of Plague in Asia," *Journal of Mammalogy* 4 (2001): 906–16; Jack F. Cully, "Plague in Prairie Dog Ecosystems: Importance for Black-Footed Ferret Management," in *The Prairie Dog Ecosystem: Managing for Biological Diversity*, Montana BLM Wildlife Technical Bulletin No. 2, (Billings, MT: Bureau of Land Management, 1989), 47–55; Kenneth L. Gage and Michael Y. Kosoy, "Natural History of Plague: Perspectives from More Than a Century of Research," *Annual Review of Entomology* 50 (2005): 505–28; Tonie E. Rocke, Susan R. Smith, Dan T. Stinchcomb, and Jorge E. Osorio, "Immunization of Black-Tailed Prairie Dog against Plague through Consumption of Vaccine-Laden Baits," *Journal of Wildlife Diseases* 44 (2008): 930–37.

25. UPDRIP, *Status Report*, 7.

26. Hoogland et al., "Pyraperm Halts Plague," 376–83.

27. Ibid., 379.

28. Ibid., 378–79.

29. Ibid., 380.

30. Sara Haas, pers. comm., May 4, 2012.

31. USFWS, *Utah Prairie Dog: Final Revised Recovery Plan*, 1.9–3.

32. Cheng, "Effects of Summer Grazing"; Cheng and Ritchie, "Impacts of Simulated Grazing,"

546–55; Elmore and Messmer, *Livestock Grazing*, 1; NRCSED (Natural Resources Conservation Service and Environmental Defense), "Utah Prairie Dog Habitat Evaluation Guide," *Utah Regional Depository* 408 (2007), 5.

33. Jake F. Weltzin, Steve L. Dowhower, and Rodney K. Heitschmidt, "Prairie Dog Effects on Plant Community Structure in Southern Mixed-Grass Prairie," *Southwestern Naturalist* 42 (1997): 251–58.

34. David L. Coppock, James K. Detling, James E. Ellis, and Melvin I. Dyer, "Plant-Herbivore Interactions in a North American Mixed-Grass Prairie: Effects of Black-Tailed Prairie Dogs on Intraseasonal Aboveground Plant Biomass and Plant Species Diversity," *Oecologia* 56 (1983): 1–9; Kirsten Kruger, "Feeding Relationships among Bison, Pronghorn, and Prairie Dogs: An Experimental Analysis," *Ecology* 67 (1986): 760–70.

35. Coppock et al., "Plant-Herbivore Interactions," 1–9; Hansen and Gold, "Blacktail Prairie Dogs," 210–14; Kotliar et al., "Prairie Dog as Keystone," 53–64; Daniel W. Uresk, "Black-Tailed Prairie Dog Food Habits and Forage Relationships in Western South Dakota," *Journal of Range Management* 37 (1984): 325–29; Weltzin, Dowhower, and Heitschmidt, "Prairie Dog Effects," 251–58; April Whicker and James K. Detling, "Control of Grassland Ecosystem Processes by Prairie Dogs," in *Proceedings of the Symposium on the Management of Prairie Dog Complexes for the Reintroduction of the Black-Footed Ferret*, ed. John L. Oldemeyer, Dean E. Biggins, and Brian J. Miller, Biological Report 13 (US Fish and Wildlife Service, 1993), 18–27.

36. Coppock et al., "Plant-Herbivore Interactions," 1–9; Ronald A. Green, "Nitrogen Distribution in a Perennial Grassland: The Role of American Bison" (PhD diss., Colorado State University, 1998); Kruger, "Feeding Relationships," 760–70; Lomolino and Smith, "Terrestrial Vertebrate Communities," 89–100; Whicker and Detling, "Control of Ecosystem Processes," 18–27.

37. For black-tailed prairie dogs, see Agnew, Uresk, and Hansen, "Flora and Fauna," 135–39; Campbell and Clark, "Colony Characteristics," 269–76; Clark et al., "Prairie Dog Colony Attributes," 572–82; Kotliar et al., "Critical Review," 177–92; Kretzer and Cully, "Effects of Black-Tailed Prairie Dog," 171–77; Lomolino and Smith, "Terrestrial Vertebrate Communities,"

89–100; Miller, Ceballos, and Reading, "Prairie Dog and Biotic Diversity," 677–81.

38. Some anecdotes on this topic can be found in Christie Aschwanden, "Learning to Live with Prairie Dogs," *National Wildlife*, April–May, 2001. See also Hoogland, *Black-Tailed Social Life*, 20–21.

39. The historical secondary range of bison encompasses all of Utah. Mary Meagher, "*Bison bison*," *Mammalian Species* 266 (1986): 3.

40. UPDRIP, *Status Report*, 7.

41. Collier and Spillett, "Factors Influencing the Distribution," 151–58; G. Donald Collier and J. Juan Spillett, "Status of the Utah Prairie Dog (*Cynomys parvidens*)," *Utah Academy of Science* 49 (1972): 27–39; G. Donald Collier and J. Juan Spillett, "The Utah Prairie Dog: Decline of a Legend," *Utah Science* 34 (1973): 83–87.

42. UPDRIP, *Status Report*, 7.

43. Steed, "Just Shoot Them," 23.

44. Ibid., 7–8.

45. Cited in Ruth Rudner, *A Chorus of Buffalo* (Ithaca, NY: Burford Books, 2000), 4.

46. Ibid., 5–6, 12; Lamb, Reading, and Andelt, "Attitudes and Perceptions," 110.

47. Rudner, *Chorus of Buffalo*, 12–14.

48. Steed, "Just Shoot Them," 18.

49. USFWS, "Proposal to Amend," 6022–24.

50. Ritchie et al., *Prairie Dog Interim Conservation*, 2–4, 9–10.

51. USFWS, "Final Rule to Reclassify," 22330–34.

52. Ibid.; USFWS, "Revised 90-day Finding," 36062–63.

53. Ritchie et al., *Prairie Dog Interim Conservation*, 3–4, 9–10; USFWS, *Utah Prairie Dog: Final Revised Recovery Plan*, 3.2–8.

54. Ritchie et al., *Prairie Dog Interim Conservation*, 2–4, 9–10.

55. The Recovery Plan released in 2012 is a revision of the original plan. It can be revised again if necessary.

56. USFWS, *Utah Prairie Dog: Final Revised Recovery Plan*, i-F10; Craig Thomas, "Habitat Conservation Planning: Certainly Empowered, Somewhat Deliberative, Questionably Democratic," *Politics and Society* 29 (2001): 105–30; Erica Wightman, "Utah Prairie Dog Habitat Credits Exchange Announced for Iron County" (Salt Lake City: KCSG Television, January 10, 2012).

57. Forest Guardians, "*Petition* to the U.S. Fish and Wildlife Service to Reclassify the Utah Prairie Dog as an Endangered Species under the Endangered Species Act," February 2, 2003, http://www.wildearthguardians.org/site/ DocServer/UPD_Uplisting_Petition.pdf?docID =784&AddInterest=1103, 1, 5, 23; USFWS, "Final Rule to Amend Special Rule Allowing Regulated Taking of *Cynomys parvidens*," *Federal Register* 56 (1991): 27438–43; WildEarth Guardians, "Protections for Imperiled Utah Prairie Dogs Improved, but Still Lacking: Amendments to Controversial 'Take' Rule Do Not Go Far Enough," August 2, 2012, http:// www.wildearthguardians.org/site/News2 ?page=NewsArticle&id=7841#.UvveomeYZjo; Williams, *Finding Beauty*, 395.

58. Elmore and Messmer, *Public Perceptions*, 11.

59. USFWS, "Revised 90-day Finding," 36063; USFWS, *Utah Prairie Dog: Final Revised Recovery Plan*, 1.7–3. Because the period for take is June–December, the cap on take applies to juveniles along with adults and therefore cannot be considered with regard to spring counts. The USFWS states that an average of 864 Utah prairie dogs (about 2–5 percent of the rangewide population, including young-of-the-year) have been killed annually, despite a limit on take of 6,000 individuals.

60. UPDRIP, *2011 Work Plan*; UPDRIP, *Status Report*, 1–15. UPDRIP was formalized in 2010 and the partnership is still in its early stages. Limited funding is available to pursue landscape-level conservation efforts for recovery of Utah prairie dogs. However, UPDRIP has already become a valuable tool for increasing coordination efforts and is making initial strides toward formulating annual and long-range work plans for Utah prairie dog conservation. In addition, the support of UPDRIP partners has already proven important in obtaining some funding from various grant programs.

61. USFWS, "Revising the Proposed Special Rule for the Utah Prairie Dog: Supplemental Notice of Proposed Rulemaking; Reopening of Public Comment Period and Notice of Document Availability," *Federal Register* 77 (2012): 24920, 46158–83;

62. Andelt, "Methods and Economics," 130.

63. Elizabeth Hanson, *Animal Attractions: Nature on Display in American Zoos* (Princeton, NJ: Princeton University Press, 2002), 46–47. Also see the preface of this book for the story of how I discovered prairie dogs in a zoo.

64. *Deseret News*, "Prairie Dogs Dig into Their New Home," July 3, 1999; USFWS, *Utah Prairie Dog: 5-Year Review*, H-15.

65. Archie F. Reeve and Timothy C. Vosburgh, "Recreational Shooting of Prairie Dogs," in Hoogland, *Conservation of the Black-Tailed Prairie Dog*, 139–56.

66. Examine, for example, the attitudes reflected in Steed, "Just Shoot Them," 1, 21–22.

67. Lamb, Reading, and Andelt, "Attitudes and Perceptions," 111.

68. Smith, "Utah Legislature."

69. Humane Society of the United States. "Today Is Prairie Dog Day!" February 2, 2011, http://www.humanesociety.org/news/press_releases/2011/02/_prairie_dog_day_020211.html.

70. The date for the report submission is listed as February 3, the day after Groundhog/Prairie Dog Day. Forest Guardians, "Petition," 1.

71. Taylor Jones, *Report from the Burrow: Forecast for the Prairie Dog* (Denver: WildEarth Guardians, 2013), 1–35.

72. Williams, *Finding Beauty*, 138.

73. NPS, "Utah Prairie Dog Day 2011," accessed June 3, 2012, http://www.nps.gov/brca/parknews/upd-day-2011.htm.

74. USFWS, "Revised 90-day Finding," 36053–68.

75. See the quote of Judge Shockey cited in Mark Jerome Walters, *Seeking the Sacred Raven: Politics and Extinction on a Hawaiian Island* (Washington, DC: Island Press, 2006), 167.

76. See Prairie Dog Coalition, "Coalition Efforts," accessed June 22, 2012 http://www.prairiedogcoalition.org/coalition-efforts.php and links therein.

77. This vaccine results from the collaboration of scientists from the US Geological Survey National Wildlife Health Center and the University of Wisconsin. Tonie E. Rocke, *Sylvatic Plague Vaccine and Management of Prairie Dogs*, US Geological Survey (2012): 3087; Rocke et al., "Immunization," 930–37.

78. Hoogland et al., "Pyraperm Halts Plague," 376–83; Hoogland, "Alarm Calling," 438–49; Hoogland et al., "Selective Predation," 546–52; Hoogland, "Black-Tailed, Gunnison's," 917–27; Manno, "Utah Prairie Dogs Vigilant," 555–63; USFWS, "Revised 90-day Finding," 36053–68.

79. Hoogland communicated a similar sentiment for black-tailed prairie dogs in "Saving Prairie Dogs: Can We? Should We?" in Hoogland, *Conservation of the Black-Tailed Prairie Dog*, 261–66.

80. Williams, *Finding Beauty*, 186–87.

81. Bill Branham, e-mail to author, January 11, 2013. For a recent example of a scientific paper with DNA analysis showing Utah prairie dogs and white-tailed prairie dogs as separate species, see Harrison et al., "Phylogeny," 249–76. According to surveys, the majority of Utahans do not distinguish between different species of prairie dog and do not think Utah prairie dogs should be considered a distinct species. Elmore and Messmer, *Public Perceptions*, 3.

82. Bill Branham, e-mail to author, January 11, 2013; southernutahradio.podbean.com/2012/11/.

83. Elmore and Messmer, *Public Perceptions*, 11.

84. Ibid., 17–19. About two-thirds of respondents in agricultural areas of southern Utah believe that farmers and ranchers should be compensated for damages, with most believing that conservation groups, and not the government or private insurance, should fund the recompense.

85. Ibid., 11.

86. Forest Guardians, "Petition," 3, 43; Nicole Rosmarino quote in Patty Henetz, "Lawsuit: Cedar City Prairie Dogs Endangered by Golf Course Relocation Bid," *Salt Lake Tribune*, April 24, 2008; Rice, "Saving Utah Prairie Dogs," 1; Williams, *Finding Beauty*, 395.

87. UPDRIP, *Status Report*, 7.

88. USFWS, *Utah Prairie Dog: Final Revised Recovery Plan*, 1.9–1, 3.5–15.

89. Ritchie et al., *Prairie Dog Interim Conservation*, 7.

90. Forest Guardians, "Petition," 3, 43; Rosmarino quote in Henetz, "Lawsuit"; Rice, "Saving Utah Prairie Dogs," 1.

91. USFWS, "Revising the Proposed Special Rule," 46169, 46179.

92. One example of limiting lethal take is the 2012 effort of Garfield County officials and Dixie National Forest to contact landowners who had 4(d) permits and ask whether they could come and translocate Utah prairie dogs from the property rather than killing them. Several landowners participated, including some in Bryce Canyon City, where some Utah prairie dogs were moved from the rodeo grounds. Another issue is that translocations are not always feasible due to the labor it takes to trap and translocate the animals. Laura Romin, e-mail to the author, January 11, 2013.

93. Elmore and Messmer, *Public Perceptions*, 6, 12.

Ackers, Steve H. "Behavioral Responses of Utah Prairie Dogs (*Cynomys parvidens*) to Translocation." Master's thesis, Utah State University, 1992.

Adams, Scott. *Dilbert 2.0: 20 Years of Dilbert*. Kansas City, MO: Andrews McMeel, 2008.

Agnew, William, Daniel W. Uresk, and Richard M. Hansen. "Flora and Fauna Associated with Prairie Dog Colonies and Adjacent Ungrazed Mixed-Grass Prairie in Western South Dakota." *Journal of Range Management* 39 (1986): 135–39.

Allen, Joel A. "Mammals from Beaver County, Utah. Collected by the Museum Expedition of 1904." *Bulletin of the Museum of Science, Brooklyn Institute of Arts and Science* 1 (1905): 117–22.

Andelt, William F. "Methods and Economics of Managing Prairie Dogs." In *Conservation of the Black-Tailed Prairie Dog: Saving North America's Western Grasslands*, edited by John L. Hoogland, 129–38. Washington, DC: Island Press, 2006.

Anderson, Stanley H., and Elizabeth S. Williams. "Plague in a Complex of White-Tailed Prairie Dogs and Associated Small Mammals in Wyoming." *Journal of Wildlife Disease* 33 (1997): 720–32.

Animal Care and Use Committee. "Guidelines for the Capture, Handling, and Care of Mammals as Approved by the American Society of Mammalogists." *Journal of Mammalogy* 79 (1998): 1416–31.

Archer, Sellers, and Clarence Bunch. *The American Grass Book*. Norman: University of Oklahoma Press, 1953.

Arnold, Walter. "The Evolution of Marmot Sociality: II. Costs and Benefits of Group Hibernation." *Behavioral Ecology and Sociobiology* 27 (1990): 239–46.

Aschwanden, Christie. "Learning to Live with Prairie Dogs." *National Wildlife*, April–May, 2001.

Asimov, Issac. *The Early Asimov: Or, Eleven Years of Trying*. New York: Doubleday, 1972.

Audubon, John J., and John Bachman. *The Quadrupeds of North America*. 3 vols. Reprinted as *Audubon's Quadrupeds of North America*. Secaucus, NJ: Wellfleet, 1989.

"Audubon of Kansas Claims Pesticides Deadly to Prairie Dogs and Threaten Imperiled Animals." *North Dakota Pesticide Quarterly* 28 (2010): 1–8.

Bailey, Vernon. *A Biological Survey of Texas*. North American Fauna No. 25. Washington, DC: US Department of Agriculture, 1905.

———. "The Ground Squirrels or Spermophiles of the Mississippi Valley." *Bulletin of the Division of Ornithology and Mammalogy* No. 4. Washington, DC: US Department of Agriculture, 1893.

Baird, Joe. "The Utah Prairie Dog Gains Useful Friends." *Salt Lake Tribune*, November 2, 2005.

Baird, Spencer F. *Mammals of the Boundary*. Washington, DC: United States and Mexican Boundary Survey, 1859.

———. *Mammals. Reports of Exploration and Surveys to Ascertain the Most Practicable and Economical Route for a Railroad from the Mississippi River to the Pacific Ocean*. Vol 8. Washington, DC: United States War Department, 1858.

Barnes, Allan M. "A Review of Plague and Its Relevance to Prairie Dog Populations and the Black-Footed Ferret." In *Proceedings of the Symposium on the Management of Prairie Dog Complexes for the Reintroduction of the Black-Footed Ferret*, edited by John L. Oldemeyer, Dean E. Biggins, and Brian J. Miller, 28–37. Biological Report 13, US Department of the Interior, US Fish and Wildlife Service, 1993.

Beebe, C. William. *The Bird: Its Form and Function*. New York: H. Holt, 1906.

Beecher, Michael D. "Successes and Failures of Parent-Offspring Recognition in Animals." In *Kin Recognition*, edited by Peter G. Hepper, 94–124. Cambridge: Cambridge University Press, 1991.

Bekoff, Marc. *Minding Animals: Awareness, Emotions, and Heart*. New York: Oxford University Press, 2002.

Benedict, Lauryn. "Offspring Discrimination without Recognition: California Towhee Responses to Chick Distress Calls." *Condor* 109 (2007): 79–87.

Biggins, Dean E., and Michael Y. Kosoy. "Influences of Introduced Plague on North American Mammals: Implications from Ecology of Plague in Asia." *Journal of Mammalogy* 4 (2001): 906–16.

Biggins, Dean E., John G. Sidle, David B. Seery, and Andrea E. Ernst. "Estimating the Abundance of Prairie Dogs." In *Conservation of the Black-Tailed Prairie Dog: Saving North America's Western Grasslands*, edited by John L. Hoogland, 94–107. Washington, DC: Island Press, 2006.

Biodiversity Legal Foundation. *Recommended Conservation Measures for Protection and Recovery of the Black-Tailed Prairie Dog* (Cynomys ludovicianus) *and its Shortgrass Prairie Ecosystem*. Louisville, CO: Biodiversity Legal Foundation, 1999.

Blumstein, Daniel T., and Kenneth B. Armitage. "Does Sociality Drive the Evolution of Communicative Complexity? A Comparative Test with Ground-Dwelling Sciurid Alarm Calls." *American Naturalist* 150 (1997): 179–200.

Bonzo, Teresa G. *Utah Prairie Dog Counts 1985–2005*. Utah Division of Wildlife Resources, 2005.

Bonzo, Teresa G., and Keith Day. *Administrative Monitoring Report, Habitat Conservation Plan for Utah Prairie Dogs in Iron County, Utah*. Utah Division of Wildlife Resources Publication No. 03-46, 2002.

———. *Utah Prairie Dog Recovery Efforts, 1999 Annual Report*. Utah Division of Wildlife Resources Publication No. 00-35, 2000.

———. *Utah Prairie Dog Recovery Efforts: 2002 Annual Report*. Utah Division of Wildlife Resources Publication No. 03-47, 2002.

Brown, Charles R., and John L. Hoogland. "Risk in Mobbing for Solitary and Colonial Swallows." *Animal Behaviour* 34 (1987): 1319–23.

Brown, Dee. *Bury My Heart at Wounded Knee: An Indian History of the American West*. New York: Sterling Publishing, 2009.

Brown, Jerram L., "Avian Communal Breeding Systems." *Annual Review of Ecology and Systematics* 9 (1978): 123–55.

Brown, Nathan. *Utah Prairie Dog Systemic Flea Control Field Study Progress Report*. Utah Division of Wildlife Resources, October 1, 2009.

Brownlee, Alec. "Animal Play." *Applied Animal Behaviour Science* 106 (2000): 307–12.

Bruce, Katherine E., and Daniel Q. Estep. "Interruption of and Harassment during Copulation by Stumptail Macaques, *Macaca arctoides*." *Animal Behaviour* 44 (1992): 1029–44.

Bryant, Richard. *Prairie Dogs at Bryce Canyon*. National Park Service, Bryce Canyon Resource Management Files, 1996.

Bureau of Land Management (BLM). *Draft Biological Evaluation: Utah Prairie Dog Biological Evaluation for Section 7 Consultation on the Milford Wind Facility—Phase II Project*. Fillmore and Cedar City Field Offices, December 17, 2009.

Burger, Joanna, and Michael Gochfield. "Vigilance in Ostriches (*Struthio camelus*): Mate Competition or Antipredator Behavior?" *Ostrich* 59 (1994): 14–20.

Burroughs, Raymond D. *The Natural History of the Lewis and Clark Expedition*. East Lansing: Michigan State University Press, 1961.

Cain, Stanley A., John A. Kadlec, Durward L. Allen, Richard A. Cooley, Maurice C. Hornocker, A. Starker Leopold, and Frederick H. Wagner. *Predator Control: 1971 Report to the Council on Environmental Quality and the Department of the Interior by the Advisory Committee on Predator Control*. Washington, DC: Council on Environmental Quality and US Department of the Interior.

Campagna, Claudio, Burney J. Le Boeuf, and Humberto L. Cappozzo. "Pup Abduction and Infanticide in Southern Sea Lions." *Behavior* 107 (1988): 44–60.

Campbell, Thomas M., III, and Tim W. Clark. "Colony Characteristics and Vertebrate Associates of White-Tailed and Black-Tailed Prairie Dogs in Wyoming." *American Midland Naturalist* 105 (1981): 269–76.

Carey, Hannah V., and Paul Moore. "Foraging and Predation Risk in Yellow-Bellied Marmots." *American Midland Naturalist* 116 (1986): 267–75.

Carr, James F. "A Rancher's View towards Prairie Dogs." In *Proceedings of the Black-Footed Ferret and Prairie Dog Workshop*, edited by Raymond L. Linder and Conrad N. Hillman, 168–71. Rapid City: South Dakota State University, 2008.

Carroll, Lewis. *Through the Looking Glass and What Alice Found There*. London: MacMillan, 1871.

Carter, Alan. "Evolution and the Problem of Altruism." *Philosophical Studies: An International Journal for Philosophy in the Analytic Tradition* 123 (2005): 213–20.

Ceballos, Gerardo, and Don E. Wilson. "*Cynomys mexicanus*." *Mammalian Species* 248 (1985): 1–3.

Cedar City Corporation and Paiute Tribe of Utah. *Habitat Conservation Plan for the Cedar City*

Golf Course and Paiute Tribal Lands. Submitted May 15, 2006.

Chagnon, Napoleon A. "Genealogy, Solidarity, and Relatedness: Limits to Local Group Size and Patterns of Fissioning in an Expanding Population." *Yearbook of Physical Anthropology* 19 (1975): 95–110.

Chancellor, Rebecca L., and Lynne A. Isbell. "Food Site Residence Time and Female Competitive Relationships in Wild Gray-Cheeked Mangabeys (*Lophocebus albigena*)." *Behavioral Ecology and Sociobiology* 63 (2009): 1447–58.

Cheng, Ellen. "Effects of Simulated Summer Grazing on Utah Prairie Dog (*Cynomys parvidens*) Growth Rates and Behaviors." Master's thesis, Utah State University, 2000.

Cheng, Ellen, and Mark E. Ritchie. "Impacts of Simulated Livestock Grazing on Utah Prairie Dogs (*Cynomys parvidens*) in a Low Productivity Ecosystem." *Oecologia* 147 (2006): 546–55.

Chesser, Ronald K. *Study of Genetic Variation in the Utah Prairie Dog*. Report prepared for US Fish and Wildlife Service. Lubbock: Texas Tech University, 1984.

Cid, Maria S., James K. Detling, April D. Whicker, and Miguel A. Brizuela. "Vegetational Responses of a Mixed-Grass Prairie Site Following Exclusion of Prairie Dogs and Bison." *Journal of Range Management* 44 (1991): 100–105.

Clark, Tim W. "Ecological Roles of Prairie Dogs." *Wyoming Range Management* 261 (1968): 102–4.

———. "Ecology and Ethology of the White-Tailed Prairie Dog (*Cynomys leucurus*)." *Milwaukee Public Museum Publications in Biology and Geology* 3 (1977): 1–97.

Clark, Tim W., Thomas M. Campbell, David G. Socha, and Denise E. Casey. "Prairie Dog Colony Attributes and Associated Vertebrate Species." *Great Basin Naturalist* 42 (1982): 572–82.

Clark, Tim W., Robert S. Hoffmann, and Charles F. Nadler. "*Cynomys leucurus*." *Mammalian Species* 7 (1971): 1–4.

Clutton-Brock, Tim H., Steve D. Albon, and Fiona E. Guinness. "Fitness Costs of Gestation and Lactation in Wild Mammals." *Nature* 337 (1989): 260–62.

Coffeen, Michael P., and Jordan C. Pederson. "Techniques for the Transplant of Utah Prairie Dogs." In *Proceedings of the Symposium on the Management of Prairie Dog Complexes for the Reintroduction of the Black-Footed Ferret*, edited by John L. Oldemeyer, Dean E. Biggins, and Brian J. Miller, 60–66. Biological Report 13, US Department of the Interior, US Fish and Wildlife Service, 1993.

Collier, G. Donald. "The Utah Prairie Dog: Abundance, Distribution, and Habitat Requirements." PhD diss., Utah State University, 1975.

Collier, G. Donald, and J. Juan Spillett. "Factors Influencing the Distribution of the Utah Prairie Dog, *Cynomys parvidens* (Sciuridae)." *Southwestern Naturalist* 20 (1975): 151–58.

———. "Status of the Utah Prairie Dog (*Cynomys parvidens*)." *Utah Academy of Science* 49 (1972): 27–39.

———. "The Utah Prairie Dog: Decline of a Legend." *Utah Science* 34 (1973): 83–87.

Collins, Allen R., John P. Workman, and Daniel W. Uresk. "An Economic Analysis of Black-Tailed Prairie Dog (*Cynomys ludovicianus*) Control." *Journal of Range Management* 37 (1984): 358–61.

Conaway, Clinton H. "Embryo Resorption and Placental Scar Formation in the Rat." *Journal of Mammalogy* 36 (1955): 516–32.

Coppock, David L., James K. Detling, James E. Ellis, and Melvin I. Dyer. "Plant-Herbivore Interactions in a North American Mixed-Grass Prairie: Effects of Black-Tailed Prairie Dogs on Intraseasonal Aboveground Plant Biomass and Plant Species Diversity." *Oecologia* 56 (1983): 1–9.

Costello, David Francis. *The World of the Prairie Dog*. Philadelphia: Lippincott, 1970.

Coues, Elliot, and Joel A. Allen. *Monographs of North American Rodentia*. Vol. 2. Washington, DC: United States Survey of the Territories, 1877.

Cresswell, William. "Interference Competition at Low Competitor Density in Blackbirds (*Turdus merula*)." *Journal of Animal Ecology* 66 (1997): 461–71.

Crocker-Bedford, D. Coleman. "Food Interactions between Utah Prairie Dogs and Cattle." Master's thesis, Utah State University, 1976.

———. "Utah Prairie Dog Habitat Evaluation." In *Proceedings of the Utah Wildlife Society Technical Meeting*, 1–7. 1975.

Crocker-Bedford, D. Coleman, and J. Juan Spillett. *Habitat Relationships of the Utah Prairie Dog*. US Department of Agriculture, Forest Service, Intermountain Region Publication No. 1981-0-677-202/4, 1981.

———. "Home Ranges of Utah Prairie Dogs." *Journal of Mammalogy* 58 (1977): 672–73.

Cully, Jack F. "Plague in Prairie Dog Ecosystems: Importance for Black-Footed Ferret Management." In *The Prairie Dog Ecosystem: Managing for Biological Diversity*, 47–55. Montana BLM Wildlife Technical Bulletin No. 2. Billings, MT: Bureau of Land Management, 1989.

Cully, Jack F., Dean E. Biggins, and David B. Seery. "Conservation of Prairie Dogs in Areas with Plague." In *Conservation of the Black-Tailed Prairie Dog: Saving North America's Western Grasslands*, edited by John L. Hoogland, 157–68. Washington, DC: Island Press, 2006.

Cully, Jack F., and Elizabeth S. Williams. "Interspecific Comparisons of Sylvatic Plague in Prairie Dogs." *Journal of Mammalogy* 82 (2001): 894–905.

Curtis, Rachel. "Factors Influencing Relocation Success of Utah Prairie Dogs (*Cynomys parvidens*). Master's thesis, Utah State University, 2012.

Daley, James G. "Population Reductions and Genetic Variability in Black-Tailed Prairie Dogs." *Journal of Wildlife Management* 56 (1992): 212–20.

Darwin, Charles R. *On the Origin of Species by Means of Natural Selection, or, the Preservation of Favoured Races in the Struggle for Life*. New York: D. Appleton, 1869.

DeBarbieri, Liliana M., and Theodore G. Manno. "Return of the Native: Black-Tailed Prairie Dogs Reintroduced to Southern Arizona." *Tucson Green Times*, July 2009.

DeCourten, Frank. *Dinosaurs of Utah*. Salt Lake City: University of Utah Press, 1998.

Deisch, Michele S., Daniel W. Uresk, and Raymond L. Linder. "Effects of Two Prairie Dog Rodenticides on Ground-Dwelling Invertebrates in Western South Dakota." *Great Basin Naturalist* 50 (1990): 347–53.

Densmore, Frances. "Northern Ute Music." *Smithsonian Institution, Bureau of American Ethnology* 75 (1922): 1–213.

Deseret News. "Prairie Dogs Dig into Their New Home." July 3, 1999.

Detling, James. "Do Prairie Dogs Compete with Livestock?" In *Conservation of the Black-Tailed Prairie Dog: Saving North America's Western Grasslands*, edited by John L. Hoogland, 65–88. Washington, DC: Island Press, 2006.

Dewsbury, Donald A. "Diversity and Adaptation in Rodent Copulatory Behavior." *Science* 190 (1975): 947–54.

Dobson, F. Stephen. "Environmental Influences on Infanticide in Columbian Ground Squirrels." *Ethology* 84 (1990): 3–14.

Dobson, F. Stephen, Ronald K. Chesser, John L. Hoogland, Derrick W. Sugg, and David W. Foltz. "Breeding Groups and Gene Dynamics in a Socially Structured Population of Prairie Dogs." *Journal of Mammalogy* 79 (1998): 671–80.

Dobson, F. Stephen, and Pierre Jouventin. "How Mothers Find Their Pups in a Colony of Antarctic Fur Seals." *Behavioral Processes* 61 (2003): 77–85.

Draganoiu, Tudor I., Laurent Nagle, Raphael Musseau, and Michel Kreutzer. "In a Songbird, the Black Redstart, Parents Use Acoustic Cues to Discriminate between Their Different Fledglings." *Animal Behaviour* 71 (2006): 1039–46.

Dunford, Christopher. "Kin Selection for Ground Squirrel Alarm Calls." *American Naturalist* 111 (1977): 782–85.

Egoscue, Harold J., and Elizabeth S. Frank. "Burrowing and Denning Habits of a Captive Colony of the Utah Prairie Dog." *Great Basin Naturalist* 44 (1984): 495–98.

Eldredge, Niles. "A Field Guide to the Sixth Extinction." *New York Times Magazine*, December 2, 1999.

Elmore, R. Dwayne, and Terry A. Messmer. *Livestock Grazing and the Utah Prairie Dog: Implications for Managing the Awapa*. Berryman Institute, Publication No. 24. Logan: Utah State University, 2006.

———. *Public Perceptions Regarding the Utah Prairie Dog and Its Management: Implications for Species Recovery*. Berryman Institute, Publication No. 23. Logan: Utah State University, 2006.

Elmore, R. Dwayne, Terry A. Messmer, and Mark W. Brunson. "Perceptions of Wildlife Damage and Species Conservation: Lesson Learned from the Utah Prairie Dog." *Human-Wildlife Interactions* 1 (2007): 78–88.

Elmore, Steve. "A Baseline Study of the Past and Present Status of the Utah Prairie Dog (*Cynomys parvidens*) in Bryce Canyon National Park." Logan: Utah State University, 1976.

Emlen, Stephen T. "Cooperative Breeding in Birds and Mammals." In *Behavioural Ecology: An Evolutionary Approach*, 3rd ed., edited by John R. Krebs and Nicholas B. Davies, 301–37. Oxford, UK: Blackwell Scientific Publications, 1991.

Emlen, Stephen T., and Lewis W. Oring. "Ecology, Sexual Selection, and the Evolution of Mating Systems." *Science* 197 (1977): 215–33.

Endangered Species Act of 1973 (ESA). 16 U.S.C.A. §§ 1531 to 1544.

Fagan, Robert. "Selective and Evolutionary Aspects of Animal Play." *American Naturalist* 108 (1974): 850–58.

Farmer, Jared. *On Zion's Mount: Mormons, Indians, and the American Landscape.* Cambridge, MA: Harvard University Press, 2008.

Fitzgerald, James P. "The Ecology of Plague in Gunnison's Prairie Dogs and Suggestions for the Recovery of Black-Footed Ferrets." In *Proceedings of the Symposium on the Management of Prairie Dog Complexes for the Reintroduction of the Black-Footed Ferret*, edited by John L. Oldemeyer, Dean E. Biggins, and Brian J. Miller, 50–59. Biological Report 13, US Department of the Interior, US Fish and Wildlife Service, 1993.

Fleischner, Thomas L. "Ecological Costs of Livestock Grazing in Western North America." *Conservation Biology* 8 (1994): 629–44.

Foltz, David W., and John L. Hoogland. "Analysis of the Mating System of the Black-Tailed Prairie Dog (*Cynomys ludovicianus*) by Likelihood of Paternity." *Journal of Mammalogy* 62 (1981): 706–12.

———. "Genetic Evidence of Outbreeding in the Black-Tailed Prairie Dog (*Cynomys ludovicianus*)." *Evolution* 37 (1983): 273–81.

Ford, Clellan S., and Frank A. Beach. *Patterns of Sexual Behaviour.* Westport, CT: Greenwood Press, 1980.

Forest Guardians. "Petition to the U.S. Fish and Wildlife Service to Reclassify the Utah Prairie Dog as an Endangered Species under the Endangered Species Act," February 3, 2003. http://www.wildearthguardians.org/site/DocServer/UPD_Uplisting_Petition.pdf?docID=784&AddInterest=1103

Forrest, Steve C., and James C. Luchsinger. "Past and Current Chemical Control of Prairie Dogs." In *Conservation of the Black-Tailed Prairie Dog: Saving North America's Western Grasslands*, edited by John L. Hoogland, 115–28. Washington, DC: Island Press, 2006.

Fox-Parrish, Lynne. "Attitudes and Opinions of Landowners and General Citizens Relative to the Black-Tailed Prairie Dog." Master's thesis, Emporia State University, 2002.

Gage, Kenneth L., and Michael Y. Kosoy. "Natural History of Plague: Perspectives from More Than a Century of Research." *Annual Review of Entomology* 50 (2005): 505–28.

Galton, Francis. *Gregariousness in Cattle and Men.* London: Macmillan, 1871.

———. *Inquiries into Human Faculty and Its Development.* London: Macmillan, 1883.

Garrett, Monte G., and William L. Franklin. "Prairie Dog Dispersal in Wind Cave Park: Possibilities for Control." In *Fifth Great Plains Wildlife Damage Control Workshop: Proceedings*, edited by R. M. Timm and R. J. Johnson, 185–98. Lincoln: Institute of Agriculture and Natural Resources, University of Nebraska, 1981.

Garrido, Jose R., Cristina G. Sarasa, and Manual Fernandez-Cruz. "Intraspecific Kleptoparasitism in the Cattle Egret." *Journal of Field Ornithology* 73 (2002): 185–90.

Gemmell, Neil J. "Kin Selection May Influence Fostering Behaviour in Antarctic Fur Seals (*Arctocephalus gazella*). *Proceedings of the Royal Society of London Series B, Biological Sciences* 270 (2003): 2033–37.

Gibbens, Robert P., and James M. Lenz. "Root Systems of Some Chihuahuan Desert Plants." *Journal of Arid Environments* 49 (2001): 221–63.

Goodall, Jane. *The Chimpanzees of Gombe.* Cambridge, MA: Belknap Press, 1986.

Goodwin, H. Thomas. "Pliocene-Pleistocene Biogeographic History of Prairie Dogs, Genus *Cynomys* (Sciuridae)." *Journal of Mammalogy* 77 (1996): 407–11.

Goodwin, Jack. "A New Look at Old Treasures." *Utah Historical Quarterly* 47–48 (1958): 283.

Grady, R. Mark, and John L. Hoogland. "Why Do Male Prairie Dogs (*Cynomys ludovicianus*) Give a Mating Call?" *Animal Behaviour* 34 (1986): 108–12.

Gratson, Michael W., Gretchen K. Gratson, and Arthur T. Bergerud. "Male Dominance and Copulation Disruption Do Not Explain Variance in Male Mating Success on Sharp-Tailed Grouse (*Tympanuchus phasianellus*) Leks. *Behaviour* 118 (1991): 187–213.

Graves, Russell A. *The Prairie Dog: Sentinel of the Plains.* Lubbock: Texas Tech University Press, 2001.

Green, Ronald A. "Nitrogen Distribution in a Perennial Grassland: The Role of American Bison." PhD diss., Colorado State University, 1998.

Gregg, Josiah. *Commerce of the Prairies.* 2 vols. New York: Henry G. Langley, 1844.

Hamilton, William D. "The Genetical Evolution of Social Behavior. I and II." *Journal of Theoretical Biology* 7 (1964): 1–52.

———. "Geometry for the Selfish Herd." *Journal of Theoretical Biology* 31 (1971): 295–311.

———. "Innate Social Aptitudes of Man: An Approach from Evolution Genetics." In *Biosocial Anthropology*, edited by R. Fox, 135–55. New York: John Wiley and Sons, 1987.

Hamilton, William D., and Robert M. May. "Dispersal in Stable Habitats." *Nature* 269 (1977): 578–81.

Hamilton, William J., and Patricia C. Arrowood. "Copulatory Vocalizations of Chacma Baboons (*Papio ursinus*), Gibbons (*Hylobates hoolock*), and Humans." *Science* 200 (1978): 1405–9.

Hansen, Richard M., and Ilyse K. Gold. "Blacktail [sic] Prairie Dogs, Desert Cottontails and Cattle Trophic Relations on Shortgrass Range." *Journal of Range Management* 30 (1977): 210–14.

Hanson, Elizabeth. *Animal Attractions: Nature on Display in American Zoos*. Princeton, NJ: Princeton University Press, 2002.

Hare, James F. "Intraspecific Killing of Pre-Weaned Young in the Columbian Ground Squirrel, *Spermophilus columbianus*." *Canadian Journal of Zoology* 69 (1991): 797–800.

———. "Juvenile Richardson's Ground Squirrels (*Spermophilus richardsonii*) Manifest Both Littermate and Neighbour/Stranger Discrimination." *Ethology* 104 (1998): 991–1002.

Hare, James F., and Brent Atkins. "The Squirrel That Cried Wolf: Reliability Detection by Juvenile Richardson's Ground Squirrels (*Spermophilus richardsonii*)." *Behavioral Ecology and Sociobiology* 51 (2001): 108–12.

Harris, Ann G., Esther Tuttle, and Sherwood D. Tuttle. *Geology of National Parks*. 5th ed. Dubuque, IA: Kendall Hunt Publishing, 1997.

Harrison, Richard G., Steven M. Bogdanowicz, Robert S. Hoffmann, Eric Yensen, and Paul W. Sherman. "Phylogeny and Evolutionary History of the Ground Squirrels (Rodentia: Marmotinae)." *Journal of Mammalian Evolution* 10 (2003): 249–76.

Hasenyager, Robert H. *Diet Selection of the Utah Prairie Dog* (Cynomys parvidens) *as Determined by Histological Fecal Analysis*. Utah Division of Wildlife Resources, submitted to Utah Cooperative Wildlife Research Unit, Logan, 1984.

Hastings, Alan, and Susan Harrison. "Metapopulation Dynamics and Genetics." *Annual Review of Ecology and Systematics* 25 (1994): 167–88.

Havnes, Mark. "Recovery Numbers for Utah Prairie Dog Strong." *Salt Lake Tribune*, November 21, 2011.

Haynie, Michelle L., Ronald A. van den Bussche, John L. Hoogland, Dennis A. Gilbert, and Robert D. Bradley. "Parentage, Multiple Paternity, and Breeding Success in Gunnison's and Utah Prairie Dogs." *Journal of Mammalogy* 84 (2003): 1244–53.

Heffner, Rickye S., Henry E. Heffner, Christopher Contos, and Dara Kearns. "Hearing in Prairie Dogs: Transition between Surface and Subterranean Rodents." *Hearing Research* 73 (1994): 185–89.

Helgen, Kristofer M., Russel F. Cole, Lauren E. Helgen, and Don E. Wilson. "Generic Revision in the Holarctic Ground Squirrel Genus *Spermophilus*." *Journal of Mammalogy* 90 (2009): 270–305.

Henetz, Patty. "Lawsuit: Cedar City Prairie Dogs Endangered by Golf Course Relocation Bid." *Salt Lake Tribune*, April 24, 2008.

Hengesbaugh, Mark Gerard. *Creatures of Habitat*. Logan: Utah State University Press, 2001.

Henzi, S. Peter. "Copulation Calls and Paternity in Chacma Baboons." *Animal Behaviour* 51 (1996): 233–34.

Hershey Archives. "History of the Hershey Zoo." Accessed May 17, 2012. http://www.zooamerica.com/about_us.php.

Hirsch, Ben. "Social Monitoring and Vigilance Behavior in Brown Capuchin Monkeys (*Cebus apella*)." *Behavioral Ecology and Sociobiology* 52 (2002): 458–64.

Hogstedt, Goran. "Adaptation unto Death: Function of Distress Calls." *American Naturalist* 121 (1983): 562–70.

Hollister, Ned. "A Systematic Account of the Prairie Dogs." *North American Fauna* 40 (1916): 1–37.

Holt, Ronald. *Beneath These Red Cliffs: An Ethnohistory of the Utah Paiutes*. Logan: Utah State University Press, 2006.

Hood, Glenn A. "Zinc Phosphide: A New Look at an Old Rodenticide for Field Rodents." *Proceedings of the Vertebrate Pest Conference* 5 (1972): 85–92.

Hoogland, John L. "Aggression, Ectoparasitism, and Other Possible Costs of Prairie Dog (Sciuridae: *Cynomys* spp.) Coloniality." *Behaviour* 69 (1979): 1–35.

———. "Alarm Calling, Multiple Mating, and Infanticide among Black-Tailed, Gunnison's, and Utah Prairie Dogs." In *Rodent Societies*, edited by Jerry O. Wolff and Paul W. Sherman,

438–49. Chicago: University of Chicago Press, 2007.

———. "The Black-Footed Ferret and the Evolution of Prairie Dog Coloniality: Reply to a Comment by Powell." *Ecology* 63 (1982): 1968–69.

———. "Black-Tailed, Gunnison's, and Utah Prairie Dogs All Reproduce Slowly." *Journal of Mammalogy* 82 (2001): 917–27.

———. "Black-Tailed Prairie Dog Coteries Are Cooperatively Breeding Units." *American Naturalist* 121 (1983): 275–80.

———. *The Black-Tailed Prairie Dog: Social Life of a Burrowing Mammal.* Chicago: University of Chicago Press, 1995.

———. "Conservation of Prairie Dogs." In *Conservation of the Black-Tailed Prairie Dog: Saving North America's Western Grasslands*, edited by John L. Hoogland, 185–266. Washington, DC: Island Press, 2006.

———. "Conservation of Prairie Dogs." In *Rodent Societies*, edited by Jerry O. Wolff and Paul W. Sherman, 472–77. Chicago: University of Chicago Press, 2007.

———, ed. *Conservation of the Black-Tailed Prairie Dog: Saving North America's Western Grasslands.* Washington, DC: Island Press, 2006.

———. "Duration of Gestation and Lactation for Gunnison's Prairie Dogs." *Journal of Mammalogy* 78 (1997): 173–80.

———. "The Effect of Colony Size on Individual Alertness of Prairie Dogs." *Animal Behaviour* 27 (1979): 394–407.

———. "Estrus and Copulation among Gunnison's Prairie Dogs." *Journal of Mammalogy* 79 (1998): 887–97.

———. "The Evolution of Coloniality in White-Tailed and Black-Tailed Prairie Dogs (Sciuridae: *Cynomys leucurus* and *C. ludovicianus*)." *Ecology* 62 (1981): 252–72.

———. "Infanticide in Prairie Dogs: Lactating Females Kill Offspring of Close Kin." *Science* 230 (1985): 1037–40.

———. "Nepotism and Alarm Calling in the Black-Tailed Prairie Dog (*Cynomys ludovicianus*)." *Animal Behaviour* 31 (1983): 472–79.

———. "Nursing of Own and Alien Offspring by Utah Prairie Dogs (*Cynomys parvidens*)." *Behavioral Ecology and Sociobiology* 63 (2009): 1621–34.

———. "Philopatry, Dispersal, and Social Organization of Gunnison's Prairie Dogs." *Journal of Mammalogy* 80 (1999): 243–51.

———. "Prairie Dog Lore." *Wall Street Journal*, September 22, 1982.

———. "Prairie Dogs Avoid Extreme Inbreeding." *Science* 215 (1982): 1639–41.

———. "Prairie Dogs Disperse When All Close Kin Have Disappeared." *Science* 339 (2013): 1205–7.

———. Preface to *Conservation of the Black-Tailed Prairie Dog: Saving North America's Western Grasslands*, edited by John L. Hoogland, xiii–xv. Washington, DC: Island Press, 2006.

———. "Saving Prairie Dogs: Can We? Should We?" In *Conservation of the Black-Tailed Prairie Dog: Saving North America's Western Grasslands*, edited by John L. Hoogland, 261–66. Washington, DC: Island Press, 2006.

———. "Sexual Dimorphism in Five Species of Prairie Dogs." *Journal of Mammalogy* 84 (2003): 1254–66.

———. "Why Care about Prairie Dogs?" In *Conservation of the Black-Tailed Prairie Dog: Saving North America's Western Grasslands*, edited by John L. Hoogland, 1–4. Washington DC: Island Press, 2006.

———. "Why Do Female Gunnison's Prairie Dogs Copulate with More Than One Male?" *Animal Behaviour* 55 (1998): 351–59.

———. "Why Do Females Mate with More Than One Male?—Insights from Long-Term Research." *Journal of Mammalogy* 94 (2013): 731–44.

———. "Why Do Gunnison's Prairie Dogs Give Antipredator Calls?" *Animal Behaviour* 51 (1996): 871–80.

———. "Why Have So Many Prairie Dogs Disappeared?" In *Conservation of the Black-tailed Prairie Dog: Saving North America's Western Grasslands*, edited by John L. Hoogland, 89–93. Washington DC: Island Press, 2006.

Hoogland, John L., Kristen E. Cannon, Liliana M. DeBarbieri, and Theodore G. Manno. "Selective Predation on Utah Prairie Dogs." *American Naturalist* 168 (2006): 546–52.

Hoogland, John L., Stacey Davis, Sarah Benson-Amram, Danielle LaBruna, Brigitte Goossens, and Margaret A. Hoogland. "Pyraperm Halts Plague among Utah Prairie Dogs." *Southwestern Naturalist* 49 (2004): 376–83.

Hoogland, John L., and Janice M. Hutter. "Aging Live Prairie Dogs from Molar Attrition." *Journal of Wildlife Management* 51 (1987): 393–94.

Hoogland, John L., and Paul W. Sherman. "Advantages and Disadvantages of Bank Swallow (*Riparia riparia*) Coloniality." *Ecological Monographs* 46 (1976): 33–58.

Hoogland, John L., Robert H. Tamarin, and Charles K. Levy. "Communal Nursing in Prairie Dogs." *Behavioral Ecology and Sociobiology* 24 (1989): 91–95.

Houck, Oliver A. "On the Law of Biodiversity and Ecosystem Management." *Minnesota Law Review* 81 (1997): 869.

Hrdy, Sarah B. "Infanticide among Animals: A Review, Classification, and Examination of the Implications for the Reproductive Strategies of Females." *Ethology and Sociobiology* 1 (1979): 13–40.

———. *The Langurs of Abu: Female and Male Strategies of Reproduction.* Cambridge, MA: Harvard University Press, 1977.

Humane Society of the United States. "Today Is Prairie Dog Day!" February 2, 2011. http://www.humanesociety.org/.

ICC (Iron County Commission) and UDWR (Utah Division of Wildlife Resources). "Habitat Conservation Plan for Utah Prairie Dogs in Iron County, Utah." Amended November 9, 2006. http://www.ironcounty.net/departments/Clerk/forms/ICHCPNov2006.pdf.

Irving, Washington. *A Tour on the Prairies.* London: John Murray, 1835.

Jameson, William C. "On the Eradication of Prairie Dogs: A Point of View." *Bios* 44 (1973): 129–35.

Johnsgard, Paul A. *Prairie Dog Empire: A Saga of the Shortgrass Prairie.* Lincoln: University of Nebraska Press, 2005.

Johnson, Whitney C., and Sharon K. Collinge. "Landscape Effects on Black-Tailed Prairie Dog Colonies." *Biological Conservation* 115 (2004): 487–97.

Jones, Taylor. *Report from the Burrow: Forecast for the Prairie Dog.* Denver: WildEarth Guardians, 2013.

Kay, Katty. *Utah Loves Jell-O—Official.* BBC News, February 6, 2001. http://news.bbc.co.uk/2/hi/americas/1156021.stm.

Kendall, George W. *Texan Santa Fé Expedition.* London: Sherwood, Gilbert, and Piper, 1846.

King, John A. "Historical Ventilations on a Prairie Dog Town." In *The Biology of Ground-Dwelling Squirrels*, edited by Jan O. Murie and Gail R. Michener, 447–56. Lincoln: University of Nebraska Press, 1984.

———. "Social Behavior, Social Organization, and Population Dynamics in a Black-Tailed Prairiedog [sic] Town in the Black Hills of South Dakota." *Contributions from the Laboratory of Vertebrate Biology, University of Michigan*, no. 67 (1955).

Kiyota, Masashi, and Hiroshi Okamura. "Harrassment, Abduction, and Mortality of Pups by Nonterritorial Male Northern Fur Seals." *Journal of Mammalogy* 86 (2005): 1227–36.

Knowles, Craig J. "Observations on Prairie Dog Dispersal in Montana." *Prairie Naturalist* 17 (1985): 33–40.

———. "Population Recovery of Black-Tailed Prairie Dogs Following Control with Zinc Phosphide." *Journal of Range Management* 39 (1986): 249–51.

———. "Reproductive Ecology of Black-Tailed Prairie Dogs in Montana." *Great Basin Naturalist* 47 (1987): 202–6.

———. "Some Relationships of Black-tailed Prairie Dogs to Livestock Grazing." *Great Basin Naturalist* 46 (1986): 198–203.

Koford, Carl B. "Prairie Dogs, Whitefaces, and Blue Grama." *Wildlife Monographs* 3 (1958): 1–78.

Kotliar, Natasha B., Bruce W. Baker, April D. Whicker, and Glenn Plumb. "A Critical Review of Assumptions about the Prairie Dog as a Keystone Species." *Environmental Management* 24 (1999): 177–92.

Kotliar, Natasha B., Brian J. Miller, Richard P. Reading, and Timothy W. Clark. "The Prairie Dog as a Keystone Species." In *Conservation of the Black-Tailed Prairie Dog: Saving North America's Western Grasslands*, edited by John L. Hoogland, 53–64. Washington, DC: Island Press, 2006.

Kretzer, Justin E., and Jack F. Cully. "Effects of Black-Tailed Prairie Dog on Reptiles and Amphibians in Kansas Shortgrass Prairie." *Southwestern Naturalist* 46 (2001): 171–77.

Kruger, Kirsten. "Feeding Relationships among Bison, Pronghorn, and Prairie Dogs: An Experimental Analysis." *Ecology* 67 (1986): 760–70.

Kruuk, Hans. "Predators and Anti-Predator Behavior of the Black-Headed Gull." *Behaviour* 11 (1972): 1–129.

Lacey, Eileen A., John R. Wieczorek, and Priscilla K. Tucker. "Male Mating Behaviour and Patterns of Sperm Precedence in Arctic Ground Squirrels." *Animal Behaviour* 53 (1997): 767–79.

Lack, David. "The Significance of Clutch Size. Parts 1 and 2." *Ibis* 89 (1947): 302–52.

Lamar, Howard R. *The Far Southwest—1846–1912: A Territorial History.* Rev. ed. Albuquerque: University of New Mexico Press, 2000.

Lamb, Berton L., Richard P. Reading, and William F. Andelt. "Attitudes and Perceptions about

Prairie Dogs." In *Conservation of the Black-Tailed Prairie Dog: Saving North America's Western Grasslands*, edited by John L. Hoogland, 108–14. Washington, DC: Island Press, 2006.

Lande, Russell. "Extinction Thresholds in Demographic Models of Territorial Populations." *American Naturalist* 130 (1987): 624–35.

Le Boeuf, Burney J., Ronald J. Whiting, and Richard F. Gantt. "Perinatal Behavior of Northern Elephant Seal Females and Their Young." *Behavior* 43 (1972): 121–56.

Lehmer, Erin M., and Dean E. Biggins. "Variation in Torpor Patterns of Free-Ranging Black-Tailed and Utah Prairie Dogs across Gradients of Elevation." *Journal of Mammalogy* 86 (2005): 15–21.

Lima, Steven L. "Back to the Basics of Anti-Predatory Vigilance: The Group-Size Effect." *Animal Behaviour* 49 (1995): 11–20.

Lomolino, Mark V., and Gregory A. Smith. "Terrestrial Vertebrate Communities at Black-Tailed Prairie Dog (*Cynomys ludovicianus*) Towns." *Biological Conservation* 115 (2004): 89–100.

Long, Dustin, Kristy Bly-Honnes, Joe C. Truett, and David B. Seery. "Establishment of New Prairie Dog Colonies by Translocation." In *Conservation of the Black-Tailed Prairie Dog: Saving North America's Western Grasslands*, edited by John L. Hoogland, 188–209. Washington, DC: Island Press, 2006.

Long, Kim. *Prairie Dogs: A Wildlife Handbook*. Boulder, CO: Johnson Books, 2002.

Luce, Robert J., Rob Manes, and Bill Van Pelt. "A Multi-State Plan to Conserve Prairie Dogs." In *Conservation of the Black-Tailed Prairie Dog: Saving North America's Western Grasslands*, edited by John L. Hoogland, 210–17. Washington, DC: Island Press, 2006.

Mackley, James W. "The Effects of Habitat Modifications on Utah Prairie Dog (*Cynomys parvidens*) Density, Survival, and Reproduction in an Established Colony." Master's thesis, Brigham Young University, 1988.

MacWhirter, Robert B. "Vocal and Escape Responses of Columbian Ground Squirrels to Simulated Terrestrial and Aerial Predator Attacks." *Ethology* 91 (1992): 311–25.

Manes, Rob. Does the Prairie Dog Merit Protection via the Endangered Species Act? (with box by Nicole Rosmarino). In *Conservation of the Black-Tailed Prairie Dog: Saving North America's Western Grasslands*, edited by John L. Hoogland, 169–84. Washington, DC: Island Press, 2006.

Manning, Richard. *Grassland: The History, Biology, Politics, and Promise of the American Prairie*. New York: Viking Penguin Books, 1997.

Manno, Theodore G. "Mating Behavior of Columbian Ground Squirrels." PhD diss., Auburn University, 2008.

———. "Social Networking in the Columbian Ground Squirrel." *Animal Behaviour* 75 (2008): 1221–28.

———. "Squirrel-esque!—The Natural Wonders of Columbian Ground Squirrel Breeding Season in Kananaskis Country." *Nature Alberta*, Summer 2007.

———. "Why Are Utah Prairie Dogs Vigilant?" *Journal of Mammalogy* 88 (2007): 555–63.

Manno, Theodore G., Liliana M. DeBarbieri, and Jocelyn Davidson. "Why Do Columbian Ground Squirrels Copulate Underground?" *Journal of Mammalogy* 89 (2008): 882–88.

Manno, Theodore G., and F. Stephen Dobson. "Why Are Male Columbian Ground Squirrels Territorial?" *Ethology* 11 (2008): 1049–60.

Manno, Theodore G., F. Stephen Dobson, John L. Hoogland, and David W. Foltz. "Social Group Fission and Gene Dynamics among Black-Tailed Prairie Dogs (*Cynomys ludovicianus*)." *Journal of Mammalogy* 88 (2007): 448–56.

Manno, Theodore G., Anna P. Nesterova, Liliana M. DeBarbieri, and F. Stephen Dobson. "Why Do Female Columbian Ground Squirrels Give an Estrus Call?" *Canadian Journal of Zoology* 86 (2008): 900–909.

Manno, Theodore G., Anna P. Nesterova, Liliana M. DeBarbieri, Stuart E. Kennedy, Kelsey S. Wright, and F. Stephen Dobson. "Why Do Male Columbian Ground Squirrels Give a Mating Call?" *Animal Behaviour* 74 (2007): 1319–27.

Martin, Paul, and Patrick Bateson. *Measuring Behavior: An Introductory Guide*. 2nd ed. Cambridge: Cambridge University Press, 1993.

McComb, Karen. "Roaring by Red Deer Stags Advances the Date of Oestrus in Hinds." *Nature* 330 (1987): 648–49.

McDonald, Kenneth P. *Analysis of the Utah Prairie Dog Recovery Program, 1972–1992*. Utah Division of Wildlife Resources Publication No. 93-16, 1993.

———. *Utah Prairie Dog Recovery Efforts, 1996 Annual Report*. Utah Division of Wildlife Resources Publication No. 97-24, 1997.

McElligott, Alan G., and Thomas J. Hayden. "Post-Copulatory Vocalizations of Fallow Bucks: Who Is Listening?" *Behavioral Ecology* 12 (2001): 41–46.

McLean, Ian G. "Paternal Behaviour and Killing of Young in Arctic Ground Squirrels." *Animal Behaviour* 31 (1983): 32–34.

McNulty, Faith. *Must They Die? The Strange Case of the Prairie Dog and the Black-Footed Ferret.* New York: Doubleday, 1970.

Meagher, Mary. "*Bison bison.*" *Mammalian Species* 266 (1986): 1–8.

Meerburg, Bastiaan G., Grant R. Singleton, and Aize Kijlstra. "Rodent-Borne Diseases and Their Risks for Public Health." *Critical Reviews in Microbiology* 35 (2009): 221–70.

Mellado, Miguel, Abundio Olvera, Adrian Quyero, and German Mendoza. "Dietary Overlap between Prairie Dog (*Cynomys mexicanus*) and Beef Cattle in a Desert Rangeland of Northern Mexico. *Journal of Arid Environments* 62 (2005): 449–58.

Menkens, George E., and Stanley H. Anderson. "Mark-Recapture and Visual Counts for Estimating Population Size of White-Tailed Prairie dogs." In *Proceedings of the Symposium on the Management of Prairie Dog Complexes for the Reintroduction of the Black-Footed Ferret*, edited by John L. Oldemeyer, Dean E. Biggins, and Brian J. Miller, 67–72. Biological Report 13, US Department of the Interior, US Fish and Wildlife Service, 1993.

Menkens, George E., Dean E. Biggins, and Stanley H. Anderson. "Visual Counts as an Index of White-Tailed Prairie Dog Density." *Wildlife Society Bulletin* 18 (1990): 290–96.

Merriam, C. Hart. "The Prairie Dog of the Great Plains." *Yearbook of the United States Department of Agriculture* (1902): 257–70.

Michener, Gail R. "Field Observations on the Social Relationships between Adult Female and Juvenile Richardson's Ground Squirrels." *Canadian Journal of Zoology* 15 (1973): 33–38.

Michener, Gail R., and Jan O. Murie. "Black-Tailed Prairie Dog Coteries: Are They Cooperatively Breeding Units?" *American Naturalist* 121 (1983): 266–74.

Midgley, Mary. *Animals and Why They Matter*. Athens: University of Georgia Press, 1983.

Milgram, Stanley. "The Small-World Problem." *Psychology Today* 1 (1967): 61–67.

Miller, Brian J., Gerardo Ceballos, and Richard P. Reading. "The Prairie Dog and Biotic Diversity." *Conservation Biology* 8 (1994): 677–81.

Miller, Brian J., and Richard P. Reading. "A Proposal for More Effective Conservation of Prairie Dogs." In *Conservation of the Black-Tailed Prairie Dog: Saving North America's Western Grasslands*, edited by John L. Hoogland, 248–60. Washington, DC: Island Press, 2006.

Miller, Brian J., Richard P. Reading, Dean E. Biggins, James K. Detling, Steven C. Forrest, John L. Hoogland, Jody Javersak, Sterling D. Miller, Jonathon Proctor, Joe Truett, and Daniel W. Uresk. "Prairie Dogs: An Ecological Review and Current Biopolitics." *Journal of Wildlife Management* 71 (2007): 2801–10.

Miller, Brian J., Richard P. Reading, and Steve C. Forrest. *Prairie Night: Black-Footed Ferrets and the Recovery of Endangered Species*. Washington, DC: Smithsonian Institution Press, 1996.

Mitchell, Brian, and G. A. Lincoln. "Conception Dates in Relation to Age and Condition in Two Populations of Red Deer in Scotland." *Journal of Zoology (London)* 171 (1973): 141–52.

Møller, Anders P. "Mixed Reproductive Strategy and Mate Guarding in a Semi-Colonial Passerine, the Swallow *Hirundo rustica*." *Behavioral Ecology and Sociobiology* 17 (1985): 401–8.

Montgomerie, Robert, and Randy Thornbill. "Fertility Advertisement in Birds: A Means of Inciting Male-Male Competition?" *Ethology* 81 (1989): 209–20.

Murie, Jan O. "Mating Behavior of Columbian Ground Squirrels. I. Multiple Mating by Females and Multiple Paternity." *Canadian Journal of Zoology* 73 (1995): 1819–26.

Nesterova, Anna P., Shirley Raveh, Theodore G. Manno, David W. Coltman, and F. Stephen Dobson. "Pre-Mating Behavioral Tactics of Columbian Ground Squirrels." *Journal of Mammalogy* 92 (2011): 861–70.

Neuhaus, Peter. "Timing of Hibernation and Molt in Female Columbian Ground Squirrels." *Journal of Mammalogy* 81 (2000): 571–77.

Newton, Ian, and Mick Marquiss. "Seasonal Trend in the Breeding Performance of Sparrowhawks." *Journal of Animal Ecology* 53 (1984): 809–29.

Noriega, Jose. *Dixie National Forest, Powell Ranger District, Biological Assessment for Threatened, Endangered, and Proposed Species for the Utah Prairie Dog Research Project*. May 18, 2001.

Nowak, Ronald M. *Walker's Mammals of the World*. Vol. 1. Baltimore: Johns Hopkins University Press, 1999.

NPS (National Park Service). *Bryce Canyon Visitors Guide*. Washington, DC: National Park Service, 2012.

———. *The Hoodoo: Park Planner, Hiking and Shuttle Guide*. Washington, DC: National Park Service, 2005.

————. "Mission Statement." Accessed June 3, 2012. http://www.nps.gov/brca/parkmgmt/index.htm.

————. "Utah Prairie Dog." Accessed June 3, 2012. http://www.nps.gov/brca/naturescience/upd.htm.

————. "Utah Prairie Dog Day 2011." Accessed June 3, 2012. http://www.nps.gov/brca/parknews/upd-day-2011.htm.

————. "Utah Prairie Dog Stewardship Plan Development." Accessed June 3, 2012. http://www.nps.gov/brca/parknews/bcnpupdstewardplan.htm.

NRCSED (Natural Resources Conservation Service and Environmental Defense). "Utah Prairie Dog Habitat Evaluation Guide." *Utah Regional Depository* 408 (2007).

O'Connell, Sanjida M., and Guy Cowlishaw. "Infanticide Avoidance, Sperm Competition and Mate Choice: The Function of Copulation Calls in Female Baboons." *Animal Behaviour* 48 (1994): 687–94.

O'Melia, Michael E., Fritz L. Knopf, and James C. Lewis. "Some Consequences of Competition between Prairie Dogs and Beef Cattle." *Journal of Range Management* 35 (1982): 580–85.

O'Neill, Deborah M., Teresa G. Bonzo, and Keith Day. *Utah Prairie Dog Recovery Efforts, 1998 Annual Report.* Utah Division of Wildlife Resources Publication No. 99-23, 1999.

O'Neill, Deborah M., Kenneth P. McDonald, and Keith Day. *Utah Prairie Dog Recovery Efforts, 1997 Annual Report.* Utah Division of Wildlife Resources Publication No. 98-2, 1998.

Ord, George. "North American Zoology." In *A New Geographic, Historical, and Commercial Grammar.* Vol. 2. 2nd ed. Edited by W. Guthrie, 291–361. Philadelphia: Lippincott, 1815.

Orians, Gordon H. "On the Evolution of Mating Systems in Birds and Mammals." *American Naturalist* 103 (1969): 589–603.

Oswald, Michael Joseph. *Your Guide to the National Parks: A Complete Guide to All 58 Parks.* Whitelaw, WI: Stone Road Press, 2012.

Palombit, Ryne A., Dorothy L. Cheney, and Robert M. Seyfarth. "Male Grunts as Mediators of Social Interaction with Females in Wild Chacma Baboons (*Papio cynocephalus ursinus*). *Behavior* 136 (1999): 231–42.

Pappas, Stephanie. "Groundhog Day and Phil's Myth Stretch Back Centuries." Accessed February 2, 2012. http://www.msnbc.msn.com/id/46238878/ns/technology_and_science-science/t/groundhog-day-phils-myth-stretch-back-centuries.

Pierotti, Raymond "Infanticide versus Adoption: An Intergenerational Conflict." *American Naturalist* 138 (1991): 1140–58.

Pizzari, Tomasso, and Tim R. Birkhead. "For Whom Does the Hen Cackle? The Function of Postoviposition Cackling." *Animal Behaviour* 61 (2001): 601–7.

Pizzimenti, John J. "*Cynomys gunnisoni.*" *Mammalian Species* 25 (1973): 1–4.

————. "Evolution of the Prairie Dog Genus *Cynomys.*" *Occasional Papers of the Museum of Natural History, University of Kansas* 39 (1975): 1–73.

Pizzimenti, John J., and G. Donald Collier. "*Cynomys parvidens.*" *Mammalian Species* 52 (1975): 1–3.

Pizzimenti, John J., and LeRoy R. McClenaghan Jr. "Reproduction, Growth and Development and Behavior in the Mexican Prairie Dog, *Cynomus mexicanus.*" *American Midland Naturalist* 92 (1974): 130–45.

Player, Rodney L., and Philip J. Urness. "Habitat Manipulation for Reestablishment of Utah Prairie Dogs in Capitol Reef National Park." *Great Basin Naturalist* 42 (1982): 517–23.

Powell, Kenneth L., Robert J. Robel, Kenneth E. Kemp, and M. Duane Nellis. "Aboveground Counts of Black-Tailed Prairie Dogs: Temporal Nature and Relationship to Burrow-Entrance Density." *Journal of Wildlife Management* 58 (1994): 361–66.

Prairie Dog Coalition. "Coalition Efforts." Accessed June 22, 2012. http://www.prairiedogcoalition.org/coalition-efforts.php.

PRCDC (Panoramaland Resource Conservation and Development Council). *Area Plan: 2006–2011.* Richfield, UT: US Department of Agriculture, 2006.

PRCDC (Panoramaland Resource Conservation and Development Council) and USFWS. *Programmatic Safe Harbor Agreement for Utah Prairie Dogs,* 1–9, June 2009.

Proctor, Jonathan, Bill Haskins, and Steve C. Forrest. "Focal Areas for Conservation of Prairie Dogs and the Grassland Ecosystem." In *Conservation of the Black-Tailed Prairie Dog: Saving North America's Western Grasslands,* edited by John L. Hoogland, 232–47. Washington, DC: Island Press, 2006.

Pulliam, H. Ronald. "On the Advantages of Flocking." *Journal of Theoretical Biology* 38 (1973): 419–22.

Punxsutawney Groundhog Club. "Groundhog Day History." Accessed June 28, 2012. http://www.groundhog.org/groundhog-day/history/.

Radcliffe, Matthew C. "Repopulation of Black-tailed Prairie Dog (*Cynomys ludovicianus*) Colonies after Artificial Reduction." Master's thesis, Frostburg State University, 1985.

Rafinesque, Constantine S. "Museum of Natural Sciences. 9. Synopsis of Four New Genera and Ten New Species of Crustacea, Found in the United States." *American Monthly Magazine* 2 (1817): 40–46.

Randall, D. "Poison the Damn Prairie Dogs!" *Defenders* 51 (1976): 381–83.

———. "Shoot the Damn Prairie Dogs!" *Defenders* 51 (1976): 378–81.

Raynor, Linda S., and Kenneth B. Armitage. "Social Behavior and Space-Use of Young of Ground-Dwelling Squirrel Species with Differing Levels of Sociality." *Ethology, Ecology and Evolution* 3 (1991): 185–205.

Reading, Richard P. "Attitudes toward a Proposed Reintroduction of Black-Footed Ferrets (*Mustela nigripes*)." *Conservation Biology* 7 (1993): 569–80.

Reeve, Archie F., and Timothy C. Vosburgh. "Recreational Shooting of Prairie Dogs." In *Conservation of the Black-Tailed Prairie Dog: Saving North America's Western Grasslands*, edited by John L. Hoogland, 139–56. Washington, DC: Island Press, 2006.

Reiger, James F. "Body Size, Litter Size, Timing of Reproduction, and Juvenile Survival in the Uinta Ground Squirrel, *Spermophilus armatus*." *Oecologia* 107 (1996): 463–68.

Rice, Nathan. "Saving Threatened Utah Prairie Dogs—On Private Property." *High Country News*, August 20, 2008.

Ridley, Matt. *The Red Queen: Sex and the Evolution of Human Nature*. New York: Penguin Putnam, 1993.

Rioja-Paradela, Tamara, Laura Scott-Morales, Mauricio Cotera-Correa, and Eduardo Estrada-Castillon. "Reproduction and Behavior of the Mexican Prairie Dog (*Cynomys mexicanus*)." *Southwestern Naturalist* 43 (1998): 147–54.

Ritchie, Mark E. "Biodiversity and Reduced Extinction Risks in Spatially Isolated Rodent Populations." *Ecology Letters* 2 (1999): 11–13.

———. *Utah Prairie Dog Recovery: Impacts of Habitat and Grazing—1997 Progress Report*. Logan: Utah State University, 1998.

Ritchie, Mark E., and Ellen Cheng. *Effects of Grazing and Habitat Quality on Utah Prairie Dogs—1998–1999 Final Report*. Logan: Utah State University, 2001.

Ritchie, Mark E., Marilet Zablan, Michael Bodenchuck, Ron Bolander, Rebecca Bonebrake, Kate Grandison, and Ken McDonald. *Utah Prairie Dog Interim Conservation Strategy*. Salt Lake City: US Fish and Wildlife Service, 1997.

Rocke, Tonie E. *Sylvatic Plague Vaccine and Management of Prairie Dogs*. US Geological Survey Fact Sheet (2012). http://www.fs.usda.gov/Internet/FSE_DOCUMENTS/stelprdb5426465.pdf.

Rocke, Tonie E., Susan R. Smith, Dan T. Stinchcomb, and Jorge E. Osorio. "Immunization of Black-Tailed Prairie Dog against Plague through Consumption of Vaccine-Laden Baits." *Journal of Wildlife Diseases* 44 (2008): 930–37.

Rudner, Ruth. *A Chorus of Buffalo*. Ithaca, NY: Burford Books, 2000.

Salzman, James. "Evolution and Application of Critical Habitat under the Endangered Species Act." *Environmental Law Review* 14 (1990): 311.

Sayler, Anne, and Michael Salmon. "An Ethological Analysis of Communal Nursing by the House Mouse (*Mus musculus*)." *Behaviour* 40 (1971): 62–85.

Schaller, George B. *The Serengeti Lion*. Chicago: University of Chicago Press, 1972.

Scheffer, Theo H. "Historical Encounter and Accounts of the Plains Prairie Dog." *Kansas Historical Quarterly* 40 (1945): 527–37.

Schwagmeyer, Patricia L., and David W. Foltz. "Factors Affecting the Outcome of Sperm Competition in Thirteen-Lined Ground Squirrels." *Animal Behaviour* 39 (1990): 156–62.

Scott-Morales, Laura, Eduardo Estrada, Felipe Chavez-Ramirez, and Mauricio Cotera. "Continued Decline in Geographic Distribution of the Mexican Prairie Dog (*Cynomys mexicanus*)." *Journal of Mammalogy* 85 (2004): 1095–1101.

Scrattish, Nicholas. *Historic Resource Study: Bryce Canyon National Park*. Denver: US Department of the Interior, National Park Service, Rocky Mountain Regional Office, Branch of Historical Preservation, 1985. http://www.cr.nps.gov/history/online_books/brca/hrs.htm.

Scully, Matthew. *The Power of Man, the Suffering of Animals, and the Call to Mercy*. New York: St. Martin's Press, 2002.

Semple, Stuart. "The Function of Barbary Macaque Copulation Calls." *Proceedings of the Royal Society of London Series B, Biological Sciences* 265 (1998): 287–91.

Seton, Ernest T. *Lives of Game Animals*. New York: Doubleday, 1929.

———. "The Prairie Dogs (*Cynomys ludovicianus*) at Washington Zoo." *Journal of Mammalogy* 7 (1926): 229–330.

———. *Wild Animals at Home*. New York: Grosset and Dunlap, 1913.

Severson, Kieth E., and Glenn E. Plumb. "Comparison of Methods to Estimate Population Densities of Black-Tailed Prairie Dogs." *Wildlife Society Bulletin* 26 (1998): 859–66.

Sharps, Jon C., and Daniel W. Uresk. "Ecological Review of Black-Tailed Prairie Dogs and Associated Species in Western South Dakota." *Great Basin Naturalist* 50 (1990): 339–45.

Shepard, Paul. *Thinking Animals*. Athens: University of Georgia Press, 1998.

Sherman, Paul W. "Natural Selection among Some Group-Living Organisms." PhD diss., University of Michigan, 1976.

———. "Nepotism and the Evolution of Alarm Calls." *Science* 197 (1977): 1246–53.

———. "Reproductive Competition and Infanticide in Belding's Ground Squirrels and Other Animals." In *Natural Selection and Social Behavior*, edited by Richard D. Alexander and David W. Tinkle, 311–31. New York: Chiron Press, 1981.

Shields, William M. *Philopatry, Inbreeding, and the Evolution of Sex*. Albany: State University of New York Press, 1982.

Shine, Richard, David O'Connor, and Robert T. Mason. "Sexual Conflict in the Snake Den." *Behavioral Ecology and Sociobiology* 48 (2000): 392–401.

Side, John G. "PPS Prairie Dog Patrol: GPS Aerial Surveys of Dog Towns." *GPS World* 10 (1999): 30–35.

Sidle, John G., Gregory L. Schenbeck, Eric A. Lawton, and Daniel S. Licht. "Role of Federal Lands in the Conservation of Prairie Dogs." In *Conservation of the Black-Tailed Prairie Dog: Saving North America's Western Grasslands*, edited by John L. Hoogland, 218–31. Washington, DC: Island Press, 2006.

Slobodchikoff, Constantine N. *Prairie Dogs: Communication and Community in an Animal Society*. Cambridge, MA: Harvard University Press, 2009.

Smith, Josh. "Utah Legislature: Murray Students Push for Praises of Prairie Dogs." *Deseret News*, February 2, 2010.

Smithson, Carma Lee, and Robert C. Euler. *Havasupai Legends: Religion and Mythology of the Havasupai Indians of the Grand Canyon*. Salt Lake City: University of Utah Press, 1994.

Sommer, Volker, and Paul L. Vasey. *Homosexual Behavior in Mammals: An Evolutionary Perspective*. New York: Cambridge University Press, 2006.

Stanley, Thomas R., Jr. "Ecosystem Management and the Arrogance of Humanism." *Conservation Biology* 9 (1995): 255–62.

Steed, Brian C. "Why Don't We Just Shoot Them?: An Institutional Analysis of Prairie Dog Protection in Iron County, Utah." Y673 Fall Mini-Conference (2005): 1–33.

Steenbeek, Romy, Ruben C. Piek, Marleen van Buul, and Jan A. R. A. M. van Hoof. "Vigilance in Wild Thomas's Langurs (*Presbytis thomasi*): The Importance of Infanticide Risk." *Behavioral Ecology and Sociobiology* 45 (1999): 137–50.

Stegner, Wallace. *Mormon Country*. Lincoln: University of Nebraska Press, 1981.

Stenten, Joanne. *Biological Assessment for the Outfitter and Guide Special Use Permits on the Teasdale, Escalante, Cedar City, Loa, and Richfield Ranger Districts, Dixie and Fishlake National Forests*. March 15, 2001.

Stevens, Scott D. "High Incidence of Infanticide by Lactating Females in a Population of Columbian Ground Squirrels (*Spermophilus columbianus*)." *Canadian Journal of Zoology* 76 (1998): 1183–87.

Sugg, Derrick W., Ronald K. Chesser, F. Stephen Dobson, and John L. Hoogland. "Behavioral Ecology Meets Population Genetics." *Trends in Ecology and Evolution* 11 (1996): 338–42.

SWCA (environmental consultants). *Habitat Conservation Plan for the Issuance of an Incidental Take Permit Under Section 10(a)(1)(B) of the Endangered Species Act for the Utah Prairie Dog by Connell Gower Construction, Inc*. Prepared for the US Fish and Wildlife Service Utah Field Office, Salt Lake City, 1996.

———. *Habitat Conservation Plan for the Issuance of an Incidental Take Permit Under Section 10(a)(1)(B) of the Endangered Species Act for the Utah Prairie Dog* (Cynomys parvidens) *to Applicant the Church of Jesus Christ of Latter-Day Saints*. Prepared for the US Fish and Wildlife Service, Salt Lake City, 1997.

Tamura, Noriko. "Postcopulatory Mate Guarding by Vocalization in the Formosan Squirrel." *Behavioral Ecology and Sociobiology* 36 (1995): 377–86.

Thomas, Craig. "Habitat Conservation Planning: Certainly Empowered, Somewhat Deliberative, Questionably Democratic." *Politics and Society* 29 (2001): 105–30.

Tolkien, Barre. *The Anguish of Snails: Native American Folklore in the West.* Logan: Utah State University Press, 2003.

———. "Coyote, Skunk, and Prairie Dogs." In *Coming to Light: Contemporary Translations of the Native Literatures of North America,* edited by Brian Swann. New York: Random House Digital, 1996.

Towne, E. Gene, David C. Hartnett, and Robert C. Cochran. "Vegetation Trends in Tallgrass Prairie from Bison and Cattle Grazing." *Ecological Applications* 15 (2005): 1550–59.

Travers, Jeffrey, and Stanley Milgram. "An Experimental Study of the Small World Problem." *Sociometry* 32 (1969): 425–43.

Treves, Adrian. "Theory and Method in Studies of Vigilance and Aggregation." *Animal Behaviour* 60 (2000): 711–22.

Treviño-Villarreal, Julián. "The Annual Cycle of the Mexican Prairie Dog (*Cynomys mexicanus*)." *Occasional Papers of the Museum of Natural History, University of Kansas* 139 (1990): 1–27.

Tufts, Lorraine Salem. *Secrets in the Grand Canyon, Zion, and Bryce Canyon National Parks.* 3rd ed. North Palm Beach, FL: National Photographic Collections, 1998.

Turner, Bonnie. *An Evaluation of Utah Prairie Dog* (Cynomys parvidens) *Transplant Success.* Friends of the Zoo and Utah Division of Wildlife Resources Publication No. 79-7, 1979.

University of Nebraska Press/University of Nebraska-Lincoln Libraries-Electronic Text Center. *The Journals of the Lewis and Clark Expedition.* Accessed February 5, 2005. http://lewisandclarkjournals.unl.edu/.

UPDRIP (Utah Prairie Dog Recovery Implementation Program). *2011 Work Plan.* Cedar City: Southern Utah University, 2012.

———. *Utah Prairie Dog Issues Status Report.* Cedar City: Southern Utah University, 2012.

Uresk, Daniel W. "Black-Tailed Prairie Dog Food Habits and Forage Relationships in Western South Dakota." *Journal of Range Management* 37 (1984): 325–29.

———. "Effects of Controlling Black-Tailed Prairie Dogs on Plant Production." *Journal of Range Management* 38 (1985): 466–68.

Uresk, Daniel W., and Deborah D. Paulson. "Estimated Carrying Capacity for Cattle Competing with Prairie Dogs and Forage Utilization in Western South Dakota." In *Management of Amphibians, Reptiles, and Small Mammals in North America: Proceedings of the Symposium,* General Technical Report, 387–90. Fort Collins, CO: US Forest Service, Rocky Mountain Forest and Range Experiment Station, 1988.

USFWS (US Fish and Wildlife Service). "90-day Finding on a Petition to Reclassify the Utah Prairie Dog from Threatened to Endangered and Initiation of Five-Year Review." *Federal Register* 72 (2007): 7843–52.

———. "Amendments to List of Endangered Fish and Wildlife." *Federal Register* 38 (1973): 14678.

———. "Final Rule to Amend Special Rule Allowing Regulated Taking of *Cynomys parvidens.*" *Federal Register* 56 (1991): 27438–43.

———. "Final Rule to Reclassify Utah Prairie Dog as Threatened with Special Rule to Allow Regulated Taking." *Federal Register* 49 (1984): 22330–34.

———. "Proposal to Amend Special Rule Allowing Regulated Taking of the *Cynomys parvidens.*" *Federal Register* 55 (1990): 6022–24.

———. *Recommended Translocation Procedures for the Utah Prairie Dog.* US Fish and Wildlife Service, 2009.

———. "Revised 90-day Finding on a Petition to Reclassify the Utah Prairie Dog from Threatened to Endangered." *Federal Register* 76 (2011): 36053–68.

———. "Revised Recovery Plan for the Utah Prairie Dog: Notice of Document Availability." *Federal Register* 77 (2012): 24975.

———. "Revising the Proposed Special Rule for the Utah Prairie Dog: Supplemental Notice of Proposed Rulemaking; Reopening of Public Comment Period and Notice of Document Availability." *Federal Register* 77 (2012): 24915–24, 46158–83.

———. *Safe Harbor Agreements for Private Landowners.* February, 2004.

———. *Utah Prairie Dog* (Cynomys parvidens) *Draft Revised Recovery Plan.* Denver: US Fish and Wildlife Service, 2009.

———. *Utah Prairie Dog* (Cynomys parvidens) *Final Revised Recovery Plan.* Denver: US Fish and Wildlife Service, 2012.

———. *Utah Prairie Dog* (Cynomys parvidens) *Recovery Plan.* Denver: US Fish and Wildlife Service, 1991.

———. *Utah Prairie Dog: 5-Year Review, Summary and Evaluation.* West Valley City, UT: Utah Field Office, Ecological Services, 2012.

USFWS and UDWR (Utah Division of Wildlife Resources). *Safe Harbor Agreement: Allen Henrie*. West Valley City, UT, 2005.

Utah Division of Wildlife Resources (UDWR). "Utah Prairie Dog." Accessed June 30, 2012. http://dwrcdc.nr.utah.gov/rsgis2/Search/Display.asp?FlNm=cynoparv

Utah State Institute of Fine Arts (USIFA). *Utah: A Guide to the State*. Salt Lake City, 1941.

Vanderhye, Alberta V. R. "Interspecific Nutritional Facilitation: Do Bison Benefit from Feeding on Prairie Dog Towns?" Master's thesis, Colorado State University, 1985.

Vermeire, Lance T., Rod K. Heitschmidt, Patricia S. Johnson, and Bok F. Sowell. "The Prairie Dog Story: Do We Have It Right?" *BioScience* 54 (2004): 689–95.

Vogel, Steven, Charles P. Ellington Jr., and Delbert L. Kilgore Jr. "Wind-Induced Ventilation of the Burrow of the Prairie-Dog, *Cynomys ludovicianus*." *Journal of Comparative Physiology* 85 (1973): 1–14.

Walker, Tom. *The Way of the Grizzly*. New York: Voyageur, 1993.

Walters, Mark Jerome. *Seeking the Sacred Raven: Politics and Extinction on a Hawaiian Island*. Washington, DC: Island Press, 2006.

Wedel, Waldo R. *Prehistoric Man on the Great Plains*. Norman: University of Oklahoma Press, 1961.

Weltzin, Jake F., Steve L. Dowhower, and Rodney K. Heitschmidt. "Prairie Dog Effects on Plant Community Structure in Southern Mixed-Grass Prairie." *Southwestern Naturalist* 42 (1997): 251–58.

Werner, Jane. *Walt Disney's Vanishing Prairie: A True-Life Adventure*. New York: Simon and Schuster, 1955.

Whicker, April, and James K. Detling. "Control of Grassland Ecosystem Processes by Prairie Dogs." In *Proceedings of the Symposium on the Management of Prairie Dog Complexes for the Reintroduction of the Black-Footed Ferret*, edited by John L. Oldemeyer, Dean E. Biggins, and Brian J. Miller, 18–27. Biological Report 13, US Department of the Interior, US Fish and Wildlife Service, 1993.

White, Gary C., and Kenneth P. Burnham. "Program MARK: Survival Estimation from Populations of Marked Animals." *Bird Study Supplement* 46 (1999): 120–38.

Whitford, Walter G. "Desertification and Animal Biodiversity in the Desert Grasslands of North America." *Journal of Arid Environments* 37 (1997): 709–20.

Wightman, Erica. "Utah Prairie Dog Habitat Credits Exchange Announced for Iron County." Salt Lake City: KCSG Television, January 10, 2012.

Wilcox, Bruce A., and Dennis D. Murphy. "Conservation Strategy: the Effects of Fragmentation on Extinction." *American Naturalist* 125 (1985): 879–87.

WildEarth Guardians. "Protections for Imperiled Utah Prairie Dogs Improved, but Still Lacking: Amendments to Controversial 'Take' Rule Do Not Go Far Enough." August 2, 2012. http://www.wildearthguardians.org/site/News2?page=NewsArticle&id=7841#.UvveomeYZjo.

Williams, Brooke. "Saving School Trust Lands." *Wild Earth* 12 (2002): 89–93.

Williams, George C. *Adaptation and Natural Selection*. Princeton, NJ: Princeton University Press, 1966.

———. *Sex and Evolution*. Princeton, NJ: Princeton University Press, 1975.

Williams, Terry Tempest. *Finding Beauty in a Broken World*. New York: Pantheon, 2008.

Winterrowd, Michael F., F. Stephen Dobson, John L. Hoogland, and David W. Foltz. "Social Subdivision Influences Effective Population Size in the Colonial-Breeding Black-Tailed Prairie Dog." *Journal of Mammalogy* 90 (2009): 380–87.

Worster, Donald. *A River Running West: The Life of John Wesley Powell*. New York: Oxford University Press, 2001.

Wright-Smith, Mary A. "The Ecology and Social Organization of *Cynomys parvidens* (Utah Prairie Dog) in South-Central Utah." Master's thesis, Indiana University, 1978.

Wuerthner, George. "Viewpoint: The Black-Tailed Prairie Dog: Headed for Extinction?" *Journal of Range Management* 50 (1997): 459–66.

Yoder, Don. *Groundhog Day*. Mechanicsburg, PA: Stackpole Books, 2003.

Young, Peter J. "Hibernating Patterns of Free-Ranging Columbian Ground Squirrels." *Oecologia* 83 (1990): 504–11.

Zeveloff, Samuel I. *Mammals of the Intermountain West*. Salt Lake City: University of Utah Press, 1988.

Index